W9-BGN-856

MARGIN OF TERROR

SINGH M								STATUS RESERV
NOT GOOD FOR PASSAGE / NON VALABLE POUR TRANSPORT		CARRIER TRANSPORT	FLIGHT VOL	CL	DATE	TIME HEURE		
VANCOUVER		CP	060		22JUN	0900		OK
TORONTO		AI	181		22JUN	1835		RQ
MONTREAL -MIRABEL		AI	182		22JUN	2020		RQ
DELHI			VOID		VOID	VOID		
VOID								
TAD 1682.00								

SINGH L MR								STATUS RESERV
NOT GOOD FOR PASSAGE / NON VALABLE POUR TRANSPORT		CARRIER TRANSPORT	FLIGHT VOL	CL	DATE	TIME HEURE		
VANCOUVER		CP	003	Y	22JUN	1315		OK
TOKYO-NARITA		AI	301	Y	23JUN	1705		OK
BANGKOK			VOID		VOID	VOID		
VOID			VOID		VOID	VOID		
VOID								
TAD 1293.00								

MARGIN OF TERROR

A REPORTER'S TWENTY-YEAR ODYSSEY
COVERING THE TRAGEDIES OF
THE AIR INDIA BOMBING

SALIM JIWA

& DONALD J. HAUKA

KEY PORTER BOOKS

Copyright © 2006 by Salim Jiwa

All rights reserved. No part of this work covered by the copyrights hereon may be repro-
duced or used in any form or by any means–graphic, electronic or mechanical, including
photocopying, recording, taping or information storage and retrieval systems–without
the prior written permission of the publisher, or, in case of photocopying or other repro-
graphic copying, a licence from Access Copyright, the Canadian Copyright Licensing
Agency, One Yonge Street, Suite 1900, Toronto, Ontario, M6B 3A9.

Library and Archives Canada Cataloguing in Publication

Jiwa, Salim

Margin of terror : the twin tragedies of the Air India bombing / Salim Jiwa and Donald
J. Hauka. Includes bibliographical references and index.

ISBN 1-55263-772-7

1. Air-India Flight 182 Bombing Incident, 1985. 2. Trials (Murder)–British Columbia–
Vancouver. 3. Trials (Conspiracy)–British Columbia–Vancouver. 4. Bombing
investigation–British Columbia. 5. Terrorism–Canada. I. Hauka, Donald J. II. Title.

HV6433.C3J58 2005   363.12'465'0916337   C2005-903938-8

The Canada Council | Le Conseil des Arts
FOR THE ARTS | DU CANADA
SINCE 1957 | DEPUIS 1957

ONTARIO ARTS COUNCIL
CONSEIL DES ARTS DE L'ONTARIO

The publisher gratefully acknowledges the support of the Canada Council for the Arts
and the Ontario Arts Council for its publishing program. We acknowledge the support of
the Government of Ontario through the Ontario Media Development Corporation's
Ontario Book Initiative.

We acknowledge the financial support of the Government of Canada through the Book
Publishing Industry Development Program (BPIDP) for our publishing activities.

Key Porter Books Limited
Six Adelaide Street East, Tenth Floor
Toronto, Ontario
Canada M5C 1H6

www.keyporter.com

Text design: Marijke Friesen
Electronic formatting: Jean Lightfoot Peters

Printed and bound in Canada

06 07 08 09 10 5 4 3 2 1

This book is dedicated to the victims of terrorism everywhere in the world. In particular, this dedication is to the families of the 329 people who died aboard Air India Flight 182 and the same-day explosion in Tokyo that took two lives.

CONTENTS

Acknowledgements

I am indebted to countless people whose assistance enabled me to work within the Sikh community for twenty-five years while investigating the growth of militancy and in particular the bombing of Air India Flight 182 and the same-day explosion in Tokyo. There were police officers, fellow reporters, management at *The Province* newspaper, and sources in the Sikh community who risked their own lives to help me get information.

There are countless people who I cannot name publicly. My gratitude extends to RCMP officers John Schneider, Doug Henderson and to his son Tom, "Doctor" John Hoadley (Inspector), Ron Dicks, Don Brost, Bob Stubbings, Jim Cunningham, Bob Wall, Bob Solvason, Peter Montague, Lorne Schwartz, Gary Bass, Rocky Rockwell, Peter Eakins, Sandy Sandhu and Dan Bond. I am grateful to those Vancouver Police officers as well who helped protect my life in collaboration with other law enforcement officials.

I am indebted to my father and my mother, to my wife Mina and my children Farouk, Hafeez and Aliya for endless tolerance and love.

My special friend Don Hauka encouraged me and assisted me in writing this book. As well, I have to thank him for escorting me to my car during periods of heightened threats and starting the car, offering to be a "small sacrifice" for me.

I pray for the victims of this tragedy. I have seen no courage greater than theirs.

Preface

There is a place by the sea at the southern tip of Ireland where twenty years ago, a slender woman stood like a pillar whipped by wind; deaf to the cry of the gulls and blind to everything save the choppy surface of the grey-green waves before her. She had brought with her from India a suitcase to this strange land where she had never been before. It was for her husband; when he came. He was a pilot. His plane had crashed beneath the waves some 142 miles beyond her sight, and his body had not been found. Satwinder had been such a strong swimmer: surely there was some hope he would make it to shore? Amarjit Kaur Bhinder continued her lonely vigil, her heart starting at every whitecap, and every fleck on that unforgiving sea that would keep her husband's body locked in the embrace of his plane's cockpit some six thousand feet under the sea. At that moment in time, her mind had blocked all thoughts that she would face the journey of life alone. It was only after two long years that she finally acknowledged she was indeed to be without him. She stopped carrying his clothes everywhere she went.

Amarjit Bhinder's vigil was one of hundreds of scenes of grief that took place in isolation all over the globe on June 23, 1985. On that infamous day in Canadian history two bombs exploded about one hour apart. Both had been concealed inside bags checked in at Vancouver Airport. One bomb blew up Air India Flight 182 after it departed Toronto. Some 329 victims died in that tragedy. One bag-bomb flew to Tokyo and exploded before it could connect with a waiting Air India Flight. The premature explosion killed two baggage handlers.

There were two tragedies here. The first was the sequence of events that led to the bombings at Tokyo and aboard Air India

Flight 182. The second was the subsequent investigation into those bombings. The Canadian Security Intelligence Service had failed to defuse the plot because of a lack of imagination and an abject failure to see the gathering clouds of threat forming in front of their eyes. As the RCMP took over the biggest mass murder probe in Canadian history, they too were lost in a swamp of cultural differences between a pre-dominantly white force and the suspects, who held on to their secrets and a holy oath of silence.

At the end of twenty years this failure to thoroughly investigate their own witnesses and the suspects resulted in a judicial debacle during the trial of Ripudaman Singh Malik and Ajaib Singh Bagri. They had fallen markedly short in gathering convincing evidence. RCMP had chased shadows and characters against whom they could prove nothing, while the real masterminds were walking around.

The families of the victims had felt a strange alienation in their own country from the very beginning of this tragedy. They felt isolated. They felt their fellow Canadians had not joined them in their grief. Even though the destruction caused to their lives had come from Canada, they made annual pilgrimages to Ireland, because politicians had forgotten that 165 victims were our own people. It took twenty long years before a Canadian leader would make a pilgrimage to the same spot where Amarjit Kaur had stood waiting for her husband. On June 23, 2005, then Prime Minister Paul Martin became the first Canadian head of government to travel to Ireland to pay his respects to the victims. In doing so, he tried to exorcise the ghost of alienation that the Canadian victims of the Air India tragedy had felt for twenty years.

"Today, as we share this moment of tranquility—and in the future, in the hard days yet to come, when the mind ponders what might have been—never forget that remembrance is in itself a timeless act of love," said Martin. "In so doing, we keep alive the memory of those who are missed. We feel them in our hearts. We mourn them; we celebrate them. And always, and forever, we remember."

My own journey into the cesspool of extremism began four years before Amarjit Kaur Bhinder made her pilgrimage to Ireland. At that time I was unaware that I was at the beginning of the story that would later bring Amarjit Kaur to the shores of Ireland in search of her husband.

Like any enthusiastic young reporter I was after a headline story. I had no idea this journey would last twenty-five years. This is my story.

Salim Jiwa

ONE

MONKS WITH MACHINE GUNS:
October 1981

It was absurd, standing alone at the foot of a flight of rickety wooden stairs, a nest of revolutionary urban guerrillas and who-knew-what sort of reception waiting for me at the top, cursing my own curiosity and my foolish decision to pitch a story about Sikhs training their own army in Vancouver.

All I could think about was Fatso and *senene*.

It had been one of the formative moments of my childhood back in Bukoba, Tanzania. We'd been eating *senene* (fried grasshoppers we considered a delicacy) and playing the Italian card game Scopa, which we called Sweep, in Salim's restaurant. We were all Muhindis (the local Swahili word for Indians), a mix of Hindus, Sikhs, Muslims and Christians, and we all got on well enough, except for Fatso. He was a trouble-maker and as he entered the restaurant, he said something to Kugi, a local Sikh who owned a fleet of trucks. Kugi slapped Fatso so hard, his glasses smashed against the far wall.

"What did you do?" I asked.

"I made a joke about his turban," Fatso sputtered. "I asked him what was inside his turban."

"You are never supposed to make fun of a Sikh's turban. Don't you know that?"

I pondered this childhood lesson as I looked for 45 Kingsway in Vancouver, in an area littered with used car dealerships and run-down buildings. I'd met a lot of Sikhs in Tanzania. They were renowned as warriors; many of their religious symbols, including the *Khanda*, a double-edged sword, were holy weapons. It marked them as saint-soldiers. As saints, their first spiritual task was to be tolerant, democratic, just, and kind. But the birth of their faith during the Muslim Mogul rule in India also meant they were a religion of resistance. One of the famous maxims of Guru Gobind Singh is, "To commit injustice is a sin, but it is a greater sin to tolerate injustice."

And here I was, alone, looking for monks with machineguns. That—and the quest for a front page story—propelled me up the stairs of the two-storey wooden building in East Vancouver. My journey had begun after a recent article in *News India*, a small weekly publication, had caught my eye. Correspondent Ratu Kamlani had written about a band of Sikh militants who had started a separatist movement in their homeland of the Punjab. Kamlani had interviewed Dr. Jagjit Singh Chauhan, who claimed the title of President of the Republic of Khalistan, a nation which would provide Sikhs a religious shelter from India's dominant Hindu majority. Kamlani had quoted the self-styled president of the unborn republic as saying, "Takeover is never without arms. We shall continue to pursue peaceful methods, yet we are training our young—in Canada and the U.S.—in martial prowess. We shall raise our own army, our own units."

Pure bluster? Bravado? At that point it was hard to tell. But this was a story no one in the mainstream media had caught on to yet and I was intrigued, to say the least, that a leader of Sikh separatists was claiming to be raising a guerrilla force in Canada. Vancouver was home to the biggest Sikh population anywhere in North America. The white-domed temple on Ross Street in Vancouver alone boasted the largest Sikh congregation on the continent with thirteen thousand members. Some sixty thousand Sikhs lived across the province and many of them had century-old roots in B.C.

I had to find this nest of rebels, but my inquiries into the Sikh community and the temples had failed to turn up any information about a separatist movement in Vancouver. The answer had finally come from an immigration consultant—a man of many political colours known as Malkit Singh Parhar—who led a group of locals deeply involved in the Overseas Congress Party. Parhar prided himself on being in the group, which ardently supported Indian Prime Minister Indira Gandhi's Congress party. That an immigration consultant would know the precise location of a Vancouver-based office of the consulate of Khalistan was a bit of a surprise. It was also a surprise that a not-insignificant number of Indo-Canadians identified so intimately with the political scene in India and were running a political party in Canada called the Overseas Congress. I would run into Parhar many times in the future. I would discover that I was dealing with a person who was able to straddle both sides of the fence, having friends at the Indian consulate, and intimates within the circles of Sikh militants.

I knocked on the door of the so-called Khalistan Consulate and was met by a big man with a long beard, wearing a turban and a long, black gown on which I would later see emblazoned the inscription "Death to Gandhi." I reached out to shake hands with the ambassador of an unborn state: Surjan Singh Gill.

I put on a big smile for Gill and the two men who were standing with him. The office was furnished simply with a large mahogany desk and a few chairs. A Sikh flag was hanging on the wall behind the desk. Gill had looked at me suspiciously at first, asking me if I was a cop, then appeared reassured that I was armed only with a pen. He finally smiled as he motioned me over to a chair on the other side of the desk. Malaysian-born, a travel agent by trade, Gill's English was very good.

"You must be from Pakistan," he said.

I could sense where he was going with that. He knew I had a Muslim name and he was about to play the religion card. Because I was a Muslim, I would be a natural enemy of India and an ally of Pakistan: the enemy of my enemy is my friend. His next line confirmed my suspicions.

"Muslims and Sikhs are brothers," he said.

I wanted to push him back a little from this patronizing chatter. But this was not the time to appear to be objecting too strenuously. I wanted to keep the door open for future interviews. There was much to find out about this movement and I knew I wouldn't gain Gill's confidence on the first day I met him. I could make a single hit with this story by burning the bridge behind me, but it was far better to light several smaller fires. I wanted the truth, but I was willing to be patient to get it.

"I am not from Pakistan, I am from Tanzania–Africa, East Africa," I said, looking straight into his eyes. "I am a Muslim. But no

one in my family has ever visited India or Pakistan since my grand-
father left India eighty-one years ago and settled in Africa." Gill
looked unconvinced. I kept going. "But, tell me. If Muslims and
Sikhs are brothers, why is it that the Muslim Mogul rulers of India
executed at least two Sikh gurus?"

"Times were different then, but even Muslim saints contributed
to Sikhism. One of the heroes of the Sikh faith is Baba Farid."

Gill was referring to a Sufi who had greatly influenced the path
of Sikhism as it emerged as a religion of love, equality and resistance
of saint-soldiers who defied the tyranny of Muslim rulers of four
hundred years ago. Gill had his geography, history, and oratory
down pat. He was determined to make an impression.

"Pakistan is with us," he said. "And one Sikh is good to fight
thirty-five Hindus."

I fished my notebook from my back pocket. It is best to smile
broadly as you do this, for sometimes this action can have the same
impact as slapping a loaded gun on the table. Anything you say
from now on can and will be recorded and held against you, it
proclaims. Some interviewees clam up immediately. Gill's eyes,
however, lit up in anticipation and he beamed at the two Sikhs who
were standing there watching us. He seemed proud his words
would be recorded and might even get into a newspaper. But just to
be sure, I floated a soft one to him.

"That is the Sikh flag behind you," I observed.

"Yes, the Nishan Sahib. This is our flag. It is the flag of Khalistan."

"And in the centre is the Khanda," I said, referring to the Sikh
emblem.

"You know a lot about Sikhism, Salim Sahib."

Gill was undeterred by the notebook. He appeared only too
delighted to talk, even risking comments a reporter might interpret as
provocative. Perhaps, I wondered, they do not fear negative publicity.
Could that explain the September 5, 1972 massacre of Israeli athletes
in Munich, and Abu Nidal's October 7, 1985 hijacking of the Italian
cruise ship Achille Lauro? Terrorism—even support for terrorism—may
shock the world, but it invariably forces the public to pay attention. It
brings exposure to a cause, I reasoned. Clearly, Gill wanted to bring
media attention to the cause of an independent Khalistan.

"Gajinder Singh recently hijacked a plane from India to Lahore. I know him personally," continued Gill. "There were no plans to hurt anyone," he added, by way of clarification. "It was designed to tell the government of India that we mean business."

Was Gill, I wondered as he talked, attempting to establish his militant credentials by association?

Gajinder Singh was a member of the Dal Khalsa, the Sikh Army and a terrorist group in the formative stages. The hijacking Gill was applauding in his comfortable perch at 45 Kingsway had catapulted Dal Khalsa to the next rung in the terrorism ladder. I suspected Gill understood that such approving talk anywhere but in Canada may very well have landed him in some secret dungeon.

Gill had played no role in the hijacking. But it had served his cause, he explained. It had rattled the Indian government. By approving of the hijacking Gill was staking a claim of collective victory for the Sikh *kaum* (community). The hijacking had come on the heels of the Indian government issuing an arrest warrant for Sikh rebel leader Jarnail Singh Bhindranwale. The hijacking had only reverberated regionally, however. The rest of the world paid scant attention to what was then considered a regional issue. In fact, two Canadians had been on board that Indian Airlines plane that was commandeered to Lahore, Pakistan in September 1981 while on a domestic Indian flight. They escaped unhurt when Pakistani troops stormed the aircraft and flushed out the band of Sikh hijackers.

They became the first Canadian targets of Sikh terrorism. Many more were to follow.

When Gill endorsed the hijacking of aircraft, I could almost see the first paragraph of my story flashing in red. I showed no excitement, but nodded my head, encouraging him to go on. He cheerfully obliged.

"We can't forgive the Hindu government of India anymore," Gill continued, launching into a long list of complaints of his peoples' treatment by New Delhi.

According to Gill, India had allowed Sikh grievances to accumulate since Punjab had missed the opportunity to separate from India at the end of British rule. What would trigger the rise of Sikh militancy, particularly in the years following 1981, was Punjab's rapid economic growth. The state prospered, particularly because of the miraculous "green revolution," which made India not only self-sufficient in food production for the first time in many years, but allowed it to become an exporter of food. This newfound prosperity would bring renewed demands for greater attention to the Punjab by the central government in New Delhi.

A month earlier, in September 1981, the Akali Dal, the mainstream political party in the Punjab, had sent a set of forty-five demands to Prime Minister Indira Gandhi's government. Broadly speaking, they fell into three categories: religious, economic, and political, including–but not limited to–demands for increased Punjab autonomy. It was demanded that Amritsar, the seat of the Holy Shrine of the Golden Temple, be declared a Holy City (a declaration which would result in banning the sale of alcohol, tobacco, and meat within the walled city) and that an independent radio transmitter be installed at the temple to relay *kirtan* (prayers). At the time, radio stations in India were state-owned. Further, the Sikhs wanted the right to wear the *kirpan* (ceremonial dagger) on domestic and international airline flights, as well as a new law to bring all historic Sikh temples in the country under a single administration.

Not surprisingly, New Delhi objected. If they met the demands from Punjab, what would stop other states demanding similar rights? Nevertheless, some of the demands were agreed to. The central government agreed to ban the sale of offending items in an area close to the Golden Temple. Declaring Amritsar a Holy City, however, would go against the nation's secular policy. Sikhs had a constitutional right to wear the ceremonial dagger, it was agreed. But carrying the *kirpan* (and all other ceremonial weapons) was banned aboard aircraft. In any case, New Delhi argued, how could they change international airline regulations which strictly forbade the carrying of weapons? As for the centralized control of all Sikh temples under an umbrella organization, there was considerable opposition to the proposal from prosperous and powerful Sikhs living outside Punjab.

There were other problems. The central government and the Akali Dal also clashed over the distribution of river waters, crucial to Punjab's flourishing agricultural industry. The transfer of the city of Chandigarh to Punjab, promised by Gandhi in the 1970s, got bogged down over the conditions set by New Delhi: an agreement had to be reached to transfer some Hindi-speaking areas in the Punjab to the state of Haryana in exchange. But the central problem was the prime minister's refusal to surrender central government powers to states like Punjab, something she said was against the interests of national unity.

Negotiations faltered, and the Akali Dal began a series of agitation movements, which included work stoppages, shutting down railways, and demonstrations aimed at clogging the jails and courts–classic tactics used by Mahatma Gandhi during India's long struggle against the British Raj. Extremists soon exploited the situation. Among the hard-liners were the All India Sikh Students' Federation and Bhindranwale, who was courted by New Delhi until he became an uncontrollable rebel.

Tensions were exacerbated by a passionate feud between traditional Sikhs and an offshoot–the Nirankaris–who believed in a formless God who can only be realized by the presence of a living guru. Traditional Sikhs suspected the New Delhi government of actively supporting what they regarded as a heretical sect to erode the Sikh faith. Clashes between fundamentalist Sikhs and the Nirankaris had started in 1978 and climaxed two years later with the killing of Gurbachan Singh, spiritual leader of the Nirankaris.

Bhindranwale launched a guerrilla war on New Delhi and plunged the Punjab into a vicious circle of violence. The resulting insurrection would pose the worst threat to India's national security since its independence and the 1947 partition with Pakistan. By 1982, the saint-soldier Bhindranwale had turned the Golden Temple into a fortress and openly incited communal violence between Sikhs and Hindus. Bands of his followers roamed the state, shouting slogans like "*Khalistan Zindabad*," meaning "Long Live the State of Khalistan." During this time, Lala Jagat Narain, a newspaper editor who had criticized the killings of Nirankaris, was himself murdered.

Bhindranwale was arrested by police in connection with the Narain killing, prompting massive violence in the streets of the Punjab, which in turn prompted the police to fire on a crowd of protesters. The violence in the Punjab escalated, fuelled from within and without India by small pockets of militants living in Western countries. Even so, in 1981 the vast majority of Sikhs living overseas remained unaffected by the turmoil that was embroiling their home province.

Gill's mission was to transform that indifference into a passionate embrace of the cause: an independent Khalistan. The theme he returned to again and again was Sikh survival. He claimed that the dominating influence of the majority Hindu population was destined to marginalize—even wipe out—Sikhism. He had the numbers to prove it. Sikhism is a minority religion in India. There are just thirty-five million Sikhs, compared to 820 million Hindus, and 130 million Muslims. In Gill's mind, the only solution was the creation of Khalistan—a religious state for Sikhs. Such a country already had a model in Israel.

"No religion can exist without state protection," he said.

Gill then turned to the two Sikhs who had been standing there nodding approvingly. Gill introduced them as "secret couriers" of the president of the Republic of Khalistan. They had allegedly arrived with a message for Gill from his friends in the militant movement. I doubted they were secret couriers. But I was here to listen. Gill said they were also refugees in Canada. Balbir Singh Changera and Hardial Singh Thiara nodded their heads when Gill said they would face death if returned to India. Both claimed they had been forced to flee India, after their work for Khalistan independence had come to the attention of the Indian government, leaving their families behind.

Stories of such persecution among Sikhs were common.

Officially, the Indian government had insisted there was no cause for any Sikh to fear persecution in his home country. Instead, they blamed unscrupulous smugglers who, they claimed, charged money to pipeline illegal migrants into Canada. The smugglers, mainly travel agents and "immigration consultants," routinely exploited Canada's open-door refugee policies. Typically, Sikhs who wished to immigrate to Canada paid a fee for a plan to get on the fast-track to a new life. The smugglers booked the immigrants' tickets to Canada and instructed them to destroy their passports while in flight by flushing the documents down the aircraft's toilet. The immigrants then claimed to be refugees–persecuted Sikhs. They were told their applications for refugee status would gain credence if they followed the smugglers' advice and participated in anti-India protests once here. They would also claim they were being hunted by police for participating in pro-Khalistan rallies in India. Just two weeks before this interview, Canada's Immigration Minister, Lloyd Axworthy, had been so concerned by a sudden influx of 1,700 Sikh refugees who had poured into Canada that he undertook a fact-finding trip to India.

Indian government officials informed him that it was a scam.

The bizarre web of connections linking the founders of Sikh militancy in Canada with travel agents and refugee-smugglers based in Vancouver, Seattle, and the Punjab was astonishing. It was an immigration consultant who had quietly directed me to the office of the Khalistan "consulate." The man was a relative of a local travel agent, whom I would identify at a later date as a ticketing agent for terrorists. The immigration consultant and a shadowy contact of his in Seattle–a man I would interview years later and know as Mahinder Singh Sidhu–were both arrested by the FBI and the Immigration and Naturalization Service for pumping dozens of so-called refugees into Canada and the United States. American authorities said the scam involved bogus marriages between Sikhs and legal residents of the U.S. Each phoney marriage minted tens of thousands of dollars for the smugglers.

One of the two men whom I had seen that day, Hardial Singh Thiara, would soon enter the United States, using the Khalistan office as a stepping-stone to a better life in sunny California. The other secret courier, Balbir Singh Changera, remained in Canada and was later allowed to bring his wife and children over.

The preliminaries were over. I was ready to move on to the heart of the story, namely, finding out about the so-called Sikh army allegedly being raised in Canada. When I put the question to him, Gill deferred to Dr. Chauhan–the president of the as-yet-uncreated Republic of Khalistan. It was a shame, he said, that I had missed Chauhan's visit to Vancouver (in July 1981). On that trip, Chauhan had attended a strategy meeting with his followers in New York before a stopover trip to Vancouver. Chauhan could have told me about military training, Gill said.

Could this be true? I wondered. Or was it simply that Gill did not know any details and mentioned Chauhan only as a way of passing the buck on a tricky issue?

Chauhan—a.k.a. the Doctor—had been stripped of his passport by New Delhi in the spring of 1981. How he had entered Canada without one was not clear. Chauhan was a former Punjab politician and a physician who had been living in exile in England since the late 1970s for inciting trouble in the Punjab with his call for a separate Sikh state. He had become a serious headache for India. He was busy galvanizing the forces of separation not only in Canada but the United States, England, and France. However, from my investigation it seemed unlikely he had an army in training in B.C. At least, I figured, not yet.

I closed my notebook and was about to leave the Khalistan "consulate" when Gill reached into a drawer and flashed a wad of Khalistan currency. Apparently he did double-duty as the governor of the Bank of Khalistan, as his signature stood out on the fake money. He said he'd caused a stir by sending some of this fake cash to parliamentarians in New Delhi. It was little wonder India was so agitated about "hostile foreign nations" who were fuelling the fires of insurgency. The protest was a shot at Pakistan and its masters in Washington, D.C. Gill also pulled out an impressive black-and-gold passport of the Republic of Khalistan.

"So now you are an honorary citizen of Khalistan," he said, and handed it to me.

"And I wonder where I can use this passport," I said, looking at the worthless document. "I should change my name to Salim Singh Jiwa."

"Oh, you can soon use that passport, maximum two years, when you visit Khalistan," said Gill.

The ambassador insisted his cause was spreading and the clergy in B.C. temples would back him up. I must have looked sceptical, because he volunteered another name.

"Talk to Ajaib Singh in Kamloops," he said. "He will tell you there is support for the cause."

I was about to make a graceful exit when two more men entered the consulate. Both, I was to learn, had offices in the building. Gill introduced the first as Tara Singh Hayer, publisher of the Punjabi-language newspaper, *The Indo-Canadian Times*. A former Indian army captain, Hayer had become a passionate advocate of a full-blown war against India. The other man was Wazir Singh Kahlon. His beard flowed majestically all the way to his waistband. He ran an organization called Panth Khalsa ("Path of the Pure") yet another group dedicated to Sikh separatism. Hayer and Kahlon claimed the Sikh Diaspora supported agitation for a separate homeland in Punjab.

I left, having promised to call Ajaib Singh Bagri.

I walked out of the stuffy office and onto the sidewalk, breathing in the exhaust-laden air of busy Kingsway. I had a good story, but to make it a great story, I had to cover a few more bases. I started with the Kamloops clergyman, Ajaib Singh Bagri, who was born and raised in the Punjab and attained a college-level education. He had immigrated to Canada in 1971, and by 1975 had become a citizen. He had been sponsored by his fiancé Surinder Kaur, of Kamloops. Shortly after his arrival in Canada, they married.

They raised five children together. Bagri worked as a forklift operator in a local plywood mill. When I telephoned him, it was obvious that he'd been tipped that a reporter would be calling. He had prepared his polemic on the oppression of the Sikhs in India and support for a secessionist movement. An immigrant who came from a small village in India, he had managed to grab the pulpit at the Kamloops Sikh temple. A firebrand preacher, Bagri was an energetic orator, wiping the sweat from his brows and gesturing with his hands as he fired up the faithful. He didn't hesitate to say yes when asked if he and members of the Kamloops congregation supported Sikh independence.

It was one thing for a radical preacher from a small city in B.C.'s interior to endorse the Khalistan cause. But would anyone in Vancouver, the heart of the Indo-Canadian community, back him up? I called the Vancouver Sikh temple. A recently arrived priest, Mohinderpal Singh, confirmed there was support in Vancouver for the movement.

For the Indian government's side of the story, I contacted a senior spokesman in New Delhi, J.N. Dixit (later to become India's

National Security Advisor) and ran the claims of the local Sikh militants past him. He said the Khalistan issue was simply a way to funnel refugees into Canada. He suggested an awful lot of people were becoming rich by using the issue as a refugee pipeline.

I had covered every angle. I was headed for the *Province* newsroom at the south end of the Granville Street Bridge. True, I hadn't found my monks with machine guns, but I had uncovered a nascent network of devoted supporters who preached the militant creed. I had enough to write a great story about organized Sikh separatists located in Vancouver plotting independence from India. The really hard part now was to try and explain the story to the Brits who ran the paper.

Fortunately, the international scope of the piece was not lost on Don MacLachlan, an assistant managing editor. *The Province* at that time was a dying broadsheet losing the struggle to survive against its newly-purchased sister-paper, the *Vancouver Sun.* "MacLach" was wringing his hands with glee at the prospect of running a sensational international scoop. He had his glasses half-way down his nose as he began editing my copy on the green-screened video terminal.

"This is incredible stuff," he said from time-to-time. "This is dynamite."

As MacLach tweaked my story, I looked around the newsroom: a vast space compared to the *Abbotsford News*, the weekly where I worked, and imagined which desk I would choose when I was offered a job here.

When the story finally appeared on the front page on October 21, 1981, the waves were felt all the way to New Delhi. The Indian government took one look and saw red, immediately filing protests with Ottawa. Soon afterwards, at a Commonwealth meeting in Nairobi, Indian prime minister Indira Gandhi shared her concerns about Canada being used as a base for Sikh "terrorism" with her Canadian counterpart, Pierre Trudeau.

Any fears that an exposé on the movement would dissuade the militants from talking to me vanished shortly afterwards when I called Gill again from the offices of the *Abbotsford News*. He and his rebels were thrilled with the coverage their cause was getting. Gill would soon discover, however, that there was a downside to publicly supporting hijackings.

Newspaper accounts are called "open source" material in the world of intelligence. The Royal Canadian Mounted Police Security Service was deeply mired in the scandal emanating from the McDonald Commission of Inquiry. The commission had been set up to look into allegations of wrong-doing (including illegal wiretaps and break-ins) by the RCMP Security Service. Because of this lawlessness that had been demonstrated during the McDonald Commission, the government began the task of forming a civilian secret service to be known as the Canadian Security Intelligence Service (CSIS). The functions of the RCMP Security Service would be absorbed by the new organization, which would have tough Parliamentary oversight to make sure fundamental rights of Canadians were not being violated under the guise of national security interests. The days of the Mounties taking care of national security were numbered, and they knew it.

Even so, RCMP officers could not ignore mounting accounts of militants organizing in Vancouver. Gill said two agents armed with my story paid him a visit, asking what was going on. He named one of the agents as Raymond Kobzey, who had brought the article with him and asked a lot of questions. He'd even left his card. Gill was worried, but I later learned that Gill's activities had caused no more than a chuckle at RCMP headquarters. No serious effort was made to keep track of him or any other Sikh militants. They seemed to merit only sporadic checkups.

Oddly, Sikh militants were not perceived by the RCMP as a threat. Sikh militancy in its formative stages was going unchallenged, falling between the cracks of a transition period—the decommissioning of the RCMP's Security Service and the planned establishment of CSIS, which would not come into being until June 16, 1984. Between the demise of the former and the birth of the latter, much was being lost in transition.

Token pressure from the RCMP did nothing to dissuade the militants. Eager to maintain momentum, they brought their top radical to town.

One afternoon Gill phoned to inform me that Dr. Chauhan was in Vancouver and wanted to visit with me. I had no problem with that. I asked Gill to bring him to my home, as my Abbotsford office was forty-five miles east of Vancouver.

The President of the Republic of Khalistan showed up at the door of my West End apartment with no secret service people in tow and only a small entourage of friends and associates who addressed him as "Doctor." He grinned, exposing a single missing tooth, and shook my hand with a firm, bony handshake. His other arm, I noticed, was a plastic prosthetic. I welcomed him in and introduced him to my wife Mina and three-year-old son, Farouk, who was busy trying to hide behind his mother's skirt.

"Come, come," Chauhan said to Farouk, trying to encourage him.

Farouk fled to the bedroom. In Dr. Chauhan's opinion, my son looked skinny for his age and his eye-rubbing was clearly a sign of allergies. He suggested an herbal remedy, which I promised to try. During our chat, he didn't talk much about politics, but did suggest I had done the Sikhs a great favour by publicizing their plight on the paper's front page. Over a cup of Indian chai, he spoke of his "just struggle" for Sikh rights. He had concluded it was impossible to get justice for Sikhs within Hindustan. It was a religious obligation for Sikhs to support Khalistan. Sikhs prayed every day to God to grant them sovereignty. "*Raj Karega Khalsa*" (Khalsa shall rule) is their daily mantra, he said.

I pointed out that this prayer might have already been granted. Less than one hundred years after Guru Gobind Singh galvanized the Sikhs, they conquered Lahore, threw out the Afghan ruler, and proclaimed their own king, Ranjit Singh. The Khalsa Raj stretched from Punjab to Kashmir and beyond to the Khyber Pass. Those had been the glory days of iron-fisted rule and of the legendary Sikh Akalis, the "immortals." They were Ranjit Singh's elite soldiers who wore blue uniforms with knife-edged quoits around their turbans. It seemed to me Chauhan wanted a return to those glory days. He was waiting for the second Kingdom to come. We said our goodbyes and Farouk finally came out from behind his mom's dress.

My story of Chauhan's visit to Canada that appeared in *The Province* again touched a nerve with the Indian government. In Ottawa, officials at the Department of External Affairs were lambasted by Indian diplomats who demanded and got a hastily-called meeting to discuss this flagrant protocol violation of allowing an enemy of the state of India to enter Canada. India reminded its fellow member of the Commonwealth of Nations that Sikh separatist forces in Canada posed a greater threat to New Delhi than those operating in Punjab.

The protest had its effect. Later, Chauhan phoned from the U.K. to tell me officials at Canada's High Commission in London had refused to renew his visa to enter the country. They had brandished the newspaper article with my name on it about his visit and bluntly told him he was not welcome in Canada.

Chauhan said he was not deterred. He had powerful friends in Washington, D.C., he hinted: two right-wing, diehard anti-communist Republican senators, Jesse Helms of North Carolina and Dan Burton of Indiana. The two senators had been assiduously courted both by Chauhan and a succession of separatist Sikh leaders. The senators' logic was as simple as Chauhan's when it came to the politics of the time. To Helms and Burton, Sikh militants and the United States were natural allies. If they succeeded in creating an independent state in the Punjab that would help form a wedge between Soviet communism and their perceived satellite states, such as India. The two senators had been ardent supporters of the Afghan fighters, whose cause they deemed noble since they had been fighting the Soviets.

So when Canada refused Chauhan entry, I was not surprised that his reception in the United States was decidedly more welcoming. . Nor was I amazed when Gill and Hayer relayed news that Chauhan was at the U.S. border town of Blaine, Washington. At the time, Blaine had more gas stations per capita than anywhere else in the world. Canadians habitually went there to fill up on cheap gas just seven hundred metres from the B.C. border, fifty kilometres south of Vancouver.

I made the journey to see Chauhan and found his presidential quarters in an old motel. The parking lot was full of cars and several Sikhs stood around in small circles. Seeing me they raised their hands together and brought them in front of their faces in welcoming *namaste*-style.

"*Wahe guru ji ka Khalsa Salim Bhai*," they chanted in unison. "The Khalsa belong to God."

"*Wahe Guru ji ki fateh*," I replied. "Victory belongs to God."

More than a dozen Sikhs were milling in and around Chauhan's tiny room. Hayer occupied the single chair, while the president was seated on a bed. All the founders of Sikh militancy in Canada were there, including Gill, Kahlon (the man with the long beard I had met at the consulate during my first trip there), and the two refugees I had met at Gill's office, Changera and Thiara. One of them told me he was now living in Yuba City, California, and had been appointed Khalistan's "governor" for the Golden State. It was all very surreal; he appeared to actually believe he had some kind of legitimate diplomatic status. It seemed to me titles were being bestowed to everyone and anyone.

Conducting an interview in such a small room was difficult, so Gill, Chauhan and I made our way to a restaurant next door. Over coffee, I asked Chauhan how he had managed to get into the United States. Senator Jesse Helms, he explained, had invited him to come to Washington to attend a Senate agricultural committee hearing. After all, the Punjab was India's breadbasket. I was still looking for those monks with machine guns, so I pressed for details about military training for Sikhs in Canada. Chauhan still refused to clarify the issue, and gingerly avoided clarification when I pressed for details. He said he would rely on the goodwill of the United States and Pakistan to stop the spread of communism south from Afghanistan. He was repeating the message he'd given Helms–the Punjab would be an effective buffer against communist expansion.

"You have said that no nation was born on the conference table," I said. "What are your thoughts about terrorism?"

A master of counter spin, he took a sip of coffee, wiped his lips and said, "You can come here and shoot all these people in this restaurant. Or you can have the same impact by simply shooting at the windows."

The aim, he said, was to create fear.

I took my leave, crossing the Canada–U.S. border with absurd ease in those pre–9/11 days. Along with a tank full of cheap gas, I had another great story in Chauhan's audacious trip to Canada's border. Chauhan was betting on things heating up with India, that the ripple effects would be felt overseas, bringing the majority of Sikhs in Canada and other Western nations into the separatist camp.

Revelations about Chauhan's presence in the United States (and how easily he was able to travel without a valid travel document sanctioned by the government of India) printed in *The Province* created more diplomatic firestorms. The U.S. ambassador in New Delhi was hauled over to the foreign ministry and told that allowing the separatist Sikh leader to enter the U.S. by waiving visa requirements was considered an "unfriendly act." In turn, Chauhan loudly blamed the "Soviet lobby" in India for the protests, saying it was an attempt to discredit the U.S. He'd spoken as a true friend of Jesse Helms, bashing India as the disciple of the evil Soviets.

Chauhan was also playing the role of champion of Sikh refugees—including seventy-eight who were in custody in Toronto. He told me by phone from the U.S. that he was going to put Canada to shame in front of the United Nations. He was going to file a complaint claiming Canada was violating UN conventions on refugees by jailing dissidents who would face political and religious persecution in their homeland.

Canadian Sikhs were, by and large, unaffected by events in India. Many of them didn't like my coverage of the militants. I was "invited" to a Sikh temple in New Westminster where I was lectured about listening to Chauhan's propaganda and assured by the temple committee that the Sikhs remained loyal to India. Some prominent Vancouver Hindus called to admonish me for betraying the "motherland."

"When Canada throws you out, India will be the only place you can call home," said one powerful Hindu businessman who ran a large concrete manufacturing plant.

The political picture in Vancouver-area Sikh temples was shifting, though. While those leading the New Westminster temple decried the rise of militancy and said there was no support for separatism, the Ross Street Temple in Vancouver was being overtaken by a more fundamentalist faction that favoured a resolution demanding the UN grant Sikhs observer status at the General Assembly and recognition of Khalistan as a distinct nation.

As I worked on my stories chronicling the growth of Sikh militancy, I could not picture the future. Nor could I guess that in a few years at least a half dozen people with whom I had face-to-face contacts would be murdered by suicide bombers or machine guns or be cut down by contract killers. That I would be playing mind games with agents of the government of India or shaking hands with terrorists who would bloody fellow Canadians and threaten my own life. This was the farthest thing from my mind. Up until now, it had all seemed as absurd as the fight between Kugi and Fatso—surreal and almost comic. But as the year ended, there was a new arrival on the stage of Sikh politics in Vancouver. A man who spoke in the temples with such passion, women would throw their jewellery at his feet. A man his fellow militants would call a "Living Martyr" who carried his own shroud with him—a man unafraid to die for his cause. The Tigers of the True Faith were about to roar into the arena. And this man—this "Living Martyr"—was the leader of the pack of ferocious cubs.

TWO

ENTER THE TIGER

I could not shake the notion that this quixotic quest for an independent Khalistan was bizarrely comic. The Sikh extremists sounded farcical, incapable of creating serious chaos in India or here in Canada by using this country as a base for guerrilla warfare. I was meeting with them almost every day now. Was I giving voice to some kind of Frankenstein? If I had, I was about to meet the monster's new mouthpiece. The caller on the line again was Surjan Singh Gill, the consul of the Republic of Khalistan, and he wanted me to go to the Khalistan consulate to meet a B.C. man who had a harrowing tale of a desperate escape from India. Despite my niggling doubts, I couldn't pass up what promised to be a big story.

The man who greeted me had a silly smile playing on his lips, but there was no mirth in his eyes. He was introduced as commander of the Tigers of True Faith (Babbar Khalsa), which was already outlawed in India as a terrorist group. He wore a massive blue turban of a special style that I was not used to seeing on a Sikh. A steel band ringed the dome and a fluffed fan of cloth adorned the top. His blue, knee-length gown was, I was told, the dress of the seventeenth century Nihang warriors, who had defended their fellow Sikhs with legendary ferocity: fearless fighters who readily embraced death in the service of the gurus. Just four years earlier, he had been an ordinary mill worker. Today, Talwinder Singh Parmar, born in the village Panchhat in the Punjab in 1944, was the Babbar Khalsa's chief. Postcards with his picture on them bore a famous quotation from the gurus, "Lifting of the sword is justified when all else fails."

I shook his hand, not realizing that many years later I would look at this as my introduction to Canada's Osama bin Laden, and

33

then sat on a wooden chair provided by Gill, moving it opposite Parmar's. With our knees barely six inches away from each other, I looked keenly into the Tiger's eyes to see if I could penetrate those very dark, almost emotionless black circles, crowned by bushy eyebrows.

I had heard much about Parmar. He had a high school education and had worked for a decade as a sawmill machine operator. He would later become a building contractor, buying and selling real estate. A few months earlier, in January 1982, I had been told he was being sought by the Indian police for his purported role in the murder of two police officers and a village elder in Dehru, Punjab, during a police sweep for militants. Wanted posters with his face on them offering a fifty thousand rupee reward were plastered on every power pole in Punjab. His road from humble mill worker to self-proclaimed "Rebel of Rebels, India's Most Wanted Man" had started in 1978 when he'd left his wife and three young children in the Vancouver suburb of Burnaby to preach a fundamentalist form of the Sikh faith in India. Parmar had been motivated by the massacre that April of several Sikhs belonging to a faction known as the Akhand Kirtani Jatha (AKJ) during a confrontation with the heretical Nirankari group, which preached doctrines considered incompatible with the traditional form of Sikhism. AKJ leader Bhai Fauja Singh had been killed in the incident and the Babbar Khalsa (BK) had been set up to avenge his death. Sukhdev Singh Babbar, a Punjab Sikh, is widely acknowledged as the man who formed the BK as the military wing of the AKJ.

But now, seated safely in the Khalistan consulate in Vancouver, Parmar claimed he had founded the separatist group, which he would later incorporate as a charity with the stated aim of creating a homeland for Sikhs. Babbar Khalsa, a terrorist group whose leader was wanted in India for murder, would soon be registered by the B.C. government under the Societies Act as a charitable organization. In the near future, the "charity" would help the families of Sikh guerrillas who had died in action in the struggle for Khalistan–and finance terror in India through a weapons pipeline originating in lawless Peshawar, Pakistan. There, Afghan Mujahideen had set up bazaars that sold everything from rocket-propelled grenades to the

Soviet Kalashnikov AK-47, the weapon of choice for guerrilla armies around the globe.

Gill's introduction of Parmar was elaborate. He wanted to tell me a story that I could not yet print about how this wanted man with a price on his head was spirited out of India. The first attempt to smuggle Parmar out with the help of a friend from Kamloops had failed. So Gill claimed to have personally gone to Nepal and then entered India posing as a truck driver. He and Parmar had made their way back to Kathmandu, Nepal, by truck before catching a flight to safety. Gill said the exact escape route had to remain a secret since other Sikhs might have to use it. A Nepal exit stamp on Parmar's passport confirmed at least part of the story.

Sitting like a king, proud as a peacock, Parmar insisted that he was innocent; he added, there were no innocent Sikhs in India as far the government in New Delhi was concerned. He was being framed, he explained to me, simply because he was a Sikh preacher. He had hidden in the northern Indian state of Uttar Pradesh for five months before escaping with Gill. During that time, in a bid to find him, Indian police had beaten his father and burned the family's home in Punjab.

His daughter, Rajinder Kaur, and his wife, Surinder Kaur, had pleaded with the Canadian government months earlier to help get him out of India safely. They said his life was in danger because the government of India believed he was linked with the Sikh separatist movement (something the family did not wish to admit while he remained in India and in danger of being arrested). Rajinder Kaur was now happy that her father was home. It was, she said later in a telephone interview, the best gift she could have received for her fifteenth birthday, which had fallen on the day her dad arrived at Vancouver International Airport. Gill had staged the homecoming carefully. There had been dozens of chanting supporters on hand at the airport bowing to Parmar, among them Punjabi-language *Indo-Canadian Times* newspaper editor Tara Singh Hayer, who would tell me that many Sikhs now feared going to India; that they were now being regarded as the enemy of the state.

The story of Parmar's escape to Canada was greeted with chagrin by India's high commission in Ottawa. On April 29, 1982, the government of India formally requested Parmar's extradition to India to face murder charges. The Canadian government was concerned about its relations with a fellow Commonwealth nation and didn't want to appear insensitive to India's security needs. But with no extradition treaty in place, Canada was forced to officially deny India's request in July 1982. In the absence of a treaty, he could not be extradited without dusting off old legal codes which allowed rendition of a person to a Commonwealth country which recognized the Queen as head of state. Even then, Parmar could not be handed over since India did not accept the Queen as head of state, but only as the head of the Commonwealth. It would not be until early 1987 that External Affairs Minister Joe Clark would finally sign an extradition treaty with India. The treaty was roundly condemned by the militant group known as the International Sikh Youth Federation (ISYF). Members of this group accused Joe Clark of "sitting down with murderers"–a reference to Clark's Indian counterparts.

Parmar, who had become a Canadian citizen in 1976–six years after immigrating on a sponsorship offered by his sister–had won a reprieve. He had also learned something about the ineffectiveness of Canadian law. He was content to use his nicely appointed residence on Howard Street in Burnaby as home base while preaching hatred for India and collecting thousands of dollars in funds for his cause.

Knowing he was untouchable in Canada, Parmar grew more audacious every day as he travelled across the country, recruiting Tigers. The BK was tight-knit, committed to its beliefs, secretive, and daring. In the interior B.C. city of Kamloops, about two hundred miles from Vancouver, Parmar found at least three of the top men in his cadre: chief lieutenant Ajaib Singh Bagri (the fiery preacher and Gill supporter) and saint-soldiers Gurmit Singh Gill, Avtar Singh Narwal, and Satnam Singh Khun Khun. Bagri laid on an elaborate reception for Parmar at the Kamloops Sikh Temple. It was a temple that Bagri, a forklift operator at a saw mill had helped build with his own sweat. This holy labour is considered to be divinely rewarding *sewa*, or religious service, in the Sikh faith. Parmar was introduced to the congregation as a hero, honoured and allowed to make a speech condemning India's treatment of their Sikh brethren in Punjab. Hayer was quick to report on how Parmar had been lionized in Kamloops and coined a new cognomen for him: *Jinda Shaheed*, the "Living Martyr."

But this romancing the "Living Martyr" would not last for Hayer, who was disturbed by Parmar's fundraising and how the money was being spent. Further, the editor was still loyal to Dr. Jagjit Singh Chauhan in the U.K., who he considered a well-educated intellectual who gave the Sikh cause credibility on the world stage with his finesse and polish. Hayer told me Parmar was attempting to usurp the leadership of the Sikh community from legitimate representatives like Chauhan: Parmar had proclaimed himself a leader second in rank only to Jarnail Singh Bhindranwale, who was the icon of Sikh militancy in Punjab. Hayer was not unenthusiastic for violence, and he fully endorsed a war against India. It was the beginning of many schisms in the militant movement, based mostly on the issue of leadership.

While Parmar raised money and assembled his covert force, Gill continued to find ways to keep the struggle for Khalistan on the front pages. The ambassador of the fledgling republic could scarcely contain his glee when he called me in January 1982, and asked me to come to the consulate to see something special. Gill proudly produced a New Year's greeting card from Pakistan strongman General Zia ul-Haq, wishing him and his "nation" prosperity. Gill was literally wringing his hands as he described how much this would anger Prime Minister Gandhi, who was already having a diplomatic row with the U.S. over Chauhan's visit the previous year.

This piece of mischief by Zia was a sign of the political times. The Cold War was still on full nuclear throttle and beating back and containing the Soviets was America's primary objective. A key piece of U.S. foreign policy was to create a Vietnam for the Soviets in Afghanistan by arming and financing hardline Muslim Jihadists. Zia was playing a pivotal role in keeping the cash and weapons flowing through Pakistan. In turn, Washington appeared to be unofficially encouraging Zia to stir up trouble for his arch-enemy, India. Although India was a member of the Non-Aligned Movement (NAM), it was seen as being misaligned by the U.S. and a de facto Soviet ally. With Sikh disaffection growing in the Punjab, conditions were right for Pakistan to sponsor their own proxy war. It was payback for India's role in tearing East Pakistan away from Islamabad's control: India had armed and trained the Bengali guerrilla force, the Mukti Bahini that had fought to liberate Bangladesh during the Indo-Pakistan war of 1971. This greeting card was an unmistakable message from the dictator that disaffected Sikhs could count on his country if they chose to rebel against New Delhi's rule. It was an open invitation, this courting of Sikh separatists through a greeting card.

The rising tide of unrest and dissatisfaction in Punjab was mirrored in the politics of Canada's Sikh community, particularly at the largest temple in North America; the Ross Street *Gurudwara* (temple) was now under the control of a man who sympathized with those who felt that Sikhs were being dealt with unfairly. In December 1981, Daljit Singh Sandhu, a soft-spoken realtor who always wore a saffron turban, had been elected president of the Khalsa Diwan Society, which boasted a membership of thirteen thousand, much larger than any other temple outside of India. His election had been foreshadowed by resolutions pushed through the society by his supporters, asking the United Nations to recognize Sikhs as a "nation." It was not an outright call for secession, but more a call to give them observer status at the world body, like the PLO. It signalled a change in the mood of the community. Surjit Singh Gill—no relation to the Khalistan consul—told me, "A year ago nobody talked about a separate state. But now a lot of people are talking about it because they feel the government (of India) is not listening to them."

The Indian government's hardline policy towards Sikh unrest played into the hands of extremists like Parmar and Gill, sending the most unlikely converts into their camp. Gill made sure I was introduced to his star revolutionaries, taking me to Abbotsford in the Fraser Valley to meet "the defence minister of Khalistan." Avtar Singh Toor was a giant of a man, the size of his massive head accentuated by his turban. He had stern eyes, a long black beard, and a barrel chest. Toor had been a tank driver for the Indian Army during the 1965 war with Pakistan over Kashmir, which had seen one of the fiercest tank battles since the end of ww II. For his courage in the face of fire and military services to his former homeland, he'd been decorated several times. He wore his medals proudly during the interview and showed me other war mementos in his living room. These included several swords, which both Gill and I gingerly admired. I noticed rivet-like dents on the sharper bottom edge and asked what they were.

"Those are the number of heads cut off by these swords, which belong to past warriors of the Sikh faith," replied Toor, with little change in expression.

"Chopped off heads?"

"These are just museum pieces, Salim Bhai," Gill said hastily, sensing my discomfort. "We can't fight the government of India with swords anymore."

Toor had exchanged his swords for the ploughshare and was now a farmer, but his words were sharp and bitter as he described his treatment at New Delhi airport just a few days previously during a visit to India. He had been stopped and detained after a Khalistan "banknote" printed in Vancouver was found in his pocket. He was only freed after Canadian diplomats intervened. Released, he made his way to the Punjab, where the police turned up to search the home where he was staying in, sending the message, "We're watching you." An Indian Tank Corps hero, Toor, had apparently been blacklisted as a separatist over a bogus banknote. He had expected his former homeland to show him some respect. Instead, he said, he'd been treated like an enemy. It was perfect fodder for Gill.

"This is so typical of the government of India," Gill said. "Every Sikh is now treated as an enemy."

A picture of Toor—his massive chest studded with medals—accompanied the story in *The Province*, with the headline, "Holiday in India Terrifying," in big, bold type.

Events in India fuelled Sikh anger in Canada and, even at this early stage, the Vancouver militants played a prominent role. In April 1982, representatives of twenty-four Sikh temples delivered a protest note to India's consulate, condemning the shooting of twenty-two Sikhs in the Punjab twelve days earlier. Spokesman Avtar Singh Samra warned Gandhi that Sikhs were capable of launching a "red" revolution in Punjab (contrasting the "green" revolution, which had turned the state into India's breadbasket). Feelings ran high, but the RCMP rarely intervened. On May 9,

India's high commissioner to Canada, Dr. Gurdial Singh Dhillon, was met by a crowd of twenty-five protesters at the Vancouver airport and was pelted with eggs during his visit to the rapidly emerging centre of Sikh militancy. No charges were laid. Nor was there any serious attempt to stop Singh Sahib Giani Sahib Singh, one of the head priests of the Golden Temple, who visited Vancouver to rally support for the evolving *dharam yudh* (holy war). The movement was given further impetus in May 1982, when India declared the militant groups Dal Khalsa and Chauhan's U.K.-based National Council of Khalistan unlawful organizations. Shortly thereafter, Amrik Singh, president of the Sikh Students Federation, was taken into custody and this prompted another wave of violence in Punjab. By now Hindu extremist organizations such as the Hindu Surakhsha Sumiti, a Hindu defence committee (akin to the Protestant Ulster Defence League in Northern Ireland), in turn began sacrilegious actions against the Sikh religion. In one instance the militant Hindu unit damaged a model of the Golden Temple and defiantly burned a picture of a Sikh guru. That led to further divisive conflict between Hindus and Sikhs, who had for generations lived side by side in Punjab.

In August 1982, another Indian aircraft was hijacked from India to Pakistan. Newspapers in India reported that B.C. Sikh rebel Parmar paid for five of the hijackers' tickets. There was no attempt in Canada to establish whether the man who was already wanted for murder in India had actually paid hijackers to commandeer an aircraft. Parmar's links to terror in the Punjab were clear. His wife, Surinder Kaur, and his sister travelled to Pakistan in the spring of 1985 (at the behest of Parmar) to cheer the hijackers during a court appearance. India described the court session as a circus. It contended Pakistan really had no intention of punishing the hijackers. Those present at the court said the hijackers were thrilled their "sisters" from Canada were there to support their cause.

As the political situation in India deteriorated, the influence of Parmar's cabal of Tigers of True Faith grew. Mainstream Punjab politicians, like Harchand Singh Longowal, leader of the Shromani Akali Dal Party, were getting nowhere in negotiations with Gandhi, who was still clinging to her Congress Party's traditional policy of secularism. Fundamentalist Sikhs in Canada saw Parmar as a man they could use to exert pressure on New Delhi to negotiate with their people. Parmar, for his part, did his best to undermine Longowal and the moderates every chance he got. In October 1982, Parmar asked me to visit his Howard Street home in Burnaby. His young son, Jaswinder, opened the door, took one look at my head and gasped, "You have to cover your head. God is upstairs!"

"Oh, okay. God is upstairs," I said, and took the cloth he offered me.

Jaswinder looked relieved as I put it on. He had probably meant that in Parmar's home, everyone covered their head as a sign of respect for the Almighty. Upstairs, Parmar told me he had sent a bank draft worth one hundred thousand rupees about $13,000 CAD, to support Longowal in Amritsar. But the money had been seized by India's external spy agency, the Research and Analysis Wing of the cabinet secretariat (R&AW). This might have been an attempt by Parmar to deflect criticism that none of the money he had collected was making it to Punjab. The R&AW had forced Longowal to write Parmar, telling him his support for the struggle for more autonomy in the Punjab was not needed.

In reality, Longowal needed all the help he could get. Every day he was stone-walled by Gandhi's government strengthened the hand of the extremists. By 1983, a desperate Longowal would resort to peaceful disobedience. Some of his supporters would pay with their lives when Indian police fired on groups of Sikhs who were blockading roads to press their demands, killing twenty-four people.

Every death in Punjab translated into a small fortune to Parmar and his growing movement. He used each death and each report of an imprisonment as highly-charged fodder in his constant pleas for donations to the Sikh cause, particularly for orphans of martyrs of the Punjab religious war. His flair for public speaking quite moved devotees to orgies of generosity. Donations poured in to Parmar. On several occasions, he ran full-page ads in Hayer's newspaper whose depictions of supposed government brutality and discrimination blatantly appealed to Sikh outrage. The ads evoked a powerful description of the suffering of Sikhs who had been arrested and tortured by Indian security forces.

"Today's Hindu Empire is inflicting unspeakable and intolerable brutality against the Sikhs that are raising their voices for freedom of religion and the Khalsa's (Sikhs) prosperity," read a typical appeal.

It was claimed that outspoken or militant Sikhs had been hauled into police stations on trumped up charges and subjected to vicious brutality and torture. The charges included incidents in which victims had their fingernails pulled out and salt added, electric shocks, blinding as a result of bright light shined continuously into the eyes, beatings that resulted in broken legs and arms, and being hung upside down. There were even charges that some Sikh's had been murdered while in police custody.

Those who had died were martyrs to the cause of Sikh independence, Parmar declared. His appeal focused on the plight of the martyrs' wives and children who survived. He said they lived in terrible poverty and suffered horribly. He begged the community to establish a fund to help sustain the families.

It proved to be a startlingly successful campaign. Exactly how much cash Parmar raised—and where it went—was never made clear. Parmar proved very clever at covering his tracks. Hayer later claimed that Parmar had raised $50,000 for the Martyrs' Fund.

In accounting for the funds, Gill later reported in another open letter to Sikh leaders that he himself had contributed $3,000 to the fund, but that all the money donated had been intercepted and seized by India.

No proof of this seizure was ever provided or accounted for by Parmar.

As support for extremism grew, Parmar spread his message of separatism by the sword to a wider and wider audience. By early June 1983, he travelled to Holland to preach to Sikh communities there. Following a three-week stay in Holland, he boarded a train from Amsterdam for West Germany. But authorities there had received an INTERPOL notice issued by India to arrest Parmar on a warrant for murder. As Parmar arrived at a border town near Düsseldorf, a policeman boarded the train and demanded his passport. Parmar was promptly taken into custody and the West Germans immediately notified New Delhi. India rushed documents to German prosecutors so they could push the extradition through.

Parmar was picked up on June 29, 1983, but it wasn't until July 6 that Surjan Singh Gill called from Bonn to tell me the news. I asked him if his diplomatic credentials were working in West Germany, but Gill sounded sombre as he told me about Parmar's arrest.

"I suspect Indian intelligence has been tailing him and tipped police here," he said.

Clearly, someone had told the police that Parmar was on the train, but just who passed on the tip was never discovered. Surinder Kaur, Parmar's wife, was worried he'd be extradited to India where he would face certain execution. Family members of Parmar and Gill asked the Canadian government to intervene, but not much could be done apart from offering consular services. India was eager to rush lawyers to Bonn to fight the case, but West German authorities said they needed more paperwork first. The legal fight to get Parmar released would go on for months and his sympathizers in West Germany, the United Kingdom, the United States, and Canada would rally to his cause. At the now-militant Ross Street Temple in Vancouver, a three-day prayer session involving the continuous reading of the scriptures on Parmar's behalf began on July 7, 1983.

Hayer reported in the *Indo-Canadian Times* that wealthy Vancouver businessman Ripudaman Singh Malik–best known at the time in the Sikh community for selling religious trinkets and books laid out on a small table at the Ross Street Temple–had arranged for sixty protest telegrams to be sent to the prime minister of Canada, Pierre Trudeau. Malik had recently founded a charitable organization, the Satnam Trust, and every weekend either he or devoted friend and fellow traditionalist Surjit Singh Gill would be selling. I saw them both at these tables during my later visits to the temple. I also learned at the time that both Malik and Daljit Singh Sandhu, past-president of the Ross Street Temple, had visited the West German consul in Vancouver to appeal for Parmar's release.

It was customary in most Indian-based societies to aid community members in trouble. There was tremendous loyalty to clan, extended family, people from home villages also counted as relatives and the minority of Sikhs in Vancouver who were baptized stood up for each other. And in that sense neither Malik nor Sandhu was doing anything out of the ordinary by going to plead for Parmar's release. Aiding a brother in trouble was part and parcel of being in position of leadership in the community. In Bonn, some three hundred Sikhs chanted and carried placards telling the West German government not to send Parmar back to face execution. The placards proclaimed: "Do not enslave the Sikhs" and "Talwinder is our Religious Leader."

Once again, despite the mysterious seizure by India of money from the Martyrs' Fund, another fund was set up. Yet, again, Hayer, despite his misgivings, allowed Parmar's wife Surinder Kaur to insert another appeal on behalf of her jailed husband in his paper.

"In this religious war, my husband, the humble servant of the Guru's nation, Group Leader Talwinder Singh Babbar (Parmar's nom de guerre) too has contributed as much as he possibly could," wrote Surinder Kaur. "Countless men have sacrificed themselves for the rising spirits of the Sikh nation and some are still sacrificing themselves. Blood has been shed.

"Life and death are in the hands of the God and a true Sikh is never afraid to sacrifice himself for the glory and liberation of religion, race, guru, and humanity."

In this appeal for financial help from the community to defend her husband, she reminded them, "You all know that the Indian government has placed a price of fifty thousand rupees on the Group Leader's head."

But it would take many more months to secure Parmar's release. He had once claimed to be immortal because he had "baptized ten thousand people in the Punjab and all of them are Talwinders (sympathizers)," and if one Talwinder was killed, a thousand more would rise. But for now, the original article, the prototype Talwinder Singh Parmar, would have to cool his heels in a cell in Düsseldorf.

While Parmar languished in jail, the situation in India was rapidly getting worse. There were virtually daily incidents of shootings, despite a massive deployment of army and police contingents. Bhindranwale had by now moved his headquarters into the Akal Takht—a highly symbolic act. The ornate structure, within the

Golden Temple, built by Guru Hargobind in 1609, is described as "the nerve centre of Sikhism." It is the Vatican of Sikhs. Edicts affecting the daily lives of Sikhs are issued from here. It is also a shrine to Sikhism's heroes. From this post, Bhindranwale directed his campaign of defiance.

Gandhi soon placed Punjab under direct rule, dissolving the state assembly and appointing a governor. The harsh crackdown further radicalized many in Vancouver and Toronto, the two major centres of Canada's two hundred thousand–strong Sikh community. Cries for a *dharam yudh* were now being heard. The crowds attending demonstrations against Gandhi's government were getting louder, their protests more violent, and there was a distinct overtone of a cultural clash between Sikhs and Hindus. Many of the chants I heard during this period mocked Hindus and their *dhotis*, the white loin cloth of the type Mahatma Gandhi had worn. References to the government of India were invariably called the "Hindu *sarkar*", or the "Hindu government."

The tracks of RCMP Security Service were visible to me as I worked on Sikhs. They had noticed my article on the arrival of Parmar in Vancouver, as they had noticed my earlier write-ups about Gill. The flip side of giving the extremists publicity was the perfect excuse it gave the RCMP to visit the Sikh militants and keep tabs on their activities—the old "open source material" routine where they would bring a copy of an article with them on a visit to those perceived as threatening Canadian security or the security of other nations.

But as Sikh militancy in Canada grew, the RCMP Security Service was in its own death throes. The McDonald Commission of Inquiry was investigating so called dirty tricks; illegal activities of a spy agency that was a law unto itself, autonomous and out of control. The commission had heard an astonishing litany of violations of rights of legitimate organizations, barn burnings in Quebec, and illegitimate bugging of groups in B.C.

Faced with a flood of blistering condemnation from civil rights groups and a mountain of damning evidence, the Liberal government proposed in 1981 the formation of a new civilian secret service that would have tight reigns over its activities. Work began on the drafting of the *Canadian Security Intelligence Service Act*, which would lead to the formation of a weaker, more controlled spy agency with Parliamentary oversight. The bill was still going through Parliament in April 1984 as tensions were escalating among Canadian Sikhs and militancy was rocketing out of control.

RCMP officers were bitter that what they saw as one of their highest and most sacred tasks—protecting the nation from internal and external threats was being taken away. With the knowledge that CSIS would be created by June 16, 1984, the Mounties had a lot of housecleaning to do: papers to destroy, others to preserve to pass on to the civilian agency. But the file on Sikh extremists was thin. The RCMP Security Service's monitoring of the militants seemed to have been conducted more out of curiosity rather than any sense that Parmar, Gill, and their followers posed a threat. Community interviews continued, but increasingly Sikh militancy was falling through the cracks created by the acrimonious divorce of the RCMP from national security work.

The intelligence vacuum was being filled by India. While our RCMP spies were busy answering charges of wrongdoing, India was rapidly bolstering its abilities inside Canada to monitor Sikh radicals they considered a grave risk to their national security. By 1983–84, Indian consulates in Vancouver and Toronto and the High Commission in Ottawa were well-staffed by members of the R&AW—the highly efficient and ruthless external spy agency of India. Some members of the Indian Police Service (IPS) and the internal security agency known as the Intelligence Bureau (IB) were also seconded to Canada as diplomats. Up to now, the R&AW had dealt with the obvious threats India faced from CIA infiltration, from Pakistan's elite, military-run Inter-Services Intelligence Agency (ISI), and other hostile neighbours. But now the government had decided to send their top spies to Canada to counter the growing threat posed by Sikh militancy.

Much of the infiltration of Indian spies into Canada went unnoticed as the RCMP Security Service began to disband. The mandate of the Indian intelligence agents was to confuse, deceive, disrupt, and discredit members of Sikh militant organizations. As the agents fanned out into major cities like Toronto, Vancouver, New York,

London, and other European centres with significant Sikh populations, one of their primary jobs was to recruit sympathetic Sikhs and
paid informants who could keep a close eye on movements and
activities of people like Parmar, Gill, and others. I'd soon learn just
how quickly these agents accessed information within the Sikh
community and would meet many of these Indian operatives as militancy grew into a dangerous force in Canada.

For veteran agents of the R&AW, working within the Canadian
Sikh community was a piece of cake. They had cultural and racial
advantages over Canadian spies. Brown-skinned agents who spoke
Punjabi fluently had no problem mixing and blending into the Sikh
populations, or even being present in Sikh temples to listen to the
daily rant against India. Contrast that with the overwhelmingly
white Canadian intelligence service of the time (and even now) and
the handicap this country had in gathering information becomes
quite apparent. This inability to penetrate (or even begin to understand) a different culture would prove disastrous. Just hiring a Punjabi
translator would take CSIS months. A speech made one day at the
Ross Street Temple in Vancouver or in the Sikh temple in Markham,
Ontario, was available to Indian agents and diplomatic staff soon
after it was delivered. Ciphers located in a locked room with a large
black metal door at the consulate in Vancouver would begin humming and within hours, External Affairs in Ottawa would hear one
protest after another from Indian diplomats about incendiary
speeches or other activities of Sikhs hostile towards New Delhi.

The R&AW employed classic espionage methods to divide and
conquer. New Punjabi–language newspapers were set up with the
help of sympathizers while existing journals were co-opted with
offers of lucrative advertising contracts. Lies and innuendo were
used to destroy the reputations of militants considered to be threats.
Money was paid to an editor and an unflattering account of the targeted person appeared in print, quickly spreading the word
throughout the community. A favourite tactic was to portray a loyal
Sikh as an Indian government agent. It was a sure-fire way of discrediting and rendering him useless to a militant organization that
relied on secrecy and absolute loyalty. Rumour is enough to cast
doubt on the operational reliability of even the staunchest militant

when terrorism is being planned. By 1984, the penetration of the Sikh community by Indian government agents and community based recruits was massive and pervasive. While Canada was still in the process of creating a civilian spy service, India had a free hand to mess with "our Sikhs."

In February 1984, I went on a vacation visit to the homeland of my ancestors. It had been eighty-four years since any member of my family had set foot in India. I spoke the languages of India—Hindi, Gujarati, and another more obscure tongue from the Kutch region of north-western India—thanks to my parents and my grandmother. But nothing could have prepared me for the culture shock I suffered as I walked along a narrow alley in Karol Bagh in New Delhi. Out on the street, a constant tide of people swept relentlessly forward. I feared being swept away in this flood of humanity if I did not move at a similarly synchronized fast clip, so I melted into the human wave, barely able to glimpse at the shopping arcades dotting this predominantly Sikh area of New Delhi, three kilometers from the city centre.

I found some respite in a little restaurant. I seated myself and a turbaned young Sikh came over to my table and put down a glass of cold water.

"How do you like India so far, sir?" he asked.

I looked at him, wondering how he knew I wasn't from here. How could he possibly tell? Was it the way I carried myself? The way I walked when I came in or what? How did he recognize a foreign "Indian" so fast?

"Man," I said with a sigh. "Too many people. There are just too many people."

He moved his head from side to side as only Indians can—that rotation as though the skull were balanced like an upside-down pendulum on a pivot. That shake of the head is supposed to say yes.

"They are just people, sir," he said.

Karol Bagh was a microcosm of the Punjab where many of New Delhi's Sikhs lived. Punjab itself was out of bounds for foreigners at this time and most Sikhs I talked to here whispered about the possible fate Gandhi faced if she continued an increasingly violent confrontation with Sikh radicals. It had only been a few weeks since the once-moderate Akali Dal, now taken over by extremist groups, had burned copies of the Indian constitution. I did a random survey of opinion; a take of what the people in the street were thinking. There was no shortage of opinions. In journalism we call it a "streeter."

"They will kill her for sure, sir," said one man.

I had no idea then how right this man would be proven a few months later. I returned to Canada and wrote an analysis of tensions in the Punjab, the growing alienation between Sikhs and Hindus, and the great distrust between many Sikhs and Gandhi's government The spokesman for the president of India was putting the best foot forward when he pointed out to me that the president of India was a Sikh, the mayors of New Delhi and Bombay were Sikhs and the chief of the air force was also a Sikh. There was no mistreatment of Sikhs or discrimination, he said: the militants did not have the heart and minds of Sikhs who lived in harmony all across the length and breadth of India.

By March 25, 1984, as Indian paramilitary forces began ringing Sikh holy places inside the Punjab, over one thousand angry Sikhs issued a manifesto and burned and beheaded Prime Minister Gandhi's effigy in front of the consulate of India in Vancouver on Howe Street. The manifesto, by the Punjab Holy War Action Committee, an ad hoc group formed by Sikhs from various temples, claimed the government had "martyred" some four hundred Sikhs by oppressive and brutal practices inside the Punjab. Khalistan protagonist Surjan Singh Gill, wearing a black gown emblazoned with the inscription "Death to Gandhi," trampled on her effigy as it burned. He then dramatically lifted up the head on the tip of his sword as hundreds cheered. Among those cheering were Parmar's wife, Surinder, and their children. They were there to demand his release from jail in Germany.

There was nothing comical about these characters anymore. Just two years ago, I had climbed those rickety wooden steps of the consulate of Khalistan and written a story about rebels plotting separatism for the Punjab. Then, they had looked like a bunch of clowns with nothing better to do. But this was no circus. I could sense more trouble ahead: big trouble.

Friday, June 1, 1984, was a busy time at the Golden Temple. Pilgrims in their thousands started to arrive for the celebrations marking the martyrdom of Guru Arjan Dev on June 3. The next day, New Delhi launched "Operation Blue Star," Gandhi's final solution to the Sikh problem. Within twenty-four hours, the entry of foreigners into Punjab was banned and the border with Pakistan sealed. The Siege of the Punjab had begun. A thirty-six-hour curfew was announced as troops moved into position around the Golden Temple, where Bhindranwale had already made preparations for battle. Fortifications were built around several areas within the temple, with sandbagged battle stations manned with machine guns and an assortment of other weapons. The Indian Army would soon discover—at their cost—how professional those preparations had been, including effective communications between Bhindranwale's forces deployed within the temple. The stage was now set for turning the most sacred shrine of the Sikhs into a battlefield.

On the evening of June 5, the Indian army addressed the militants within the temple, demanding their surrender, but only 129 came out with their arms raised. By nightfall, Operation Blue Star kicked into high gear and its forces attacked with tanks. The temple became a slaughterhouse, for both the army units attacking it and the Sikhs holed up inside. In the first few hours as the battle raged for control of the periphery of the temple area, the relatively moderate Akali Dal boss Harchand Singh Longowal was arrested by the army along with three hundred others. Bhindranwale was determined to stand his ground.

Early on the morning of June 6, as the world watched in horror, the heavy armour, including an armoured personnel carrier, moved into the sacred grounds. But this was immobilized by anti-tank rockets fired from within the Akal Takht fortification. The army had moved into the Akal Takht itself, using the searchlights of a tank to blind militant gun positions. Even now, Bhindranwale would not give up. There was room-to-room fighting and by morning the superior training, armour and fire power of the Indian army had overcome determined Sikh resistance.

Mopping-up operations continued the next day. Bhindranwale's bullet-riddled body was discovered in the basement along with that of Amrik Singh, president of the Sikh Students' Federation, who had been arrested earlier and then released, only to be killed in the fighting. Also killed in the action was former Indian army General Subheg Singh, who had teamed up with Bhindranwale. The main seat of the Sikh religion, the Akal Takht, was badly damaged. Simultaneously with the operation against the Golden Temple, other raids were launched against other Sikh temples in different cities throughout the Punjab.

The casualties were enormous. The army had suffered eighty dead and more than 250 wounded. The death toll among those defending the temple was much, much higher. The official White Paper on the Punjab conflict listed a few hundred, but Sikhs who witnessed it would later say more than one thousand died. Among the dead were innocent pilgrims caught in the crossfire. The Vatican of the Khalsa (Pure Ones) was covered in blood and the Akal Takht was nearly destroyed. The Golden Temple itself was riddled with bullets. Hundreds of militants were taken into custody and arms and ammunition of all descriptions were seized. Inside, the army also found a crude hand-grenade factory.

Months in the planning, Operation Blue Star forever seared the psyche of Sikhs. In death, Jarnail Singh Bhindranwale would pose a greater threat to India than he had ever had in life. It had been a reckless adventure, this attack that struck at the very heart, the very soul of Sikhism. Gandhi would pay heavily for it.

I witnessed grown men weeping in Vancouver in helpless rage and impotent fury. They threatened revenge. Were the threats real? I was about to find out.

THREE

PLAYING WITH FIRE

"Indira bitch! Shame, shame!"

The screams came from behind a door that was shuddering and quaking–mirroring the motions of my own intestines. At least the portal appeared to be holding, despite the efforts of the men hurling themselves against it, desperate to break in. The radio reporter standing beside me with her back to the wall clutched her notebook close to her chest and looked helplessly at me. I don't know if the look on my face exuded the calm, nonchalance I was hoping to achieve, or simply made her more terrified, seeing as I was inwardly petrified, heart pounding, mouth dry. There seemed to be no escape. Around us, shards of glass carpeted the floor. Shattered pictures of Mahatma Gandhi and Indira Gandhi had been thrown down and covered by shoes: a symbolic insult to both the founder of India and the current prime minister. Someone had already trashed this office. Now, as the front door vibrated and the cries of "Indira bitch! Shame, shame!" alternated with the chanted battle cry, "*Bole soh nihal*!" it appeared they were coming back for seconds.

It was June 6, 1984, and we were trapped in the lobby of the Indian consulate in Vancouver. As word of the attack on the Golden Temple had spread in the Sikh community, a crowd had begun to gather in front of the consulate on Howe Street, the upscale downtown business sector of Vancouver. The mob shouted insults and a steady chant of "*Indira Kuti! Hai, hai*!" (Indira bitch! Shame, shame!") was getting louder and more frenzied. I'd arrived just in time to see two screaming, chanting Sikhs being pushed into a paddy wagon and rushed away. With the police on scene, I had assumed it was safe to enter the building and the radio reporter and

52

I had climbed the stairs to the second floor lobby. We'd scarcely had time to survey the damage before two Vancouver policemen rushed out of the inner offices, slammed the outside door, and bolted it shut. Without explanation, they had then disappeared back into the offices, leaving us stranded when the hammering and banging on the door began. Who wants to protect reporters in war zone?

After a few terrifying moments, the shouting and pounding was replaced by the sounds of a scuffle on the other side of the door. Then, behind us, I could hear a police radio from inside the consulate offices. An office door opened and a policeman walked into the lobby, smiling at us. I didn't return the gesture. I just wanted to get out of there and my radio-reporter friend was in as much of a rush to do the same. The officer opened the door leading to the landing and I was out, taking the stairs downwards two at a time.

Outside on the street, the crowd was, by now, in a fine frenzy. The paddy wagon had returned. There on the pavement, flanked by a couple of uniformed officers, tears streaming down their faces, were Balbir Singh Changera and Wazir Singh Kahlon, the two men I had met at the consulate of Khalistan in late 1981.

"Was that you trying to get into the consulate?" I asked them.

They nodded; their eyes were red from weeping.

"Indira attacked our Golden Temple," Changera said. "Many, many Sikhs are dead."

"Yes, I understand," I said. "But I almost died of fright up there."

The crowd of Sikhs was getting bigger. Chants of "Indira bitch!" were giving way to "Death to Indira!" Police officers were surrounding the consulate and the street was being blocked off. I was surprised when two men were let out of the paddy wagon. The first one out raised his fist in the air and screamed at the top of his lungs; his adrenalin appeared to be pumping overtime. I recognized Sodhi Singh Sodhi, a local mill-worker who had joined the Sikh separatist movement as the troubles in Punjab had escalated. The second man was Jasbir Singh Sandhu, soon to be inducted into Khalistan President Chauhan's cabinet as a reward for his attack on the consulate. Sodhi and Sandhu had rushed the Indian offices without warning after hearing about the attack on the sacred Golden Temple in Amritsar; bursting inside, waving swords and scattering consular staff, who fled for their lives. They smashed pictures and overturned furniture before being overpowered by police and stuffed into the paddy wagon.

Now Sodhi and Sandhu were out of police custody. It was astonishing; two men attacking a foreign diplomatic mission walking free. Charges had been laid, and withdrawn because consulate staff, police claimed, was not prepared to testify in court. But it seemed like police had given in to appease the large crowd. It was an attempt to defuse the situation. A firehose would have worked, along with the mayor reading the riot act. But that was not to be the case, and once again, Canada had shown how weak it was when it came to enforcing the laws of this country.

It would be twenty years before Sodhi told me the entire truth of what he intended to do that day. He said he wanted to hold the consul-general of India hostage and then force him to make a call to New Delhi to ask his government to stop the army action against the Golden Temple. He confessed that he was in an emotional turmoil after hearing news about the assault on the Golden Temple on the radio at 1 pm. He went straight to the Ross Street Temple where other Sikhs had gathered. Among them was fundamentalist school janitor Hardial Singh Johal, who would later emerge as a provocateur and architect of terrorism in Canada. Soon, Jasbir Singh Sandhu arrived at the temple. The two friends set out to do something drastic, first stopping at a general store in the Punjabi Market on Main Street. They told the owner they were going to the consulate and asked for swords. The blades were given for free; apparently there was no charge for items being used to carry out a sacred duty. Then they went to Howe Street.

"I went in to the consulate first," said Sodhi. "Jasbir came up second."

Sodhi marched to the door to Consul-General Jagdish Sharma's office, but it was locked. Brandishing his sword at other consulate workers, Sodhi asked where Sharma was. He wanted to take the consul-general hostage.

"We didn't want to hurt him," he told me. "We just wanted to hold him and force him make a phone call to his government to stop the army action at the Golden Temple."

Not finding Sharma, Sodhi and Sandhu forced the consulate employees into a room. If they could not find Sharma then these clerks would be held hostage until they made the phone call. Sodhi said he and Sandhu smashed the furniture and the pictures that hung on the walls. Within minutes, the police arrived. The barrel of a gun won over the sword.

"They had big guns and they took us into custody," said Sodhi simply.

Sodhi and his partner Sandhu were bundled into the paddy wagon and taken to the police station at the foot of Main Street. Charges were laid. Meanwhile, the angry crowd outside the Indian consulate was growing and there was open talk about "killing them here since they are killing us over there in India." Police then asked Kahlon what it would take to make the crowd go away. He demanded the release of his two comrades. The police swiftly brought the Sikh swordsmen back to the scene and released them right in the middle of the chanting crowd.

Sodhi, his fist raised in defiance, stumbled out of the paddy wagon, a hero. A *Province* photographer captured the image and the paper used it on the front page. The consulate staff would not testify in court, so all charges were dropped. The Vancouver police apparently were never aware that Sodhi and Sandhu had intended to take Sharma hostage. It was a spontaneous, emotional reaction to the attack on the Golden Temple, hatched in anger. The same day the pair raided the consulate, Sharma received a threat from Parmar's Babbar Khalsa group, promising to kidnap or kill him. The caller also threatened his family.

Sodhi had been transformed from a relatively modest Sikh who was too embarrassed to grow his beard or wear the turban during a visit to the Golden Temple a few months before the attack. In January 1984, Sodhi, clean-shaven, wearing a three-piece beige suit and a cloth covering his head, looking hopelessly out of place, sat next to Bhindranwale on the rooftop of a building within the Golden Temple complex as his wife snapped pictures. Sodhi showed me these pictures at his home many years later. Behind the crowd sitting on the floor along with Sodhi and Bhindranwale, you can see the sandbag fortifications built by the saint-soldier's followers who knew

Indian police would one day come after the militant leader. Sodhi was no more than a foot away from Bhindranwale when he was asked, "Where are you from?"

"I am from Canada," replied Sodhi.

Sodhi knew he did not fit in well with this crowd of Sikhs wearing long beards and turbans. He felt a little uncomfortable that he was not a baptized Sikh and was only wearing a cloth on his head. His clean-shaven face also betrayed this lack of commitment to the traditions of his faith. Bhindranwale sensed this.

"Whose son are you?" he asked Sodhi.

"I am the son of Sikhs," he replied.

"If I go outside with you in a crowd, how would they know you're the son of Sikhs?" asked Bhindranwale.

A little awkwardly, Sodhi told Bhindranwale that many Sikhs who lived in Canada and who wore the turban and beard faced discrimination. Bhindranwale had merely smiled.

"Others who are devoted must feel the same pressure? Yet they are sons of Sikhs."

Sodhi took out a wad of about one thousand rupees to donate to the Saint, but he moved his hand away gently and smiled, "I am just an ordinary Sikh. Give this to the needy."

Sodhi then asked, "Can I take a few pictures with you?"

"But you are not listening to me," Bhindranwale had gently chided, an apparent reference to Sodhi's reluctance to put on the turban and grow his beard.

Following the Golden Temple attack and the death of Bhindranwale, whom he had met just five months before, Sodhi began wearing a turban and grew a beard. Bhindranwale's picture hangs in his home today. And an inscription on the picture says Bhindranwale was the greatest Sikh of the twentieth century. Sodhi is no longer worried that anyone will mock him about his appearance.

If the problem of militancy was a molehill before Operation Blue Star, it had now grown to Himalayan proportions. The assault had dealt a deadly blow to relations between Sikhs and their motherland, alienating the Khalsa all over the world. Thousands of previously loyal Sikh soldiers defected, many of them crossing over into Pakistan. Police officers also fled. Cries of "blood for blood" rang out around the world from Malaysia to Vancouver to Toronto to London.

I reached Dr. Chauhan at his London home by telephone and his message was ominous and blunt.

This was war.

Sikh history should have been a lesson to Gandhi, he said. Anyone who had dared to desecrate the Golden Temple, he reminded me, had not lived to the end of their natural life. *Shaheedi jathas* (martyr brigades) would be formed in Canada and Britain, he said, and then added, they would not break any laws of foreign lands. On June 10, 1984, the Sunday after the assault, twenty-five thousand Sikhs marched in the streets of Vancouver. Thousands of others marched in Toronto and in cities across the world where there were large Sikh communities. Men, women, and children filled several blocks of downtown Vancouver. Placards proclaimed their grief and their chants vented their frustration. Men had tears on their faces. Among those present on the podium were Daljit Singh Sandhu (the former president of the Ross Street Sikh Temple), BK lieutenant, Ajaib Singh Bagri, along with Surjan Singh Gill. This was no separatist rally: representation was broad. Few had probably ever heard of the Khalistan cause. Now, however, they were chanting slogans in favour of their own state and calling for Gandhi's blood. As I walked along and then listened to the passionate speeches, I had no doubt in my mind that any one of these twenty-five thousand would have gladly plunged a dagger into the Indian prime minister. She had done it to them; they would do the same to her.

Vancouver's Ross Street Sikh Temple now became the engine of enmity, a meeting place where militants shared a podium and preached to the converted. By June 29, 1984, several new men had arrived at the temple bent on harnessing the thirst for vengeance. The most fascinating and controversial of them was retired General Jaswant Singh Bhullar, a former hero of the Indian army. Accustomed to exercising his authority over soldiers, he found willing followers in these saint-soldiers wounded by India's actions. Many Sikhs were looking for guidance and were relying on their own historic valour to fuel their own bravado. One Sikh could defeat thirty-five Hindus, they boasted. There was clearly an expectation that there would be no stopping them now from getting their own homeland. Bhullar's new recruits were anxious to meet him and to learn what plans he had to strike back at India. But Bhullar's explanation of how he had arrived in Vancouver in the first place would split the community: many believed his fantastic tale while others challenged it, claiming he was a *gadhaar*–a traitor. Some asked why he had left the temple alive when Bhindranwale had given his life. Sikhs who flee to safety leaving behind those who fought and died are not appreciated. Others suggested he had been sent out earlier as part of a plan by the government of India, which had anticipated Sikh resentment worldwide over the temple attack that had been in the planning for three months of more. The theory some offered was that Bhullar wanted overseas Sikhs to react violently since that would induce intelligence and policing authorities in those countries to be on guard. They said India believed it could control insurgency within its own borders as long as other nations perceived Sikhs as terrorists and took action to control them.

Bhullar told me his version of events personally. He said he had been in the Golden Temple on the eve of the Indian army assault. But Bhindranwale himself had ordered him to leave; knowing those inside would have to lay down their lives. Bhindranwale had commanded the general to keep the cause alive in the event of his death.

Despite these misgivings about him in the community, Bhullar collected thousands of dollars as he made the rounds of temples in Vancouver, Calgary, and Toronto. Some of the more moderate figures at the temples admired his ability to present a well-educated war hero to the public as the face of resistance. He had key friends in the Sikh traditionalist camp including Daljit Singh Sandhu, the former Ross Street Temple president. Another was California millionaire Didar Singh Bains, who would later fly around in a private jet christened *Khalistan One*. These three men would become instrumental in forming the World Sikh Organization, considered at the time to be relatively moderate compared to Parmar's BK and a new organization called the International Sikh Student's Federation.

The second new man at the temple was the son of an Indian police inspector: Harjinderpal Singh Nagra, also known as Harpal

Singh Ghumman. A founding member of the International Sikh Youth Federation (ISYF) in the U.K., Nagra had come to Vancouver and married a local Sikh woman in a bid to stay here. It was his suggestion that perhaps the local group needed to change the name of the organization they had formed—from the International Sikh Student's Federation to the International Sikh Youth Federation, since many of the members were in their mid-twenties or early thirties. Within a few months, the ISYF became a potent anti-India force, growing to over four thousand members, but it was not banned as a terrorist organization by the Canadian government until after the 9/11 attacks in the U.S.

Sodhi Singh Sodhi was named treasurer of the ISYF. Canada would soon hear about terrorism unleashed by the group. Newspaper editor Hayer was enamoured by the idea of Bhullar and other educated Sikhs taking over the leadership of the movement opposed to the government of India. Bhullar was soon called to 45 Kingsway along with Sodhi. Hayer wanted to reward Sodhi and Jasbir Sandhu for their brave deed in attacking the Indian consulate. He had earlier written in his newspaper that Sodhi had made Indian diplomats "run like dogs." Hayer "handed a sword to Bhullar and Bhullar presented it to me," Sodhi told me later. A presentation sword is a salute to valour.

As the fireball of Sikh turmoil began rolling across Canada and the Punjab, CSIS was not yet born. But on June 16, 1984, former members of the RCMP Security Service moved into an unremarkable building on Broadway in Vancouver above an Indian restaurant. Overnight, gun-carrying members of the RCMP had become part of a civilian security service. As the service began to find its feet with Tedd Finn as director, it faced many challenges. The new spy service was still in Cold War mode; counter-espionage was still directed at the Soviets and Red China and Eastern-Bloc countries. Yuri Andropov had just died and Constantin Chernenko had taken over as Soviet chairman.

CSIS had, unfortunately as it would turn out, inherited the RCMP's mind-set about where Sikh terrorism stood on the scale of threats to Canada—not very high. The top of the terror ladder was occupied by Armenians; next came Middle Eastern groups which included Palestinians residing in Canada. Libyan agents and members of secretive Egyptian fundamentalist groups still accounted for much of resource allocation on the counter-terrorism front. Resources were severely lacking, policy directives were changing every day, and rules for retention of tapes of intercepted conversations were the same as those issued by RCMP brass in 1980. The rule was, in the absence of evidence of serious subversive activity, tapes were to be erased ten days after being heard and no later than thirty days. Destruction of tapes rather than retention of taped conversations was emphasized. Further, CSIS officers were aware of what had gone wrong with the RCMP and what Parliament wished to see in the new civilian security service: respect for the civil rights of Canadians and accountability. A memorandum of understanding had been drafted between the RCMP and CSIS on cooperation and how the two agencies would interact. But the divorce was acrimonious and would affect person-to-person relations between CSIS officers who were now viewed as untrustworthy civilians as opposed to the lofty, legendary, Canadian icons of culture and institution that the Mounties with their paramilitary past and rank system represented. CSIS had to negotiate for months before being given access to the police computer system containing the criminal database commonly known as the Canadian Police Information Centre (CPIC).

The nascent CSIS was finding its feet as the fury in Sikh communities across the land developed faster than a tornado. A furious and often angry struggle had begun within Canada for supremacy among Khalistani leaders. Militants wanted blood. There was bravado. Some Sikhs got a kick out of wearing t-shirts emblazoned with the word "Terrorist."

But the man who could draw blood, Parmar, was still languishing in a West German jail, and it was not until July 3, 1984, that the caged Tiger of True Faith was released. West German prosecutors decided there wasn't enough evidence to warrant an extradition–a decision perhaps also motivated by the breakdown of law and order in the Punjab and India's atrocious track record of human rights violations. Indian officials were exasperated that they had not even been told Parmar was being freed.

Happy to be home, Parmar wasted no time. In his first interview with me in early July 1984, he said bluntly, "I want to warn the Indian government they'll pay a price for attacking the temple." Parmar quickly consolidated his position in the Canadian leadership struggle. He began a cross-Canada trip to assert his supremacy; he wanted it known that it was he who would take the reigns after the death of Jarnail Singh Bhindranwale, not General Jaswant Singh Bhullar (whom he considered a do-nothing mouth piece and possibly even a government agent). To Parmar, Bhullar's very existence was a betrayal. How could Bhullar have left the Temple when Bhindranwale sacrificed his life?

It was to be a year of escalating violence. There had been an attack on India's acting high commissioner during a demonstration in Winnipeg. In Toronto, Mississauga, Markham, and Vancouver, Sikh temples began falling into the hands of militants belonging to the ISYF. Many temples now began sporting pictures of Sikh martyrs killed in the Golden Temple assault, including Bhindranwale and Amrik Singh.

There was no room for moderation in the eyes of the militants. The intimidation of moderates and the shutting down of dissent began in earnest on July 19. Sarabjit Singh Khurana ran a sari and clothing store on Fraser Street in Vancouver. At around 6 p.m., two men in the Parmar-style nihang uniform walked into his store with a gun and a sword. Three female customers were ordered to move back as they wielded the sword over Khurana. Police had to lay siege to a two-block area while Khurana desperately reasoned with the two swordsmen. An hour later the two walked out, their job of intimidating Khurana done. (Both men later were arrested, but nothing ever came of charges.)

What had Khurana done to warrant such treatment? He had aired a speech by India's President Zail Singh explaining the government's rationale for the Golden Temple attack on his local radio station. Khurana was unnerved and told me that the intimidation and threats had begun two weeks before the incident. A group calling itself the Dashmesh Regiment, the Tenth Regiment, had sent him a warning he would be "executed" for airing Indian propaganda. The windows of his home and business had been smashed and he had been living in fear ever since. Another threatening letter had arrived from an unknown group calling itself the Commando Headquarters of the Republic of Khalistan. For now, with his two assailants arrested, he was safe: "God was giving me courage....They wouldn't even let me move. I finally convinced them (to leave)."

While I was getting a unique view from behind the lines of Sikh militants, Indian government agents like Gurinder Singh of the R&AW (who was posted as vice-consul to the Vancouver consulate) had begun to call me often with information. He was a tall Sikh who wore no turban and had supreme loyalty to his nation. I wondered how he felt, being a Sikh trying to defuse the insurgency that had enveloped India and was now beginning to consume portions of Canadian society.

"I am an Indian first," he told me, looking me straight in the eyes. "I am a Sikh second."

The RCMP protected him twenty-four hours a day. A trailer manned by the RCMP's VIP protection service was parked just behind his home in southwest Vancouver. But Gurinder Singh had refused the police escort that accompanied Consul-General Jagdish Sharma everywhere. A spy does not want the company of foreign police officers, but Sharma was a diplomat who Canada absolutely insisted on protecting.

On August 15, 1984, I was invited to a flag raising ceremony Sharma was holding to mark Indian Independence Day at his home in the British Properties, a prized parcel of real estate with homes worth several million dollars each. As I arrived, I could see the RCMP VIP security trailer parked at the side of the house. Within minutes of my arrival, a busload of Sikh militants belonging to the ISYF turned up bent on disrupting the ceremony. A riot soon began on the front lawn and the small contingent of police called for reinforcements. I watched from the large, glass windows overlooking the front of the house as police in riot gear desperately tried to beat them back. Some of the rioters were bleeding, but holding their ground as police pushed back with their shields.

Sharma watched from where I was standing and appeared unmoved by the scene. He vowed to raise the Indian flag despite the violence. Providing security to a foreign diplomat's home was Canada's job, he insisted. With police clearing away the Sikhs, the guests who had been inside the house made their way out on the lawn and Sharma ran his country's standard aloft triumphantly. Evidently, the former artillery captain in the Indian army was not easily fazed.

Following the publication of my story of the riot at Sharma's home, Vancouver restaurateur Manmohan Singh, a man who had been appointed spokesman for the ISYF, wrote to *The Province* (somewhat disingenuously, I thought) claiming that the demonstration was aimed at delaying the flag raising ceremony because "according to Hindu tradition, a flag should be raised before noon, with the rising sun." On the face of it, this was an outrageous statement. But Manmohan Singh was in fact dismissing India as a state run by Hindus for Hindus, and that Sikhs had no part to play in its governance. He clearly saw this as a Hindu-Sikh conflict.

"We had no intention of causing violence," he wrote. "Delaying the ceremony was our only objective. The violence was provoked by the consul-general himself by insisting on raising the flag."

In Manmohan Singh's mind, it was all about Sikhs and Hindus. It was just one of many comments that would come from Singh, whom I would get to know well, and who would invite me often to visit his eatery, the Punjab Restaurant in Vancouver. He would become famous as a spokesman with one foot planted firmly in his mouth. On one occasion, he warned "the Canadian government is playing with fire" by going after Sikh militants. The fires had been set and they were burning furiously.

On the evening of October 30, 1984, seven months after I wrote my article on the perils Indira Gandhi faced, I received a call from city desk. Gandhi had been assassinated by her two Sikh body-guards and, despite having worked a full shift that day, I rushed back to the office to collect reaction from local Sikhs and others. It was around 9 a.m. in New Delhi when Gandhi's guards had opened fire on her. Her bullet-riddled body was taken to hospital, but she was already dead. As they were surrounded by guards loyal to the slain prime minister, the two Sikh assassins, Beant Singh and Satwant Singh, threw down their guns and offered no resistance. They had done what they had to do, they told their comrades, "Now you do what you have to do."

Beant Singh was shot dead on the spot. Satwant Singh would later hang.

While many around the world mourned Gandhi's murder, among the militants, there was a sense of jubilation. They had promised they would get her and they had kept the promise. As dawn broke over Vancouver's Punjabi Market on Main Street, Sikh militants distributed sweets and danced a macabre jig of joy as Hindu merchants watched in disgust. Similar dances were taking place in the courtyard of the Ross Street *Gurudwara* and across Canada where militants showed their pleasure at the death of a woman they had called a tyrant. Among those seen at the celebration on Main Street was Satinder Pal Gill—soon to be grand chieftain of the ISYF.

While Sikhs abroad were dancing, their brethren in India were running for their lives. Another tragedy was taking place as enraged Hindu mobs began taking revenge on innocent Sikhs. An entire community was being held responsible for the actions of two men. During four days of violence, rampaging gangs torched Sikh homes, raped and murdered Sikh women, men, and children—burning some alive. Trains arriving in New Delhi carried the bodies of Sikh travellers who had been killed with impunity in the coaches. According to *The Times of India*, three-quarters of the 450 Sikh temples in Delhi were either damaged or destroyed. All the while, police did nothing to intervene. The savagery had taken hold even as the new prime minister, Rajiv Gandhi, appealed to his nation, "We should remain calm and exercise the maximum restraint. We should not let our emotions get the better of us."

Casualty figures vary, but most estimate at least three thousand Sikhs were killed and many more injured. The massacre of Sikhs in India following Indira Gandhi's death had given the BK and the ISYF even more ammunition to fuel the seeds of religious conflict.

FOUR
LOST IN TRANSLATION

By the early 1980s, global terrorism had a different face than is has today; back then Sikh militants belonged nowhere near the top of the international terror scale of organizations being watched by security forces around the world, even though, with the death of Indira Gandhi and the Delhi riots that targeted innocent Sikhs, India had been plunged into a black hole of deadly insurgency.

As the newly formed CSIS opened its doors in many Canadian cities with its headquarters in Ottawa, Armenian terrorists had rampaged through some twenty-one countries carrying out nearly one hundred terrorist attacks in as many cities across the globe. Much of the allied international security dispatches exchanged information about the movements of Armenian terror figures as one city after another–from Paris to Ottawa to Los Angeles–reported assassinations of Turkish diplomats.

Accompanying the frenzy of global terrorism was the trademark intimidation of expatriate Armenian communities in Canada and other Western countries where ordinary members, willing or not, were being told to help finance the terror. Many Armenian families in Canada lived in fear of extortion.

CSIS commenced operations on June 16, 1984, ten days after the attack on the Golden Temple. The fact that CSIS was new did not mean their agents lacked experience. Most had worked for years with the RCMP Security Service. Some were from counter-espionage, others from counter-terrorism and many were experts in surveillance and technical intrusion; breaking in and planting bugs in homes, cars and businesses as warrants permitted. CSIS agents could not carry guns nor were they empowered to arrest; CSIS was not authorized to investigate crime.

Not surprisingly, many former Mounties decided to join the new intelligence unit, believing they could return to their old jobs if CSIS work failed to pan out.

What CSIS lacked in the early days were comprehensive policies relating to retention of intercepted conversations, resources to translate conversations from several different languages, and an adequate number of surveillance specialists who could be assigned to watch the many targets CSIS would be required to monitor every day to protect national security. Physical surveillance is labour intensive.

Much of Canada's counter-terrorism effort with the inception of CSIS was directed according to activity levels of known terrorist groups operating in Canada and allied countries. While Sikhs were not a top priority for the counter-terrorism desk, there had been work done on them and community interviews had been carried out to assess the danger levels of various Sikh militant and separatist groups. There had been periods of sporadic physical surveillance as well.

Indian government diplomats in Canada were well-informed by accounts provided by their own spies who had deeply penetrated the Sikh community. Armed with this information, the diplomats demanded action from the External Affairs Department officials to curb militancy and the export of finances for terror. Canada did not appear to fully appreciate that things were really getting out of hand.

Sikhs living in Vancouver, Kamloops, Hamilton and Toronto, though, were beginning to feel arm-twisting from extremists. One after another, Sikh temples were falling into the hands of militant organizations like the BK and the ISYF (both of which were deemed terrorist groups and banned many years later by the Canadian government). They would ultimately control the podium and the microphone as well as the coffers, where generous congregations poured in thousands upon thousands of dollars in tithe money and donations.

Gaining controlling of temple treasuries was proving a bonanza for the militant groups. Accompanying this, there had been numerous incidents of assaults on those who resisted the wresting of temples from their control. Moderates were threatened and, on occasion, assaulted–sometimes quite severely. One outspoken member, Ujjal Dosanjh, was attacked by two assailants armed with an iron bar and required hospitalization. It was only good fortune that he had survived the heavy blows to his head. (He would survive his beating and go on to become premier of British Columbia and then a federal cabinet minister.)

Familiar tactics for coercing compliance was threatening dissidents with harm to their families in India if they did not cooperate. The reach of the militants was expanding on a daily basis. Community members who had felt the pain of the Golden Temple attack but did not wish to retaliate for it–and this was the majority of the diaspora–felt almost as if their outrage had been hijacked.

While the Sikh violence in Canada still appeared to be localized, other terrorist groups had already talked through the barrel of a gun in Canada. If the 1970s belonged to anti-Castro factions bombing and murdering Cuban officials in Montreal and Ottawa, then the early 1980s marked the beginning of significant terrorist activity by Armenian nationalist elements in Canada. The known entity–the squeaky wheel–was placed at the top of counter-terrorism priorities.

In 1982, two serious attacks had taken place against Turkish interests by the international terrorist group, Justice Commandos for the Armenian Genocide (JCAG). In April 1982, a Turkish commercial attaché was left paralyzed when ambushed at his apartment in Ottawa. In August of the same year, Turkish military attaché to Canada, Colonel Attila Altikat, was assassinated in his car. In the midst of all the Armenian activity, a domestic urban terrorist group known as Direct Action bombed the cruise missile production unit of Litton Industries in Toronto in October 1982 with dynamite stolen from B.C., injuring ten people.

In June 1984, an international alert was issued by the U.S. as fears grew of a terrorist attack during the Olympics being held in Los Angeles, an alarmingly easy drive straight down the coast from Vancouver. One of the most serious threats was from an Armenian group threatening to kill all Turkish athletes. There were also fears of a strike by Palestinian elements. One year later, on March 12, 1985, in the most serious incident yet in Canada,

Armenian terrorists blew up the front door of the Turkish embassy, killing a Canadian civilian guard, seriously injuring the Turkish ambassador and taking his wife and two daughters hostage. The terrorists later surrendered. These activities caused a substantial draw on CSIS's abilities to maintain a lookout on other growing and imminent dangers.

With counter-terrorism resources stretched to the limit, and a shortage of analytical staff, CSIS put two experienced former Mounties, Raymond Kobzey and Dave Ayres, in charge of keeping an eye on Sikh militants in the B.C. region. Ayres had already done some preliminary work on Sikhs while he was with the RCMP Security Service and was familiar with Khalistan consul Surjan Singh Gill and his chief, Talwinder Singh Parmar. Some surveillance had been done by CSIS in October 1984 and several Sikhs in Vancouver had been identified as being close associates of Parmar; among them were Vancouver businessman Ripudaman Singh Malik, Kamloops priest Ajaib Singh Bagri, travel agent Amarjit Singh Pawa, and Surjan Singh Gill.

Ayres knew that Parmar was surveillance-conscious because of his previous brushes with the law. Parmar knew the ropes because he had spent time in a German jail and escaped a police dragnet in India in 1981 following the incident where two police officers and a village elder died in a shootout. The RCMP had previously found out that Parmar was also aware of his Charter rights and knew he could shut the doors on the Mounties without any repercussions. Those who had lived in corrupt and abusive police states like the Punjab knew that, if you lived in Canada, you were unlikely to be taken to a police station and be beaten up. This is something the RCMP and CSIS would often run into. Many years later, RCMP Inspector Jim Cunningham would reminisce about this: "They would tell you things like, 'you can raise your voice at me if you like, but I know you can't do things to me that Indian police can. There is nothing you can do if I don't want to talk to you.'"

In December 1982, for instance, the RCMP Security Service had arrived at Parmar's residence for an interview. He flatly refused to speak with them and demanded they leave. There was nothing the RCMP could do but meekly comply.

At this stage in the development of Sikh militancy in Canada there were two logical targets csis could pick for signs of serious subversive activity. More than any other organization, it seemed that the isyf was gaining momentum with membership and fundraising. The group used Canadian temples it controlled to send men and money to a major Sikh shrine in Lahore, Pakistan, that was becoming the headquarters of the Punjab insurgency (several Sikhs from B.C., Ontario, and Alberta were killed in firefights with India and the isyf put pictures of these machinegun-toting Sikhs on a large poster calling them heroic martyrs). The isyf in Canada was an organization with multiple leaders and no real chief. Each chapter appeared to operate and organize projects independently. Chapters sprang up in Vancouver, Abbottsford, Edmonton, Winnipeg, Toronto, Hamilton, and Montreal.

Initially the group would issue membership slips to anyone for one hundred dollars, but soon realized this was folly if it was to fuel a guerrilla war from within Canada. They quickly learned that the security of other members of the organization depended on a cell structure, with only those involved in a single operation being aware of what had to be done. Several recent arrivals in Canada took top positions in the isyf. One was Lakhbir Singh Brar. A nephew of Jarnail Singh Bhindranwale, Brar had arrived in Canada as a refugee. His blood relationship with the father of Punjab militancy would make him a revered figure and he was soon named the convener of the group. Brar would say that his uncle did not die in the Golden Temple attack and was in a "high place" from where he would come back to lead Sikhs to victory.

Much later Brar would be declared a security threat to Canada and would flee to Pakistan, where he remains to this day. India has demanded that he be repatriated to face charges of terrorism along with nineteen others as a sign that Islamabad is serious about halting support for terrorism and normalizing relations in the wake of new realities imposed by the American war on terror. But now Lakhbir Singh Brar drives around in a limo in Pakistan and the country's president, General Pervez Musharraf, has flatly rejected any idea of sending him back to India.

Another key figure was Satinderpal Gill, who was seen in the small crowd of people during the dance of death performed on

Main Street in Vancouver after Indira Gandhi's assassination. Gill would later also leave for Pakistan and not return to his home in Surrey, B.C. for many years. Once in Pakistan, he served on the executive of the Panthic Committee, an umbrella organization of terrorist groups such as the Khalistan Commando Force and the Khalistan Liberation Force. Tens of thousands of dollars were ferried via couriers to Gill in Pakistan by the ISYF in Canada. Sodhi Singh Sodhi was the treasurer of the ISYF between 1984 and 1989. Thousands of dollars of other incoming funds were in the care of Brar, Bhindranwale's nephew.

Parmar's year in jail in West Germany had put him behind in the race to consolidate his leadership of Sikhs militants. Within days of returning, he was on the move, visiting temples across Canada to convince people that he was the man who could lead a violent revolt against India. Accompanied by his deputy, Ajaib Singh Bagri, Parmar headed to New York, where General Bhullar and his World Sikh Organization group were holding a convention on July 28, 1984. Bhullar, the former war hero who claimed he had been asked by Bhindranwale to leave the Golden Temple to continue the resistance, would later be barred from entering Canada. But the U.S. seemed disinterested in curbing his activities. Later, Sikhs from many areas of Canada would meet him in Blaine, Washington, the border town near Vancouver.

Parmar was turned back by U.S. Immigration, possibly because his name turned up on government watch lists. Bagri, however, was not stopped and he carried his leader's message to New York. Bagri's job was to promote Parmar as a logical leader of the rebellion against New Delhi.

In front of nearly three thousand people, Bagri delivered a passionate and inflammatory speech in which he made no attempt to restrain his rhetoric, mocking the "Hindu" leadership of India, and flamboyantly declaring that the valiant army of the BK would extract revenge for the attack on the Golden Temple.

"More than fifty thousand young men have been killed in the Punjab. I tell you one thing. They, the Hindu dogs, have already delighted their hearts. Now it is our turn!" Bagri shouted.

"They say Hindus are our brothers, many have said that, but I give you my most solemn assurance, until we kill fifty thousand Hindus, we will not rest!"

During his speech Bagri suggested a leadership comprised of Parmar and Bhullar (who had also vowed to wage war against India during his speech at the Madison Square Garden function). But the BK went home empty handed when Bhullar was confirmed the head of the World Sikh Organization.

Bagri and Parmar travelled to the Hamilton temple four more times that year. These frequent trips into Ontario continued well into 1985. In Hamilton and in Montreal, Parmar found more support than he had in British Columbia and more than half his recruits of the time lived in Ontario.

Speeches made by Bagri and Parmar were quickly seized on by the Indian government intelligence machinery in Canada. India's network of community-based sources—some of them well paid—quickly picked up these seditious sentiments. The network reported directly to the R&AW and IB agents who worked in consulates and the high commission in Ottawa. New Delhi required visas from Canadians wishing to travel to India as part of a campaign to filter out Sikh militants. Hundreds of Sikhs who had attended demonstrations or made speeches were blacklisted and told that India was out of bounds for them. This was neither an unreasonable nor an unwarranted move by the Indian government, since many of those barred undoubtedly would have carried out attacks. But it also was a pressure tactic, providing Indian agents the opportunity for face-to-face interviews with prospective travellers who were of interest to intelligence. Visa restrictions allowed Indian spies based in Toronto, Ottawa, and Vancouver vital leverage to interrogate whomever they pleased. Intense, often brutal face-to-face "interviews" were used to coerce militants into supplying information and, in some cases, turning them into informants.

By contrast, CSIS was severely handicapped in its efforts to gather information and to act on it. It was extremely conscious that its mandate was to allow legitimate dissent and desist from interfering in the fundamental rights of Canadians to freedom of speech, of religion, peaceful association, and not emulate its predecessor, the RCMP Security Service. At the same time, it had been directed, with severely limited powers and resources, to prevent and defuse threats from violent organizations that posed a serious threat of subversion inside Canada and to protect other nations from harmful activities of such groups operating here. In a bid to impose curbs–the absence of which had led to RCMP abuse–the government was overly cautious in stating the mandate of the new spy service. Many critics and observers still think the legislation that created CSIS was flawed and too restrictive, and the acute limitations of powers given to it hamper the spy agency in doing an effective job.

To this day, a great deal of confusion exists within the general public, and even among journalists, about the major difference between CSIS and its Parliamentary mandate, and the RCMP. CSIS was specifically created to keep the government of Canada informed of any threats to national security and has no power to investigate a crime under the Criminal Code of Canada. CSIS is strictly an intelligence-gathering agency, not a crime-fighting law enforcement agency. Further, CSIS cannot and does not obtain warrants to intercept criminal activity, nor can conversations obtained by this agency be used in court because of the fundamentally different route electronic intercept authorization is obtained (to date no court in Canada has allowed its use and there is likely to be a serious charter challenge if such conversations are allowed to be entered as evidence).

When CSIS has legitimate cause to suspect significant subversive activity, it has to convince a federal court judge to authorize a wiretap or other means of electronic intercepts of the conversations of a group or an individual. It is clear to federal judges when these warrants are issued under the CSIS Act that they are for the purpose of gathering intelligence and not criminal information. The threshold for obtaining warrants to intercept conversations for the purpose of gathering intelligence for national security is much lower than what the RCMP are required to do to obtain a similar wiretap authorization. RCMP and police warrants are granted for the specific purpose of obtaining information that could be used in a court of law to prosecute a crime or to prevent a crime. Police wiretaps legally obtained are handled in a different manner and police are careful to maintain continuity of their evidence. Such wiretap authorizations are issued for short periods of time. Law enforcement agencies are also mandated to inform targets that they had been subjected to electronic intercepts once the warrant duration date has expired. This is not a requirement for CSIS, which does not have to tell a target that intercepts had been authorized. RCMP warrants enable the collection of evidence useable in a court of law as provided by the Criminal Code, which the police–not CSIS–enforce.

This important difference in the activities of the Mounties and CSIS was emphasized time and again by those charged with the transition from the RCMP Security Service to the civilian agency. Archie Barr, the director of CSIS security policy development unit in Ottawa issued a memorandum to regional offices to make CSIS's Parliamentary mandate absolutely clear on April 5, 1984, three months before the inauguration of the security service. The memo deals with recording facilities and the handling of intercepted communications:

"Discussion on the above subject has resulted in the following policy decision. As the CSIS Act contains no requirement for the collection of by the service of information for evidentiary purposes, no such capacity will be provided for within CSIS facilities."

In a nutshell, Barr told the agents: you collect intelligence, not evidence. You are not cops, you are spies.

In the fall of 1984, Barr applied for a federal warrant to intercept the communications of BK terrorist Parmar. It was withdrawn and not filed again until March 1985. But it is instructive. It provides a damning indictment of Parmar's inflammatory oratory and his propensity for violence to carry out his revolutionary plans. In his affidavit filed before a federal court judge to obtain permission to tap Parmar's phone, Barr relayed the following information to the Federal Court of Canada:

"Talwinder Singh Parmar, a naturalized Canadian citizen, is a Sikh extremist and leader of the Babbar Khalsa. The Babbar Khalsa is a Sikh terrorist group now established in Canada, Parmar founded the Babbar Khalsa in India during a visit there in 1981. Since its inception, Babbar Khalsa has claimed responsibility for more than forty assassinations of moderate Sikhs and other persons in the Punjab, India, opposed to the Khalistan movement. The Babbar

Khalsa is a militant offshoot of the Khalistan Liberation Movement (KLM). The KLM is an autonomous Sikh organization whose aim, through violent means, is the creation of an independent state in the Punjab, to be known as the Republic of Khalistan. Babbar Khalsa is fanatically dedicated to the Khalistan concept. The Babbar Khalsa in Canada consists of approximately twenty members, Parmar is their leader. This Canadian group has penned its name to threatening letters to the late Indian Prime Minister Indira Gandhi and other high officials in India. On June 06, 1984, Babbar Khalsa threatened to kidnap or kill the Indian Consul General in Vancouver. This telephone threat was also directed at members of the Consul's family.

"Parmar has openly threatened and warned the Indian government, 'that they will pay a price for attacking the temple.'" (This was borrowed by CSIS from my article written upon Parmar's return from West Germany.)

Barr listed a litany of violent speeches made by Parmar in temples in Calgary to Toronto. In Calgary he told a Sikh congregation to "unite, fight and kill" to avenge the Golden Temple attack.

Later, in Toronto on July 21, 1984, Parmar addressed Sikh congregations in several locations, urging violence, Barr's affidavit said. He is reported to have said, "Sikhs will kill fifty thousand Hindus; Sikhs will harass Hindus, Indian embassies, high commissions, and consulate personnel; Sikhs will blow up embassies; and Sikhs will not sit back, but will take revenge on the Hindu government (in India)."

"Then again, in a press conference, on August 31, 1984, Parmar described himself as, 'India's most wanted rebel.' He commented that his goal, 'is to achieve a Sovereign State. Any Sikh who doesn't ask for a Sovereign State is a traitor.'

"Babbar Khalsa is based in Vancouver but does not maintain a formal headquarters. Parmar's residence (in) Burnaby, British Columbia, where he lives with his family, is used for meetings of Babbar Khalsa, and is the focal point of Babbar Khalsa activities."

Another key point Barr made was the cell structure of Parmar's group, making introduction of a human source inside the BK highly unlikely:

"The Babbar Khalsa is a small, tight-knit, and highly secretive group. In addition to religion, members are tied together by bonds of family and long standing friendships often including common origins in a particular community in the Punjab. The introduction of a human source into such a group is thus virtually impossible."

And therein lay the major weakness: CSIS had no ability to penetrate the BK and every intelligence operative will tell you that the alternative, electronic monitoring has inherent flaws because it lacks the potency of a human source, in both interpretation and intent of a target's words or activities.

On March 14, 1985, CSIS again applied to the Federal Court of Canada under the CSIS Act to intercept the telecommunications of Parmar. By March 27, every call in and out of Parmar's home would be intercepted directly at telephone company headquarters. They were directed into the communications intercepts room at CSIS regional headquarters in Vancouver. In CSIS jargon, Parmar would now be "talking in the presence of the source", or a telephone bug. Intelligence agencies use the term "talking in the presence of a reliable source" or "talking in the presence of a source" in their transcripts of intercepts to confuse outsiders who may stumble onto lost or stolen intercepts. It's designed to camouflage the nature of the source. Therefore, both a human source and a technical source, like a bug planted in a telephone, home, or car, would be identified as a "source." Even media articles are a "source." Deception is the key to the spy trade. But this jargon would mislead a major television news station in Canada that would go to town with the incorrect story that CSIS had a mole within BK.

Betty Doak, a CSIS transcriber, would listen to the tape reels the day after they were recorded. She had been instructed by agents Kobzey and Ayres to listen for certain specifics: any travel plans Parmar might make, overseas contacts, and anything dealing with money (specifically, sending money to India and the methods of sending it). Kobzey also told her to listen for Parmar's contacts: Khalistani consul Surjan Singh Gill, Kamloops militant Ajaib Singh Bagri, Vancouver businessman Ripudaman Singh Malik, fundamentalist Vancouver Sikh Hardial Singh Johal, and Babbar Khalsa members Gurmit Singh Gill from Kamloops, among others.

Parmar's conversations were invariably in Punjabi, but CSIS in Vancouver appeared to be having trouble hiring a Punjabi-language translator; this despite the fact that B.C. at that time had a Punjabi population of sixty thousand. Doak could therefore only brief Kobzey and Ayres about English language conversations that often came from Parmar's other family members, particularly his children. Arrangements were made to send tapes to the Ottawa CSIS headquarters where a translator was available to transcribe from Punjabi. But there was soon a backlog of tapes in Ottawa and Vancouver was advised not to send any more. While eighty-three tapes had been sent to Ottawa, only thirty-one from between March 27 and April 9, 1985 had been translated. The rest sat in Ottawa for several months.

Finally the Vancouver office hired its own translator on June 6, 1985. By that time there was a backlog of 133 tapes. By June 21, the newly hired translator had transcribed tapes recorded between May 21 and June 20. Kobzey, CSIS's key investigator of Sikh extremism, had left for a vacation on June 7; one day after the Vancouver Punjabi translator was hired. He would not return until June 23, 1985. More than eighty tapes recorded in April and May were not even translated or listened to until September of that year. Parmar may have been security conscious, but given the state of affairs, it appears he could have plotted openly over the phone to bring down the Parliament Buildings in Ottawa and his chances of being caught in time were slim. Because of the lack of timely transcription of taped conversations, any early warning, if available, would not have been heard. There is also no doubt, that anyone listening carefully to what was being said would have decided there was something suspicious going on. To complicate things further, confusion reigned supreme among the spies about policies pertaining to the retention of taped conversations. Generally, most spies thought that tapes had to be erased within ten days of having been listened to by a transcriber as was the rule from RCMP directives. No one at CSIS, it seemed, was aware of what exactly they were supposed to do with tapes. They had been told that they were spies, not cops, and they collected intelligence, not evidence. As a result, most of the tapes would be erased after some of the suspicious conversations of Parmar were transcribed, often paraphrased. Only some conversations were transcribed verbatim. This crucial oversight would prove both embarrassing and extremely damaging later on.

Now as Gandhi's son Rajiv took office in India and a still-new CSIS tried to listen to Punjabi language conversations with an English-speaking transcriber, Sikh militants vowed they would not be satisfied by just Indira Gandhi's death. They wanted the blood of the whole dynasty. In the months following her death, Parmar's deputy BK leader, Bagri, would make several speeches where he would proclaim, "Your mother is dead Rajiv! Now it is your turn."

Parmar's phone was humming with calls. His children would speak in English, and sometimes their conversations would provide clues to the activities of their father or visitors from out of town. Sometimes his children would call his contacts for the purpose of passing along Parmar's messages or instructions.

Many conversations were routine in nature and aroused no suspicions.

On April 8, 1985, however, at approximately 2 p.m. CSIS tapes picked up a call from Jang Singh, a Sikh from Germany. Singh was about to make Parmar a deadly proposition. It was known among militant leaders that Rajiv Gandhi had scheduled a visit to the United States in June of 1985. The two talked in Punjabi, but CSIS translated the call:

Jang Singh: Soljer Singh came here for a visit to Germany. I have heard that the woman's son (Rajiv Gandhi, Indira's son) is coming on the sixth of June. I am presenting all my...on the ninth of April...now if you can do something–
Parmar: Keep quiet. Everything will be taken care of.
Jang Singh: Well, he is arriving, and how do I contact you...and I...somehow or other you have to–
Parmar: I said I understand. Now shut up, I shall get everything done.
Jang Singh: I am willing to serve in any way.
Parmar: Don't require this kind of service, but things will somehow work out.
Jang Singh: Something should be done...I beg you from all my family, he should not be allowed to go back...those in India, we cannot hope that they will do anything.

Parmar: No they cannot do anything.

Jang Singh:…tried in India but couldn't do anything.

Parmar: Well, don't talk on the phone here. We shall see.

Jang Singh: I beg you send somebody or something, there are three of us here, one of us can have the killer number.

Parmar: Do you have a passport? Can you move around easily?

Jang Singh: Yes, sir, there is no problem. I can come and go freely.

Parmar: Good, then maybe you'll be able to do something.

Jang Singh: Give me this chance to serve, if you can do this, because I don't think I can have any success in India. The one I had thought about has already been taken by God (Indira Gandhi)…this is the only thing that you are lacking.

Parmar: OK, OK, don't worry. Everything will be alright. Find out his complete plan (Gandhi's travel plans).

Jang Singh: But you tell me, who and when and where I have to meet somebody for instructions–

Parmar: I said keep quiet. If somebody wants to meet with you, they, they will find you.

Jang Singh: I am very happy to have talked to you.

That was the first sign something sinister was stirring during Rajiv Gandhi's visit, which was a concern to the U.S. Secret Service, the FBI, the RCMP, and CSIS. But at CSIS, no one was listening to this conversation live.

It wasn't only Sikh militants in West Germany and in Vancouver hatching assassination plots against Rajiv Gandhi. On November 16, 1984, according to intelligence reports, four Sikhs who had been militantly opposed to Indira Gandhi turned up for training at Frank Camper's mercenary and combat training school in, of all places, Dolomite, Alabama.

The Sikhs had a surprising request. According to testimony, they wanted to be trained in assassination and urban combat techniques, as well as chemical warfare and explosives instructions and training. One of the men was identified as Lal Singh.

Camper was a U.S. army veteran who had served in Vietnam. His training had included reconnaissance and he was expert who had worked with U.S. military intelligence and as an expert for the FBI.

As the training progressed, Camper took pictures of the Sikhs and sent them to an FBI agent identified as "Fox."

According to Camper, at the request of the FBI, he set up a meeting with the Sikhs at the Sheraton Center Hotel in New York on December 15, 1984. A key leader of the Dashmesh Regiment would turn up at this meeting with Lal Singh. The leader's name was Gurpartap Singh Birk. Later, Camper would email me with some amazing details of clandestine meetings he would hold with the Sikhs who, Camper claimed, had expressed an interest in, among other acts of terrorism, contaminating water supplies, creating mass panic in Indian movie houses, destroying nuclear power plants, and assassinating Indian government officials. Another meeting with Lal Singh was held in front of an FBI agent in a Hilton Hotel in New York, Camper said.

The meeting with Birk, Lal, and another Sikh was recorded. The undercover FBI agent present with Camper asked Birk if there was not a substantial risk of killing innocent Sikhs, for instance, if they went ahead with a plot to contaminate food supplies in India. Birk's response floored him.

"At this stage of the game I'm not really concerned with the number of lives lost—and even if a part of the Sikhs go with it that is the price of our revolution," said Birk.

Simultaneously, a plot to murder Indian minister Bhajan Lal was discovered by an undercover FBI team. The minister was to be killed during a public appearance he was to make in New Orleans prior to his planned eye surgery. The FBI pounced on four Sikhs, including Birk, on May 4, 1985. Lal Singh and Amand Singh, two members of the plot, escaped the FBI dragnet.

The FBI and the U.S. Secret Service (in charge of protecting American and visiting world leaders) were concerned about the two who got away and, as part of their hunt, they would look for the pair in areas of large Sikh concentrations: particularly in Vancouver, where at least one of the Dashmesh Regiment chieftains was known to have connections. U.S. law enforcement agents would subsequently visit both Parmar and his right-hand man, Surjan Singh Gill, at their homes in the Vancouver suburb of Burnaby. Both would deny knowledge of the two men who had escaped or any link with the conspirators in New Orleans. Gill would tell me around that time he had been visited. He said he had also been shown pictures of some suspects who he could not identify.

It would take me many years to confirm the FBI and U.S. Secret Service suspicions that Lal Singh and Amand Singh had come to B.C. to hide out. Amand, I discovered, had a sister in Burnaby near Vancouver. Lal assumed the alias of Manjit Singh and his hide-out was in a Vancouver–area farm owned by a radical Sikh. Lal Singh would later flee to Pakistan. But his presence in B.C. following his escape would raise some tantalizing possibilities in my investigation of Sikh militancy and some horrid events in the months to come.

The CSIS warrant application in Spring 1985 to intercept Parmar's conversations had been made just days after the FBI reported to allied agencies they had made arrests and newspaper stories sprang up about mercenary camps training Sikhs. It seemed to re-focus CSIS on the dangers of Sikh militancy and there was also a hint that some members of the BK in Canada knew some members of the Dashmesh Regiment in New York as well as New Orleans. It was also significant that on May 15, CSIS began tracking Parmar wherever he went. However, it still seemed that the focus of CSIS concern was the Rajiv Gandhi's visit to the U.S. There was also the possibility of a Sikh strike in Canada on Indian government targets and new threat assessments done by CSIS through community interviews showed the risk of an attack on Air India flying out of Canada. Nevertheless, neither CSIS nor the RCMP had yet seen any specific indications of a planned attack inside Canada.

On May 17, 1985, the High Commission of India presented a diplomatic note to the Department of External Affairs regarding the threat to Indian diplomatic missions and Air India aircraft by extremist elements. What prompted that warning was unclear and, to be fair, four RCMP officers were guarding Indian aircraft departing Toronto. One officer was stationed at the entrance to the doorway of departing airplanes and two police cruisers sat under the wings of the aircraft. In those days, hijackings were considered the main threat to aircraft, not suitcase bombs. India requested explosive-sniffing dogs to check baggage on Air India planes. Canada, seeing no need for that precaution, declined to provide them. In any case, no one had mentioned the possibility of specific targeting of Indian aircraft from Canada.

On May 6, 1985, CSIS had issued a threat assessment stating that Sikh extremist activities against the government of India would increase sharply coinciding with the first anniversary of the Golden Temple attack during June 1985 and the Gandhi visit to the U.S. during the same month. Also on May 6, 1985, a senior interdepartmental working group, or a task force, was set up in Ottawa composed of representatives from the Solicitor General's office, the RCMP, CSIS, and the Department of External Affairs to address and monitor levels of protection for Indian installations in relation to the anniversary and the Gandhi visit. On May 28, CSIS again issued a warning of a high potential for serious violence to coincide with the coming anniversary. CSIS regions were instructed to give the matter high priority. Despite its own warning of a higher risk of trouble, CSIS was still not listening live or translating Parmar's conversations in a timely manner to see if he was saying something that could point to imminent action. On June 6, at the request of the RCMP, CSIS again issued a high-threat assessment to Indian government interests, including Air India.

These assessments may have been based on rumours circulating within the community, which I had picked up as well; rumours that "something big" was going to happen. But no one I talked to knew what or how big "it" would be. Pushpinder Singh, a Sikh refugee from India living in Vancouver, reportedly told several people at a gathering at a friend's Vancouver home to "wait for two weeks and see what happens." There was also confirmation that at a Hamilton temple, several members had put out warnings that it was "not a good idea" to fly Air India. At the Ross Street Sikh Temple, hard-liners had been saying for days that Sikhs should not fly Air India, not only because it was deemed risky, but because the company's profits made its way to the government, thus contributing to the government's "war of genocide" against the Sikhs.

On June 4, 1985, CSIS agents were continuing their surveillance of Parmar and they were tailing him everywhere. On that day they were parked outside Parmar's home when former Khalistan consul and now BK member Surjan Singh Gill drove up. Two men emerged from inside Parmar's home and got into the car driven by Gill. CSIS agents Larry Lowe and Lynn McAdams clearly identified Parmar and at first mistakenly believed that the younger man with him was his son Jaswinder. Later it would become clear that the young man was not in fact Parmar's son. The man's identity never became clear and is now known only as Mr. X.

CSIS agents followed the car driven by Gill to the Horseshoe Bay ferry terminal. Here one can board a ferry to Vancouver Island. Agents observed that Gill dropped Parmar and Mr. X at the terminal. Gill, who had given them a ride to the ferry, then drove to his home in Burnaby. Gill had not accompanied his boss on this trip. Parmar and Mr. X boarded the ferry as foot passengers.

The agents decided to continue following Parmar and Mr. X on to the ferry and they boarded the vessel with their unmarked surveillance car. (CSIS has not said that there was more than one car following the two men. Generally physical surveillance requires more than one vehicle. Information I received later indicated more than one car and two agents were involved in the surveillance.)

On board the ferry, on the passenger deck level, agents were so close to Parmar they could see what telephone numbers he was dialling using the call box aboard the vessel. When the ferry docked at the Nanaimo terminal on Vancouver Island, another car picked up Parmar and Mr. X and dropped them off at a home in Duncan. Later that day, CSIS agents Lowe and McAdams, who were waiting outside the Duncan home, observed Parmar and Mr. X as they got into another vehicle with a bearded, turbaned man. This vehicle had the licence plate "I-Reyat." CSIS agents followed this car for several miles on a highway leading out of the city of Duncan. The vehicle then turned on to a side road and parked. CSIS agents parked some distance away so as not to be seen. Parmar and the car's driver—later identified as Duncan mechanic and fanatical Sikh Inderjit Singh Reyat—exited the car and walked into the woods. Mr. X remained near the car, apparently as a lookout.

Within minutes of Parmar and Reyat walking into the woods, the two agents who had remained seated in their vehicles heard a thundering boom. Lowe exited the vehicle and made a quick dash into the woods to see if he could spot something, but found nothing. He quickly got back into his car and began following the "I-Reyat" vehicle again. CSIS agents tailed the car to the ferry terminal and noticed that Parmar alone boarded the ferry for the ride back to Vancouver. Mr. X, the man who had come along with Parmar from Vancouver, was staying behind in Duncan with Reyat.

CSIS would later say that the following day, June 5, 1985, they informed Duncan RCMP that while carrying out surveillance of Parmar they had heard what appeared to be a gun going off in woods near Duncan.

RCMP Inspector Doug Henderson, whom I had known for years, confirmed the call from CSIS agent Raymond Kobzey. At that time Henderson was a corporal in the RCMP's Duncan detachment.

Henderson, however, says he was left with the distinct impression that CSIS did not want the RCMP to intervene and–in the process–blow their surveillance of Parmar. Henderson told me he confirmed for Kobzey that the vehicle with the plate number "I-Reyat" belonged to Inderjit Singh Reyat and that police records showed he owned a registered firearm.

Henderson said he filed an "incident report" with his own office about the fact that CSIS had surveillance on Parmar and that agents had heard a loud boom in the woods. However, since RCMP had not been asked to investigate further, the Mounties took no action to find out what made the booming sound. The assumption a gun had gone off would remain the mistaken belief of both organizations for the next few days. That would turn out to be a big mistake. I would learn later that some CSIS agents had stayed in Duncan overnight in a bid to further identify Reyat who they had not seen before. One agent hid herself in a ditch outside Reyat's home but was soon called off by CSIS headquarters under two working assumptions. One was that the young man with Parmar was his son, Jaswinder and he was well-known to CSIS. The second assumption was that agent Lowe was an experienced hunter and could not have made a mistake about the sound heard in the bush being a gun. This assumption was further reinforced by information from Henderson that Reyat did own a legal firearm. CSIS mistakenly concluded that like other Sikhs (those who carried out firearms training in the U.S. mercenary camp in Alabama) Parmar was shown how to shoot a weapon by Reyat.

Meanwhile, CSIS surveillance of Parmar continued until June 16, 1985.

On June 12, Vancouver RCMP and members of the U.S. Secret Service visited Parmar and Surjan Singh Gill. According to the RCMP, the visit had a two-fold purpose. The first was to ask Parmar and Gill what their intentions were relating to Rajiv Gandhi's visit to the United States. The second was to pre-empt any possible threats by the Parmar group on the life of Gandhi by sending a message to both Parmar and Gill that the RCMP and the U.S. Secret Service were aware of a plot by some extremists to kill Gandhi and that authorities were reacting to it. Despite this visit, no questions were directed at Parmar about the trip he had made with Reyat on June 4, 1985, where the loud sound had been heard. It appeared to have been forgotten. Such a query would have defused a plot in progress. The visit by RCMP and the U.S. Secret Service had not disrupted Parmar's planning, apparently, in any meaningful way. Parmar had not been disturbed by talk of a hit on Gandhi for a simple reason, I believe: he was not planning a hit on Gandhi. He had much bigger plans. The visit, however, may have backfired in at least one sense: Parmar was behaving with more discretion on the phone.

Parmar's conversations became nuanced and obscured in coded references. Of greater significance, perhaps, was that a huge time lag existed between the time the conversations were recorded and when they were transcribed by CSIS. Nevertheless, had the conversations been transcribed and analyzed in a timely fashion it is possible a very reliable roadmap of Parmar's activities could have been created, and perhaps a plot could have been intercepted and foiled. And more than anything, it seemed the analysis being done at CSIS was myopic, the most urgent priority being the potential for violence surrounding the visit to the United States by Rajiv Gandhi.

Sikh militants had dubbed the month of the raid on the Golden Temple "Black June." There was apprehension something would happen on or around the anniversary, June 6, 1985, but that week passed without trouble. When Rajiv Gandhi's trip to Washington, D.C., also ended uneventfully, CSIS and the RCMP seemed to breathe a sigh of relief. The danger appeared to have passed. CSIS headquarters cancelled the need for daily situational reports from regions and the physical surveillance of Parmar stopped on June 16. Only an observation post remained in operation, staffed only for the purpose of taking pictures of people who arrived at his home and those who left. Car license plates were recorded for identification of visitors. Surveillance was easing up. Concern over a major terrorist attack among law enforcement and intelligence agencies was diminishing.

All seemed well, at least on the surface. But underneath, dark currents were slowly swirling, currents that would end in tragedy.

FIVE
THE TERROR AND
THE TRAGEDY:
June 1985

Toronto, June 22, 5:45 p.m. (EDT)

Air India co-Pilot Captain Satwinder Singh Bhinder could be for-
given if he felt he was in a war zone as his plane powered-up on
the tarmac of Lester B. Pearson International Airport. While the
scene was not quite like Ben Gurion International Airport in Tel
Aviv, the most secure airport in the world, Bhinder, sitting in his
perch in the cockpit of the Boeing 747 aircraft sixty-three feet
above the ground, had a perfect view of the two RCMP cruisers
manned by four heavily-armed Mounties idling below the wings
of his aircraft. On his way to the plane, the former military trans-
port pilot had passed Air India security man John D'Souza and a
burly Mountie posted at the entry gate for a check of embarking
passengers.

Just seventeen days earlier, a memo from Canada's security
service to the RCMP had detailed an extraordinarily high threat
assessment for Air India aircraft.

Bhinder had been briefed, but—despite the presence of armed
personnel—seemed disinclined to worry. He and flight commander
Captain Hanse Singh Narendra conferred on pre-takeoff checks, just
as they would on any other flight on any other day. The high profile security measures had been designed as much to reassure a
nervous flying public, but for a few it had had the opposite effect.
There had been a few cancellations already.

But most passengers arrived as they would on any other day. In a few minutes, hundreds of excited passengers would board Air India Flight 182–a Boeing 747 christened *Kanishka*–for their flight to India.

PASSAGES TO INDIA
Vancouver, June 22, 7:00 a.m. (PDT)

Passengers were making their way to connect with aircraft flying to Toronto where they would ultimately link up with Air India Flight 182, but Balbir Singh Hera's son was not among them. Vancouver travel agent Amarjit Singh Pawa, who booked tickets for Talwinder Singh Parmar, had made sure of that.

Hera, who runs a security business in Vancouver, was Pawa's friend. Three days before his son was to depart on Air India 182, Pawa called and asked him to come into the offices of Friendly Travels in east Vancouver. When Hera arrived, the travel agent said, "I have changed your son's flight. He is now flying Japan Airlines instead of Air India."

Hera was surprised. "Why make the change?"

"Well, you know how there is trouble between Hindus and Sikhs these days and it is not a good idea to fly with Air India," said Pawa, offering no further explanations for the mysterious change in travel plans for his friend's son.

Hera had no idea that in a few days he would know why Pawa had cancelled his son's flight. The young man headed out to the airport on the same day as other travellers who were to connect with Air India 182, but he headed west over the Pacific to Tokyo and then Delhi via Japan Airlines.

But there was no one to warn troubled widow Sukhwinder Uppal and her two small children. She and her friend Pradeep Sidhu had gone to the Ross Street Sikh Temple prior to making their way to Vancouver Airport. Morning prayers were just ending as the four entered the main prayer hall. They walked towards the priest, seated cross-legged on the red carpet in front of the small podium. They sat down after bowing in front of the *Guru Granth Sahib*, the

Sikh holy book. Her covered head bowed, Sukhwinder asked the priest for a *hukam nama* (a divine order) for her trip to India.

The *Guru Grant Sahib* is given the reverence that would be accorded a living guru. At night, the holy book is folded in elaborately decorated cloth and carried atop the priest's head accompanied by a small procession to be laid to rest delicately on a bed resembling a throne.

Absolute respect and dignity are necessary in the monotheistic faith in bringing the *Guru Granth Sahib* back to the podium for the morning prayers, which begin at 4 a.m. The *Granthi* (priest) first bathes to cleanse himself. Then, accompanied by several people, he brings the decorated holy book downstairs, once again carrying it atop his head. With considerable solemnity the holy book is placed on the podium and a random page is opened. The writs on that page become the daily *hukam nama*, or the divine guidance for the day for the Sikh faithful. A special *hukam nama* can be obtained by people undertaking a venture, or travel, or some mission where divine guidance is required. A smile played beneath the Granthi's salt-and-pepper beard as he looked at Sukhwinder's young children. He had offered many such prayers in his years of service to the faithful. With a rhythmic voice, he read out the passage. It was about life and death.

"Man does not decide who lives on this earth and who goes away. The decision of life and death is made by God."

As Sukhwinder sat with her head bowed, contemplating the holy pronouncement, her friend Pradeep looked up sharply at the mention of death. The priest's words had made her heart skip a beat. She knew the hardship the thirty-seven-year-old widow had endured. A trail of personal disasters had shadowed her for years. The verse was a reminder to both women that we are all creatures of destiny.

The two women and the children stood up and bowed, retreating from the podium. As they walked out of the temple towards their car, Pradeep's thoughts were still on the *hukam nama*. The mention of death had taken her back to the day in May 1975, when Sukhwinder, two-months pregnant, was left a widow by a car accident. The crash was a double blow for her tight-knit family. It had claimed the life of her husband Harbhajan. It had also killed Sukhwinder's brother Dilbar Sidhu. With her daughter Parminder just learning to walk and the baby on the way, she was devastated. The young widow did not smile again until the December day when she gave birth to her son, Kuldip.

Being a widow in the community is not an easy role. She lived in the basement of her father's house in South Vancouver. She got a job with a dry-cleaning business and got on with the task of raising her two children. She led a quiet, earnest life, relying on her faith in God to keep her going. Once in a while, memories of her husband's death overwhelmed her. She would retreat into a corner and cry silently into the night. Her dream now was to take her children to the Punjab, to her birthplace, a reminder of their ancestry.

As the dream took shape, she contacted Pradeep, a travel agent with Gaba Travels in Vancouver, who had done everything she could to make the trip easier for the widow, who did not speak English well. She had initially booked Sukhwinder and her two children on an Air India flight leaving from Toronto on June 29. But Sukhwinder wanted to go a week earlier and had visited the children's principal at Walter Moberly Elementary School, close to their home, to ask permission for them to leave before the start of the summer holidays. It took several phone calls and Pradeep's influence as a travel agent to get the three seats on Air India Flight 182, which was nearly full. A day before they were to depart, Pradeep also went to the Indian consulate to pick up their visas.

As she drove them to the airport through the heavy traffic on Marine Drive in Vancouver after the visit to the temple, Pradeep still could not shake off the thoughts about the *hukam nama*. Death is not something you want to hear about when you're about to make a long trip by aircraft. Had Sukhwinder received a message of consolation for her past sorrows from the divine book? Could it be a reference to the miscarriage the widow's sister-in-law had suffered the previous week after six months of pregnancy? Or was it a warning of future disaster? Still, Pradeep managed a chuckle as she glanced into her rear-view mirror at the children sitting in the back seat of her car. Her thoughts shifted to the previous night, when a friend had dropped by the Uppal's home. Sukhwinder's workmate had brought gifts for the trip: a sari, a watch, and a box of cookies. Nine-year-old Kuldip beat his sister to the watch, putting it on before Parminder could even move.

Later, after Pradeep had gone, Parminder gave Kuldip a dirty look, turned to her mother and demanded, "Well, what did your friend bring for me?"

"She brought you this sari," Sukhwinder said, smiling, showing her the garment.

"She should know I don't wear saris. I'm too young for that," Parminder replied, looking woefully at the smug Kuldip, who was pompously checking the time as if he had an important appointment.

At the airport, Pradeep helped her friend check in the baggage and then went over to another family, which was also boarding the connecting flight, Air Canada Flight 136 to Toronto. She asked them to help her friend get around the busy airport at Toronto. The children were jumping up and down with excitement over the prospect of their summer holiday in India. But Sukhwinder was sad as she said goodbye to her seventy-year-old father, Mehnga Singh. She hugged Pradeep and cried on her shoulder.

"Will you come and pick us up at the airport when we return?" Parminder asked her. "Should we phone you to let you know when we are coming back?"

Pradeep mopped the tears from her friend's eyes and managed a smile for Parminder.

"No darling, I already know when you are coming back," she replied.

Then the three, mother and children, walked through the departure gate and disappeared. There could be no escape now from their date with destiny. The guru had already made a decision, and karma can't be altered.

Eddie Madon was nine-years-old and it was time for the youngster to go through the mandatory ceremony of initiation into his parents' Zoroastrian faith. The initiation is known as *navjote*. A child can be initiated any time between the ages of seven and fifteen. It is an elaborate ceremony in front of priests and a child is given a sacred shirt and sacred thread. The child also has to recite a solemn oath to do good deeds in this life. It is somewhat akin to "confirmation" in Christianity.

Since there were preparations to make for the ceremony, Eddie, his sister Natasha and mom Perviz Madon had flown to India in May 1985. Sam Madon, a marine college instructor from Vancouver could not get early leave from his job and had promised to be with his family in Bombay on June 24, in time for his forty-second birthday. So Madon had gone to the airport in May to see his wife and children off on their flight. With him was Air India Vancouver office manager Jehangir Parakh. At the airport, Madon had clung to Natasha, five, who was crying because her dad was not flying with her.

Parakh comforted the little girl. He brushed his hand through Natasha's hair and said: "Don't cry darling, Daddy will be with you soon."

And now on June 22, 1985, Sam Madon had turned up at Vancouver Airport to take a connecting Air Canada flight to Toronto, with his final passage to India to be made through Air India Flight 182. He had implored his friend Parakh to join him on the trip and Parakh toyed with the idea for some time. At one point he even called Toronto to tell the boss he might take a few days off to visit Bombay and received clearance. But there was business to attend to in Vancouver and promotional presentations to make on Vancouver Island to promote tourism to India. Parakh told his friend he would have to go by himself. Madon boarded the Air Canada flight out of Vancouver with the Uppal family. Less than twenty-four hours later, Perviz would receive a phone call from family members in England to tell her that her husband wouldn't be able to keep his promise to her.

Vancouver Airport, June 22, 7:30 a.m. (PDT)

Ragbhir Grewal scanned the bustling international departures area, already crowded on this early summer morning, looking for his brother-in-law. But Daljit Grewal was no where to be seen. Ragbhir knew Daljit, a Surrey sawmill worker, had mixed feelings about his trip. On one hand, he was happy to be returning to his home village near the city of Ludhiana in Punjab State. But the excitement was tempered by the reason for the journey; his seventy-year-old mother was dying and wanted to see him one last time.

Ragbhir continued to survey the area and finally, his eyes glimpsed a familiar face. But it wasn't Daljit. It was fundamentalist Sikh Hardial Singh Johal who was there, moving quickly, appearing to be looking for someone. Ragbhir greeted Johal politely and asked what he was doing at the airport. Johal said he was there to see someone. What was Ragbhir doing there? Ragbhir told Johal about Daljit's trip. Johal moved off, leaving Ragbhir by himself. He didn't have to wait long. Daljit finally arrived, surrounded by his wife and children, luggage bulging with gifts for relatives in India: clothes, a stereo cassette, and other presents. Daljit explained he had slept in.

As they moved towards the check-in counter, Johal reappeared and rounded on Daljit. The two men talked for a few minutes. Then Johal thrust an envelope, ostensibly containing a letter for Johal's mother, in Daljit's pocket. Daljit didn't know it then, and Raghbir had no reason to suspect anything sinister in Johal's presence at the airport, but for Johal this accidental run-in with someone who had recognized him was a serious problem. Who wants to be seen at the scene of a crime? That's why Johal gave Daljit the letter he probably had written after going to another part of the terminal. It would give him a tenuous alibi if he was ever questioned; a plausible reason for his presence at the airport.

But it appears Johal had said something that scared Daljit. Whether it was because of what Johal had said or whether it was just intuition, he stopped at the insurance counter and purchased $400,000 flight insurance. His wife told me she was shocked when he handed the insurance copy to her. "You might need it for the children's education," he quipped. Later, she would tell me she was surprised her husband bought the life-insurance policy just as he was about leave.

As he said his goodbyes, Daljit Grewal turned to his children. His ten-year-old daughter, Provijod, hugged him tight.

"Look, you must study hard," he told her, repeating the advice he'd given her twelve-year-old brother, Mundip.

"I'll come back and see how well my son is doing at school."

Daljit Singh Grewal waved as he walked into the boarding

lounge and passed through the security check for passengers, promising his wife he would bring back films of family members in the Punjab shot with his brand new movie camera. Then he went to board his aircraft, bearing the message for Johal's mother that would never be delivered.

Mumbai, India, June 22, 9:30 p.m. (IST)

On the other side of the world, it was a hot, noisy evening in Mumbai and Amarjit Kaur Bhinder was grateful that she had finally managed to put her children to sleep. Her daughter, eleven-year-old Jasleen, and son Ashamdip, eight, were now slumbering despite the heat and nightly noises of the sprawling city. As usual, Ashamdip had not been able to stop talking about his father, Satwinder. He wanted to be a pilot, just like Daddy, and had sworn that one day he would be his father's co-pilot. The child's promise always made Amarjit smile. Certainly, Satwinder Singh Bhinder was a hero to his son.

Amarjit had fallen head-over-heels in love with Bhinder while working on her master's in political science at Punjab University in Chandigarh. Bhinder, a dashing young military pilot, was the pride of his family and especially of his youngest sister, with whom Amarjit had gone to college. Bhinder had been flying since he was recruited as a pilot-officer by the Indian Air Force at age nineteen in March, 1963. They had plucked him right out of college while he was still completing his bachelor of science degree.

As a young military wife, Amarjit Kaur had worried herself sick. The 1971 Indo-Pakistan war had begun barely a year after the couple had married in Karnal, a colorful town filled with colleges and universities in Haryana State, midway between the garden city of Chandigarh and New Delhi. Both she and Satwinder had grown up there and Bhinder's father was a wealthy landlord in the city. Bhinder flew unarmed Dakotas and massive Super Constellation C-121 four-propeller troop transporters during the wars with Pakistan. It took a special kind of courage to pilot the huge, defenceless aircraft into the heart of the war zones and Bhinder had distinguished himself. He was squadron leader in October 1977, when Air India offered him a job flying commercial aircraft.

Amarjit was glad he took it; now, at least, no one would be shooting at him.

Amarjit thought the world of Satwinder; that God could not have given her a better husband. He was generous, good looking, bright, jovial, and loyal. And like her, he had a life-long thirst for knowledge and higher education. Bhinder had continued his studies even while flying Air India planes around the globe. He had completed his master's degree in marketing management from the prestigious Jamula Lal Bajaj institute in Mumbai and it was his dream to become the managing director of the state-owned Air India.

Amarjit wished she could be with her husband now. In April, 1985, he had flown New York to London for transatlantic flight training which would ultimately send him to Canada. Once finished, he took Amarjit and the children on an American vacation. By the end of May, the family had returned to Mumbai and Bhinder did some more schooling, finishing his final exam for taxation management.

He had wanted Amarjit to go on this flight to Canada. But she insisted on getting their children ready for school. Their American vacation had left her pressed for time and there was so much to do. Satwinder had been a little annoyed, but it had not lasted. They were still very much in love after a dozen years of marriage. But as her husband flew off to Canada where he had family and friends, there was still that lingering doubt in Amarjit's heart that just doesn't go away when you're a pilot's wife. She constantly sought reassurances from him, longed to hear his voice, to be told that he would be safe. He'd logged so many hours flying, surely he was tempting fate. Lately, there had been good reason to worry. She had seen the Air India security circulars about the potential for terrorist attacks and advising airline staff to "take all possible precautions." Bhinder had warned her not to do any favours by agreeing to take parcels or even a letter from anyone—even close friends—if she was travelling on an Air India or an Indian Airlines flight. The former air force pilot never let his guard down. Amarjit tried to take comfort from her husband's words, as she always did when she fretted.

"This is the safest aircraft in the world," he would say of the Boeing 747 he flew. "It has so many facilities and it can even land on water in an emergency."

Satwinder was right. There was nothing to be gained by worrying. Still, she could not wait for him to call. This next flight was a special one for him; his first from Canada. It would take him to London, where he would have a layover of a week. After that, he was scheduled for command training, a feather in the cap of this perfectionist flyer with an unblemished record after 7,489 hours as a military and civilian pilot. She would go to bed now: She must be well-rested when Satwinder called in the morning.

Vancouver Airport, Canadian Pacific Air counter, June 22, 8:00 a.m. (PDT)

It was a madhouse that weekend, at least at Jeanne Adams' (a.k.a. Bakermans) counter as she stood behind wicket 26. Passengers had begun crowding into the airport for weekend getaways and the morning flights to Toronto. But it was just another Saturday in Adams' ten years behind the counter as she checked in the passengers, one by one.

Wearing high heels, standing about five-feet-six, in the usual gray dress of CP Air ground personnel, she surveyed the long queue of thirty to forty people checking in at the counter. The time was shortly after 8 a.m. when she came face-to-face with a man with a "cute" little face and "sparkling eyes" whom she would soon think of as a "jerk." Usually check-ins are routine; at best they take only thirty seconds for passengers who are properly ticketed. But this time it was to be different. The passenger was a man with a very specific purpose. His ticket coupon bore the name Mr. M. Singh. He was in his mid-thirties, wore a grey suit and was about five-feet-seven. He spoke good English as he handed Adams his one-way ticket to New Delhi.

She put an orange tag on his bag, so it would get off the plane with him when he disembarked in Toronto. She gave him a seat number. The man said he wanted his bag checked in all the way to Delhi. She took a look at the computerized reservation file. He has Flight 60 to Toronto confirmed, Adams thought as she read the screen. Another flight–Toronto to Mirabel–on the holding list. And another Air India flight, Montreal to Delhi. Well, the rules were clear.

"I can't do that, sir, because you're not confirmed on the flight."

"Yes, I am confirmed," he said. "This is my ticket."

"Your ticket doesn't read that you're confirmed," she said. "I can't do it."

"But then I'll have to pick up my baggage and transfer it," said the insistent Mr. Singh.

"I realize that, but we're not supposed to check your baggage through."

"I phoned Air India. I am confirmed on it," argued Mr. Singh.

Adams, by this time slightly irritated by the man's insistence on getting his luggage sent through to India, tried to explain that he might be confirmed in Air India's computer, but her computer said otherwise. His ticket only showed he had an RQ, a requested reservation, but Singh stuck to his guns, maintaining he didn't want the hassle of transferring his bag in Toronto. The line-up behind Singh was getting longer and longer. It was getting to a point where Adams was saying to herself, "Come on, get on with it." The pushy Singh made sure she understood he was flying business class; the little bit extra you pay to get a little better service. Then he said something that made her more than just irritated.

"Wait. I'll get my brother for you."

"You gotta be crazy," Adams thought.

"I don't have time to talk to your brother," she said aloud.

As the man moved away from the counter, a desperate Adams called him back.

"Okay, I'll check it through, but you have to check with Air India when you get to Toronto," she warned him.

The man standing behind Mr. Singh was by now paying attention to the fuss; he, too, suggested that Singh should check with Air India in Toronto.

Adams ripped off the orange tag for Toronto off his bag, put on a pink "interline" tag on the bag and wrote down the destination: "Vancouver–Toronto on CP, Toronto–Mirabel and Montreal–Delhi as the final destination." She assigned him seat 10B, wrote out his boarding pass and wished him a happy flight.

Johal, the loyal cohort of Parmar and a friend of travel agent Pawa, couldn't have been far away as M. Singh succeeded in checking in his bag.

M. Singh walked out of the airport building, not bothering to board the flight over which he had made such a fuss. His mission had been accomplished. The world would learn what it was. Life would never be the same again for Jeannie Adams.

Air Canada Flight 136 and CP Flight 60 left Vancouver ten minutes apart for routine trips to Toronto. Both flights carried travellers who were on their way to connect with Air India. But CP Flight 60 also carried the bag M. Singh had checked in. No one seemed to care that the passenger had not boarded his flight after checking in a bag. That was the state of security at Vancouver Airport in those days of carefree travel.

PRELUDE TO TRAGEDY
Vancouver Airport, Gate 20, June 22, 1:15 p.m. (PDT)

The ground staff and the flight crew had waited long enough. They "buttoned up" Tokyo-bound Canadian Pacific Airlines Flight 003, closed the door of the Boeing 747 christened the *Empress of Australia*, and retracted the gangway. The airliner's crew performed their pre-takeoff tasks, making sure luggage was safely stowed and ensuring the passengers had their seatbelts fastened. But one seat, allocated to a passenger in the Royal Canadian class, remained empty. The seat had been reserved for a man whose ticket identified him as L. Singh. The flight crew had waited for him patiently as announcements rang out in the terminal building asking Mr. Singh to report to the boarding lounge.

Flight 003 to Tokyo was leaving without him. Once again an aircraft was departing on a long international flight with a missing passenger and taking his bag along. It was risky business.

The veil of cloud hanging over Vancouver International Airport all morning was parting slowly as CP Flight 003 received final clearance for takeoff for the long journey across the Pacific. The sun burned away the last vestiges of the haze, and the cool, grey day turned into a bright one with pleasant twenty degrees Celsius temperatures. The skies were brilliant blue at 1:37 p.m. as the *Empress of Australia* hurtled down the runway, its four engines thrusting it off the tarmac and into the air.

As the jumbo soared to thirty thousand feet over the sunny Pacific and turned west for the ten-hour journey to Tokyo, the 390 passengers and crew aboard settled in for the longhaul. It was odd that L. Singh hadn't made his plane: he'd paid $1,300 cash for his ticket. It was the same thing that had happened in the morning when M. Singh had made such a fuss boarding his bag on CP Flight 60, and then walked unnoticed out of the terminal building.

While M. Singh was remembered by Adams since he had made a fuss, no one seemed to be able to describe L. Singh. His check-in for Flight 003 had been routine and therefore nothing had attracted anyone to L. Singh or his appearance. He had a confirmed flight aboard CP Air Flight 003 and his connection from Tokyo to Bangkok aboard Air India Flight 301 was also confirmed. The bag was safely stowed in the belly of the 747 as it made its way to Tokyo.

Lester B. Pearson Airport, Toronto, June 22, 4:30 p.m. (EDT)

Things were running like clockwork at Lester B. Pearson Airport as a steady stream of planes touched down carrying travellers connecting with Air India Flight 182. Air Canada Flight 136 from Vancouver, carrying the Uppals, Sam Madon, Daljit Grewal, and others, had landed precisely on time. Twenty minutes earlier, CP Flight 60 had arrived from Vancouver minus a confirmed passenger but with a piece of luggage destined for New Delhi.

A long walk faced the Vancouver passengers as they entered the main terminal building and made their way towards the Air India counter. From here, they would check in for their plane, scheduled to take off at 6:35 p.m.–a two-hour wait. As they headed towards the check-in carrying their flight bags, another passenger had just made the link with the ill-fated flight.

Rahul Aggarwal was having fun in the airport lounge with three university pals who had come to see him off. A twenty-three-year-old University of Manitoba arts student, Rahul had been his usual bubbly, unhurried self when he disembarked from a noon flight from Winnipeg. He wandered out into the terminal, looking for his three friends. But Raghu Rajan, Naiyer Usmani, and Shaffique Dhamarjee were waiting at the wrong gate. After a few minutes, the trio realized their mistake and made their way to where Rahul, looking impressive in a jacket and tie, was waiting with out-stretched arms.

"Late again, eh!" joked one of his friends.

"I almost missed my flight in Winnipeg. Don't tell Dad I was late again!"

As the four friends sat in the airport lounge sipping their drinks and talking animatedly about their past together at the university, Rahul was philosophical. Ostensibly, he was returning to India to write a thesis on Indo-Canadian relations to complete his master of arts degree. But he told his friends his real reason for going to India was to rediscover himself–to find out where he came from. To min-gle with the crowds in Mumbai's dusty streets and to breathe the air of a country that evoked pride in him. Rahul excused himself and went over to a telephone to call home. He marvelled at the scene in the airport.

"I almost feel like I am in India, there are so many women in saris at the airport today. I can't wait to get there."

Lester B. Pearson Airport, Gate 107, June 22, 4:30 p.m. (EDT)

On the tarmac, as ground personnel pumped thirteen thousand litres of fuel into the *Kanishka*'s huge wing-tanks, Air Canada staff that had been contracted by Air India to perform maintenance cleaned the cabin. Technicians were also busy attaching a fifth engine to the port wing. An Air India flight had returned to Toronto on June 8 when one of its engines failed after takeoff. The plane had borrowed an engine from Air Canada. Now the aircraft was being fitted with the non-functioning engine for the trip home. Foreman M. N. Patel had flown in from India to supervise the mounting procedure, which followed strict rules: it wouldn't do to drop a three-ton engine from thirty-one thousand feet. The instal-lation had begun the moment the flight arrived, but the engine couldn't be mounted without first having its cowlings removed and the fans and compressor rotors tied up. It would turn out to be a five-hour job.

Lester B. Pearson Airport, baggage transfer area, June 22, 5:15 p.m. (EDT)

The mounting of the dud engine on the left wing of the 747 wasn't the only cause of delay and frustration that evening as the flight prepared for departure. Burns International Security officers were cursing the baggage X-ray machine, which had stopped working. It wasn't the first time it had done that to Naseem Nanji and her co-worker, Jim Post. Nanji had been given a crash course on how to operate the scanner just three weeks earlier, after being moved from her normal beat near Canada Customs. She'd seen the baggage scanner malfunction on June 8, just the second time she had used it. Today, though, the machine had worked well enough when she first began using it around 2:30 p.m. Air India had just opened its counters for passengers and the flow of bags and cases was at first slow. She had put a cart full of baggage through with no problems. But now, with the bags coming much faster as boarding time neared, the machine had quit again. Naseem looked at the huge pile of luggage and decided it was time to call in the experts.

But Air India security officer John D'Souza couldn't fix the stubborn machine either, so he asked Nanji and Post to use a portable bomb-sniffer. D'Souza watched Post use the PD-4 sniffer, and then the Air India security man decided to give him a practical lesson. He lit a match and held it near the device to show Post how it gave off a long whistle when it detected nitrate fumes, which indicate the presence of explosives like dynamite. A short time after D'Souza left, a bag being checked by Post made the sniffer beep. The beep was coming from around a slight opening in the zipper. But the sound wasn't like the long whistle D'Souza had obtained with the lighted match. Post tried the device again on the maroon vinyl bag, and again it beeped when he passed it around the lock on the zipper. The beeping bag was allowed to go through, however, because it didn't produce the specified whistling sound. No one told D'Souza about the incident as ground crew began loading baggage into the forward and rear luggage holds of the aircraft. To this day, no one is sure if Post had stumbled on the luggage bomb, and experts are divided about the accuracy of the sniffer that was being used.

Parking area, Mirabel Airport, Montreal, June 22, 5:30 p.m., (EDT)

To Subhashini Paliwal, it seemed like no time at all since her son Mukul had dismantled the family's cassette player while she was taking an afternoon nap. But time had flown since the day the small boy had grabbed a screwdriver, performed surgery, and then appeared baffled as his child's mind tried to comprehend how to put it all together again. That had been almost eight years ago. Mukul, now fifteen, had learned much since then. He could repair calculators and cassette players without difficulty and loved to make little electronic gadgets like the electric pinball machines which were greatly enjoyed by his friends at school. Only recently he had turned a pile of junk into a model train with the help of his father, doing all the electrical work including automatic switching on double tracks and lights. The fluently trilingual Ottawa high school student—he spoke English, French, and Hindi—was taking grade ten courses in computers while only in grade nine. No, thought Subhashini, the boy was almost a man; old enough to go to India on his own to see his grandmother in Agra, the city of the Taj Mahal, the famous monument to love.

One of Mukul's loves was music. He played the tabla with a maturity beyond his years and often accompanied sitar players performing complex Indian classical music. He had appeared several times on local television, delighting his audience; thrilling them with the rhythms of an art he had first learned when he was only nine. At school, Mukul was a better than average student and had missed his family's trip to India the previous year because he wanted to take courses during the summer break. He had stayed behind, living with his uncle in Ottawa. In May, Mukul's father had told him that he could go to India on his own if he wished. The teenager had agreed on the condition that he could go again with the rest of his family for the planned marriages of two other uncles in December 1986. His father had agreed and so the pair had booked a flight for June 22.

With the ticket purchased, Mukul told all his friends about the upcoming trip. In the last week, the teenager hadn't had much free time to spend with his family. First he was busy with exams in four subjects, which he finished that Wednesday. Then, for the next two days, he was packing for the journey. He included some presents for his grandmother, who was anxiously awaiting the arrival of the grandson she hadn't seen for over two years. That morning, before the family left for Montreal, Mukul had insisted on paying a visit to his uncle's house to say goodbye.

Mukul was sitting in the back of the station wagon with his older brother, Shailendra, and younger sister, Vandana, as their father, Yogesh, drove the car into a parking spot at Mirabel Airport. The family had driven the one hundred miles from Ottawa and arrived with hours to spare. Air India Flight 182 was not scheduled to depart until 8:35 p.m. but Paliwal, a federal research scientist, believed in not having to rush at the last minute. Inside the terminal, as the family waited in the queue to check in Mukul's baggage, Yogesh Paliwal recognized another Ottawa family lined up for the flight to India. Paliwal went over and shook hands with Satish Seth and his wife Sadhana. The Seths were travelling with their three children, including an infant who was still in a stroller. Mukul's mother played with the baby for a long time. Afterwards, Air India officials told the Paliwals their plane would be delayed leaving Montreal. Paliwal asked anxiously what the reason was.

"We had to do some repairs in Toronto," the official replied.

The Paliwals headed out to a restaurant for some ice cream, but Mukul had never been fond of it and refused to eat. He preferred just to sit quietly through the hours of waiting and think about the short-wave radio he was leaving at home. There was a lot he would like to do with it when he got back.

Lester B. Pearson Airport, Toronto, June 22, 5:30 p.m. (EDT)

Rahul Aggarwal and his friends had almost forgotten he had a plane to catch. Suddenly, Rahul looked at his watch and knew it was time to go. But the flight was leaving from Terminal 2, and he was still in the other terminal. Rahul ran down the corridor towards the connecting tunnel. He didn't want to be late this time. Not for the flight to India! But the young man needn't have worried. The flight wasn't leaving on time. Besides, he wasn't the only one who was late. The captain and crew were halfway to the airport before someone noticed that flight engineer, Dara Dumasia, had been left behind at the Royal York Hotel. The bus went back for the mild-mannered, fifty-nine-year-old engineer. Dumasia, who had amassed fourteen thousand hours in the air, had overslept, having missed the wake-up call for his last flight.

Lester B. Pearson Airport, cockpit of *Kanishka*, Air India Flight 182, June 22, 5:45 p.m. (EDT)

Flying was second nature to Captain Hanse Singh Narendra, the fifty-six-year-old son of a wealthy father from the Mathra district of the Indian State of Utar Pardesh. After finishing high school, Narendra had taken flying lessons at a private club and become a commercial pilot in next to no time. When Air India was formed from a number of smaller airlines in 1956, Narendra offered his services and the company hired him. Those who had flown with him over the years knew him as a perfectionist who kept his cool even when the going got rough.

His other passion was hunting, a sport that had fascinated him since his childhood days under the British Raj. His parents couldn't keep him home as a boy because of his passion for tracking tigers at his uncle's huge estate in Mathra. During his school vacations and even now, when he had a few free days on his hands, Narendra would romp over to Sahanpur Estates where he had grown up. The huge parcel of land was still the focal point of the wealthy, close-knit family, even though while on duty the captain himself lived in a plush bungalow on a hill in what Bombay residents know as the "Air India Colony" in the Bandra section of the city of multitudes. He also had acquired land in Delhi, and was considering building a house. A few months earlier, during a trip to Ottawa, where his sister Sheila Mann lived, Narendra had told her of his dream of spending his retirement years at the ranch he'd acquired in India. At home in Bombay, where two full-sized tiger skins adorned the walls of the living room, Narendra had left behind a twenty-one-year-old son, Anil. He hadn't been keeping well and Narendra and his wife Sheila had only recently discussed sending him overseas for medical treatment. But they had changed their minds, deciding that doctors in Bombay could do as good a job.

Narendra knew the airplane he was sitting in today as well as he knew the back of his hand. But twice in the last year, he'd had his wrists slapped for putting too much faith in his co-pilots. On August 25, 1984, he had slipped up while flying over the territory of India's traditional enemy, Pakistan. Air India Flight 1100 from London to Delhi deviated from its track by 170 nautical miles while being controlled by a co-pilot. The commander, responsible for the safety of his aircraft and the actions of his co-pilot, was sent back to school for a few days to re-learn instrument navigation systems and route cross-checking procedure. Narendra would not repeat that particular mistake.

The second error occurred on December 6, 1984, during a Delhi to Bombay flight. The runway in use at Bombay's Santa Cruz Airport was number 27, but the aircraft, again in control of a co-pilot, was seen approaching runway 32. Narendra's stern bosses sent him to a simulator to practice approaches and landings at runway 27 in Bombay. But that was all; there were no other blots on the captain's record. He was a check-pilot and had never recorded an accident in twenty thousand hours in the cockpit of jets of all sizes.

Narendra was now preparing patiently along with co-pilot Bhinder to begin the task of flying *Kanishka* to London before handing it over to another commander. He had flown in on Saturday, June 15, exactly a week earlier, from Frankfurt, Germany, hauling an extra engine that had been borrowed by Air India from Air Canada. This was not his usual route, but like Bhinder, he had been assigned to the flight because of staffing situations. Narendra was one year away from retirement. It was all he talked about whenever he was with family and friends.

Lester B. Pearson Airport, Gate 107, June 22, 6:10 p.m. (EDT)

The passengers for Air India Flight 182 were waiting impatiently in the boarding lounge when the longed-for boarding announcement finally came. More than two hundred passengers (many of them children) began boarding the aircraft in Toronto, including twenty-one who had arrived aboard various Air Canada flights from Winnipeg, Vancouver, Saskatoon, and Edmonton during the day. There was no sign, however, of the CP Air 60 passenger from Vancouver who had made such a fuss with the clerk at Vancouver Airport to have his bag put directly aboard Flight 182 in Toronto. He hadn't even shown up to check at the Air India counter there to see if he had a seat. But his bag was being loaded.

The boarding security was extraordinarily tough for the times. Passengers were first frisked under the watchful eyes of the Mounties and Burns Security while passing through the door frame metal detector. Then they were checked again as they boarded the flight from the holding area. Security chief John D'Souza searched each and every piece of hand baggage being taken aboard the aircraft while metal detectors were used again to check the passengers. Furthermore, the airline, sensitive to the threat of terrorism, was also using a "security numbers" system to make sure that all the passengers who had checked in were actually boarding the flight. The point was to make sure that passengers who had checked in had boarded their flights and not just their bags. Because the bag from Vancouver had arrived without a passenger the security numbers system was defeated. Boarding was finally completed at 7 p.m. (EDT).

The aircraft had already been delayed by twenty-five minutes. But there would be further delays as ground technicians encountered a problem loading parts of the non-functioning engine inside the rear cargo compartment. To facilitate the insertion of the inlet cowlings of the fifth engine, Air Canada technicians removed the door fittings. Actual procedure as outlined in Boeing manuals calls for the removal of panels from the cowling to load it into the compartment. However, neither the Air Canada technicians nor Montreal maintenance manager Thiniri Rajendra were aware of the Boeing procedure. Rajendra, however, made sure the door fittings were properly reattached. He also carried out a final check of the aircraft and handed the certificate of airworthiness to Captain Narendra, who duly accepted command of the aircraft.

Kanishka was now ready for takeoff. The time was 8:16 p.m. (EDT), a delay of one hour and forty-one minutes from scheduled time of takeoff. As it lifted off for the short haul to Montreal before embarking on its long journey to New Delhi via London, the plane was carrying 270 passengers, twenty-two crew, and hundreds of pieces of luggage, including two diplomatic bags from Vancouver. Sixty-eight of those passengers would disembark in Montreal. Also aboard for the hour-long flight to Montreal were D'Souza (who would supervise security during the boarding at Mirabel), maintenance manager Rajendra, and passenger service supervisor Divyang Yodh, who had come in from New York because the regular Toronto agent was on leave.

And, of course, the aircraft was still carrying the bag whose owner, M. Singh, had never showed up.

Mirabel Airport, Gate 68, Montreal, June 22, 9:10 p.m. (EDT)

It had been a long, long wait for Mukul Paliwal, but it was over now. The Air India plane that was to take him to his grandmother and to the Taj Mahal had finally touched down in Montreal and was parked at Gate 80. Just ten minutes before the flight arrived, Mukul had said goodbye to his family. In the age-old tradition of showing profound respect for parents, Mukul went down on his knees and kissed the feet of his father and mother. Then he embraced them and kissed them. His mother wiped tears from her eyes and gave him some last minute advice. He might be old enough to go to India on his own, but he was still "her baby," she said.

As Mukul and 104 other passengers proceeded through the security check on their way to the boarding gate, sixty-eight arriving passengers, including Air India staffers Rajendra, Yohd, and D'Souza, disembarked and were shuttled to the arrival terminal.

There had been a few problems, however, while the passengers were waiting to board. Burns Security officers Real Gagnon and Jacelyn Cardinal had put aside a bag belonging to a passenger boarding from Montreal. They had spotted wires near the suitcase opening and they weren't about to take any chances. They placed it next to the X-ray machine, which, unlike the one in Toronto, was working fine. Then they picked out two more bags that made them uneasy. The security men informed Air India service agent Janul Abid of the suspect suitcases, but Abid asked them to leave the bags aside until D'Souza arrived from Toronto on the flight. While they waited, two diplomatic pouches from Ottawa were brought over by Mohinder Singh of the Indian High Commission. After the flight arrived, he and a ground worker proceeded to the aircraft and handed the smaller pouch, which weighed a kilogram, to flight purser Inder Thakur. The other bag, weighing nine kilos, was put with the diplomatic bags from Vancouver in a container in the forward luggage hold.

The aircraft, meanwhile, had been hooked up to a ground power cable to supply electricity because its auxiliary power unit, which provides power when the engines are off, had been out of service since the aircraft left Bombay the previous day. Rajendra and three Air Canada technicians on contract to Air India were busy performing a final check on the aircraft as catering staff loaded dinner and breakfast for Montreal to London leg of the journey. Flight engineer Dumasia had also come out of the plane to take a look at the fifth engine. He discovered that one of the latches was loose and asked an Air Canada technician to take care of the problem. It was soon rectified and Dumasia, Rajendra and the three ground service men from Air Canada decided that there were no other snags.

D'Souza, meanwhile, had been informed by Abid that three suitcases had been laid aside as suspect baggage. The security man put the three bags through the X-ray machine and also used the explosive sniffer he had brought from Toronto. He decided to keep the bags in Montreal overnight. They could always be sent over on another flight if they proved to be harmless. But he and Abid made no effort to contact the passengers whose bags they had decided to keep.

Mirabel Airport, Runway, 9:50 p.m. (EDT)

Mukul and fellow passengers boarding in Montreal were on their way to the waiting plane in a bus. Sari-clad hostesses Rima Bhasin and Sharon Lasrado (who had celebrated her twenty-third birthday two days earlier in Toronto) were standing at the plane's doorway with their hands held together in front of them in the traditional Indian greeting, *namaskar*.

As the passengers from Montreal were seating themselves and stowing their hand baggage in the overhead compartments, a Mountie had been notified in the airport terminal that three suspect suitcases had been held back. He asked Air India representatives to come to the luggage holding area so the bags could be examined. But D'Souza was busy elsewhere.

Cockpit of *Kanishka*, Air India Flight 182, 10:18 p.m. (EDT)

The microphone in the cockpit of Flight 182 had just crackled and come alive with the voice of the air traffic controller. The co-pilot acknowledged:

> **Captain Bhinder**: Air India 182. Good evening.
> **Control Tower**: Air India 182, taxi to position, 06,18.
> **Captain Bhinder:** Taxi to position 06,18.
> **Control Tower:** Air India 182, airborne departure, 124.65 clear takeoff 06.

Kanishka was off and away, carrying 307 passengers, 22 crew, 539 pieces of luggage, two diplomatic bags, parts from the extra engine, 104,000 kilograms of fuel, and one bomb.

As the aircraft disappeared into the night sky, back in the terminal building, more than fifteen minutes after the flight had left, Abid and D'Souza walked into the baggage room where RCMP Sergeant J. N. Leblanc was waiting for them. The Mountie asked them to determine the owners of the bags, but the Air India security personnel informed him the flight had already left.

The three bags were then taken to a decompression chamber owned by the airline with the toughest security in the world, Israel's El Al. There, dogs sniffed the bags and when they were opened later that night, the only unusual items found were an iron, a camera, a radio, and a hair dryer.

The Boeing 747 aircraft piloted by Captains Narendra and Bhinder had been acquired by Air India on June 19, 1978, and had made its first commercial flight for the company on July 7, 1978. The plane was in its young middle-age, with 23,634 hours of service completed in its seven years of operation. Its four engines were each capable of producing a roaring thrust of 48,650 pounds maximum. It was in top-notch condition, having been thoroughly serviced on May 24. Its maintenance record was routine, showing no extraordinary problems. As high as a five-storey building, with a wingspan of 195 feet and 231 feet from the nose to tail, Kanishka was designed to carry up to 710,000 pounds of payload soaring into the sky.

Tonight, as Narendra put the aircraft into a steep climb on approach to its cruising altitude, he could be certain that the plane was in excellent shape. And it was carrying more that eight hours' worth of fuel, enough to take it to Paris in case an emergency forced it to overfly London. The passengers settled down for their dinner and in-flight movie as Moncton air traffic control cleared the big jet to fly at an altitude of thirty-three thousand feet. The plane's estimated time of arrival in London was 8:33 a.m. (GMT), six hours and fifteen minutes after takeoff from Montreal. Over Gander, Newfoundland, traffic control gave the Boeing 747 oceanic clearance at normal cruising speed. But Bhinder advised them that he needed a slower speed because of the fifth engine, which created considerable drag on the aircraft. Gander cleared him to head out over the ocean at a reduced speed of Mach 0.81.

New Tokyo International Airport, Narita, Japan, June 23, 6:20 (GMT)

Globe-trotting Woodwards Department Store merchandise buyer John Kennedy had three hours to kill before his trip home to Vancouver. He had just flown in from Taiwan after completing a shopping spree for the Vancouver store. After going through passport control at the gleaming Tokyo International Airport, Kennedy had wandered into the huge waiting area where a maze of duty-free shops offered tempting electronic fare. But the forty-year-old buyer had had enough of shopping. Instead, he meandered over to a series of clear glass windows, stretching sixty feet, which offered waiting passengers a panoramic view of the hustle and bustle of one of the world's busiest airports.

Kennedy watched CP Air Flight 003 taxi to the gate where he was to board for the flight home. When you travel a lot, three hours to spare at an airport isn't an awfully long time to wait and he was used to it. Now, as he looked out through the sparkling glass windows, he could see little forklift trucks driving up to the *Empress of Australia* and driving away again with containers of luggage for the passengers who had just arrived from Vancouver. With Pacific headwinds not as harsh as usual, the orange and white CP Boeing 747 had made good time, coming in ten minutes ahead of schedule at 2:45 p.m. Tokyo time.

Looking down through the windows, Kennedy could see the busy baggage trucks disappearing beneath him into the ground-floor terminal where handlers would sort out the bags and cases before the passengers picked them up. Deciding at this point that he had better things to do than just watch the baggage trucks or stare into the distance at the sleepy little city of Narita, sixty kilometres northeast of Tokyo, Kennedy turned away from the window.

He hadn't taken two steps when a thundering explosion almost knocked him off his feet.

"What the hell was that?" he thought. His was heart pounding. It sounded like a cement truck had come crashing through the roof of the terminal. The time was 3:20 p.m. There was a moment of stunned silence in the airport as the roar of the blast died down. Then came the outburst of human activity: babies crying, women screaming, and men running.

All hell seemed to break loose as Kennedy stood rooted to the spot. He waited, expecting to hear another massive blast. But none came. From the ventilation grille behind him, thick acrid smoke began filtering into the lounge. He was certain it had to be a bomb: nothing else could make a sound like the earth falling apart.

Amid the chaos and calamity, sirens wailed from the tarmac below as police hurled into action. From the windows Kennedy could see ambulances, fire trucks, and police cars dashing towards the scene of the explosion on the ground level, right below where he was standing. He watched, awe-struck and slack-jawed, as the scene on the tarmac below him unfolded. The first two victims, both baggage handlers, were being brought out on stretchers. Mercifully, their bodies were covered from head to toe. Then two more were brought out, their bodies covered only in blood. The ambulances sped away, sirens wailing. Other baggage handlers who had been near the explosion could be seen milling about, bloodied but still alive.

The chaos began to subside. From where he was standing, Kennedy had a panoramic view of the efficient Japanese security team in action. An armoured car arrived to probe the rest of the baggage that had been taken off CP 003. The bomb squad was taking no chances with the plane that had brought deadly cargo from Vancouver. Kennedy then saw the odd-looking figure of the chief of security, shouting orders to his men; behind him an attendant was carrying a pole with a large number on to identify the man in charge. In chaotic situations, it's imperative to know just who is issuing the orders. Also on the tarmac, Japanese press officers were briefing reporters, drawing out chalkboard diagrams for the curious newsmen. Kennedy could well imagine the kinds of questions they were asking: Was it a bomb? Where did it come from? How many dead? How many wounded? Had anybody claimed responsibility yet? The officers had few answers. The one thing they were sure about was that a bomb had caused the explosion and it had been brought to Narita by the orange and white Canadian Pacific jet.

As the *Empress of Australia* idled on the tarmac, tourists took pictures of her through the bank of windows in the waiting area: mementoes of the terror that had been played out in front of their eyes. For passenger John Kennedy, it was all like a bad dream: he had had a confirmed seat on his trip home on Flight 004.

Down on ground level, firemen had doused a small fire and forensic experts were busy clearing up and photographing the mess. The deadly blast had occurred just as luggage handlers were removing a bag from a transit container. The two men were killed instantly. The detonation of the blast was so intense it hollowed a huge crater in the thick concrete pavement. Thousands of metal and plastic particles lay scattered around. Police blocked all roads leading in and out of the airport and vehicles were being checked before leaving or entering the terminal area. A task force of three dozen policemen was immediately formed to probe the explosion.

When the explosion ripped through the terminal, some short distance away Air India Flight 301 to Bangkok was being refuelled.

No one knew it then, but the bag that had blown up "prematurely" had been destined for stowage on Flight 301. It belonged to one of the flight's confirmed passengers: the mysterious L. Singh.

COUNTDOWN TO DISASTER
On-board *Kanishka*, June 23, 6:20 a.m. (GMT)

Oblivious to events in Tokyo, passengers aboard Flight 182 had not a care in the world as the plane cruised at an altitude of thirty-one thousand feet over the North Atlantic. Four hours had passed since the Boeing 747 lifted off from runway 6 at Montreal for the six-hour-and-thirty-minute flight to London. The passengers were watching a Hindi movie with a special bonus—the flight purser was also a movie star. At age thirty-five, Inder Thakur was not only a successful screen actor, but a distinguished international model and fashion designer. Air India was keeping its promise to make passengers feel as if they were already in India the moment they boarded. Sari-clad hostesses served Indian food in an aircraft decorated like a palace reminiscent of a bygone era.

Thakur, a thirteen-year veteran of Air India, was flying with his wife and child. Only the month before, the versatile purser had displayed his exclusive Indian designs at a convention of the World Modeling Association in New York. The smiling charmer had walked away with the award for the International Fashion Designer of the Year. *The Magic Carpet*, Air India's in-flight magazine, featured a picture of Thakur with WMA president Ruth Tolman.

There had been four hours of uneventful flying and no turbulence. From the cockpit, Capt. Narendra could see the sun rising over the Atlantic and way below, at ten thousand feet, cloud blanketing the sea. The weather was no problem, either on the surface or at flight level, where *Kanishka* was cutting through the air at speeds varying from 287 to 296 knots; slightly slower than normal because of the drag factor caused by carrying the non-functioning engine. The surface temperature was thirteen degrees Celsius with a wind speed of about fifteen knots. There was no cumulonimbus cloud or thunderstorm activity. At *Kanishka*'s altitude, it was a chilly minus-forty-seven Celsius with a steady westerly wind flow. There was no sign of anything mechanically wrong with the aircraft. There was nothing Captain Narendra or co-pilot Captain Bhinder could complain about. Mechanically and weather-wise there was nothing to prevent touching down at London's Heathrow Airport at 8:33 a.m. (GMT). Unbeknownst to the captain, crew, and passengers of Air India Flight 182, however, the countdown to disaster had begun.

On-board *Kanishka*, June 23, 7:00 a.m. (GMT)

There was just time enough to serve breakfast and collect the trays before passengers readied themselves for the stopover in London. Narendra would begin his final approach in about an hour. Most of the passengers lounged in their seats with their seat belts unfastened. In the cockpit, flight purser Jamshed Dinshaw was standing with in-flight supervisor Sampeth Lazar. Dinshaw, travelling with his wife Pamela, a hostess on the flight, was listening to small talk between Bhinder and flight engineer Dumasia. The cockpit voice recorder in the back of the plane documented the cockpit crew's conversation:

Binder: Dinshaw.
Dinshaw: Yes, sir.
Binder: Do me a small favour.
Dinshaw: What's that?
Binder: *Ekdam end pe, fifty-four seat pe* (at the very end of the plane, on seat fifty-four) A boy is sitting there. Inder Thakur knows. He just wanted to have a look in the cockpit.
Dinshaw: Where is he?
Binder: Inder Thakur knows about him.
Dinshaw: Okay, fifty-four seat. Can I send him now?
Binder: After about fifteen to twenty minutes.

It was another five minutes before Bhinder spoke again, remarking sourly about all the beer the hostesses were taking home from their weeklong layover in Toronto. There is nothing so welcome in India as gifts of imported beer and Air India flight crew tended to get their hands on as much of the prized alcohol as possible. Lazar remarked it was "a hard core problem." The normally extroverted Captain Narendra, silent so far, suddenly joined in the conversation, joking that that some of the cabin crew might be carrying beer for others as well.

"Somebody ten beers, somebody six beers," said Bhinder. "Hold, hold!"

It was time to check with Shanwick Control, a joint air traffic control centre in Ireland (shared control between between Prestwick, Scotland and Shannon, Ireland.) The time was 7:06:39 a.m. (GMT) when Bhinder made contact:

Bhinder: Shanwick AI-182. Good morning.
Shannon: Station calling Shannon. Go ahead again.
Bhinder: AI-182. AI-182 is 51 N 15 W at 0705 level 310.
　　Estimate FIR 08 W 51 N 08W at 07:35.
Shannon: 182, your correct Shannon frequency is 131 15.
Bhinder: 131 15, sir.

The cockpit voice recorder next picked up Shannon communicating with TWA Flight 770, which was following Air India 182 at a distance of five miles at an altitude of thirty-five thousand feet. Trailing the TWA plane by about twenty miles was CP Air Flight 282. Shannon cleared it to fly to Amsterdam at an altitude of thirty-seven thousand feet.

At 7:08 a.m. Bhinder contacted Shannon again to report his position. Shannon asked him to "squawk 2005."

"Right, sir, squawking 2005, 182," Bhinder replied.

As Bhinder spoke with Shannon, Dinshaw was escorting the little boy up the aisle of Kanishka. The child was in for a real treat: a bright moment to break the monotony of a routine flight.

In the cockpit, flight engineer Dara Dumasia told Bhinder that purser Dinshaw wanted thirty seals for the bar for customs inspection purposes in London, and asked if he could call London Operations and tell them to have them ready for the flight's arrival.

Bhinder: Customs.
Dumasia: Custom seals. *Wo bar seal karane ke liye* (seals to close the bar). For their arrival—customs. Bar—

Those were the last words recorded from the cockpit of Kanishka. The sound of an explosion cut the conversation off. The time was 7:14:01 a.m. (GMT). Presumably, whoever had set the bomb's timer had assumed the flight's arrival time in London, and had not—or could not have—allowed for the many delays.

Time was up. The margin of terror had been crossed.

The aircraft went into wild gyrations, breaking up in the air, forming a whirling cloud of hurtling bodies, luggage, and metal in the sky.

Most of the 329 passengers and crew were dead before they hit the water, having been wrenched violently out of the aircraft's sheltered cabin and exposed to the viciously cold, oxygen-starved upper air. Their bodies were twisting around and their limbs flailing wildly as they hit the Atlantic. But at least one was still alive. An autopsy later would determine the female passenger, five months pregnant, had lived to hit the water, only to drown. No one stood a chance to survive this catastrophe.

It had been four hours and fifty-six minutes since the aircraft had left Montreal. It was now a cloud of fragments raining down into the Atlantic. Much of it sank, forming a nine-mile long field of debris on the ocean floor, over six thousand feet below the surface. Marking the beginning of the wreckage path was a bag with clothes protruding from its torn vinyl skin that had slowly sunk to the bottom of the ocean.

SEARCH AND RESCUE
Shannon Air Traffic Control, 7:14 a.m. (GMT)

As the wreckage of *Kanishka* hit the Atlantic waves, Shannon Air Traffic Control was still in the dark over the fate of the aircraft with which it had communicated just four minutes and ten seconds ago. Air Traffic controllers Mike Quinn and Thomas Lane noticed a clicking sound that lasted for just a fraction of a second. Then, the diamond-shaped blip that had been Air India Flight 182 vanished from their screens. No mayday, no sign of trouble—just gone. Lane looked at his radar for an agonized moment, hoping the diamond of light would flicker back onto the screen. Nothing. The frantic controllers called Air India 182 five times at 7:16 a.m. (GMT), but there was nothing except silence. At 7:17 a.m. (GMT), Quinn contacted TWA 770, which had been flying just behind and above Air India:

Shannon: Okay, just calling to tell you there's an Air India there with you and…he's not talking to us at this time— would you just give him a call please?

TWA 770: Air India 182 from TWA 770.

(A pause. Just a few seconds that dragged on, endlessly. There was no reply.)

TWA 770: Ah, Shannon, TWA. He won't answer us either.

Shannon: We just had him ahead of you there. Five miles just ahead of you there and his squawk is gone off the scope…that's why… Can you see anything ahead of you there?

TWA 770: Well, no, we don't see him.

Shannon: Air India 182, Air India 182.

TWA 770: We've been looking and I've been calling him on guard (an emergency frequency monitored by all air- craft) and he hasn't answered and we don't see him.

Shannon then asked CP 282 to see if the missing aircraft was vis- ible anywhere. But CP 282 could only see the TWA jet. Shannon requested TWA 770 descend and turn to see if it could spot Air India 182. The control centre also asked other airliners in the area to keep an eye out. But it was as if the lost plane had never existed.

The Atlantic Ocean, 7:30 a.m. (GMT)

Just sixteen minutes after Air India 182 vanished from radar, Shannon informed the Irish Marine Rescue Coordination Centre (MRCC) of the aircraft's disappearance and requested emergency action. The search and rescue machinery kicked into gear like clock- work. The Irish Naval Service and the Irish Air Corps were briefed about the emergency. In minutes, MRCC called the Valentia Coast Guard Radio Station to alert all marine vessels to watch for any sign of wreckage, giving the last known location of Air India 182 as approximately 180 miles southwest of Cork. One by one, ships in the area reported in, offering assistance. At 7:50 a.m. (GMT), the Irish warship *L.E. Aisling*, under the command of Lieutenant Commander James Robinson, reported to Valentia Radio that it was fifty-four miles from the last known location of the flight and proceeding to the scene. A few minutes later, the Panama-registered cargo vessel *Laurentian Forest*, owned by Federal Commerce of Montreal and headed to Dublin from Quebec, advised it was twenty-two miles from the distress area and headed towards it. MRCC then alerted the rescue coordination centre in Plymouth and was informed a Nimrod rescue aircraft was preparing to depart shortly and Sea King helicopters were already on their way to the quiet seaside city of Cork for deployment.

At 8:29 a.m. (GMT), Shannon advised Valentia Radio that aircraft passing over the site were picking up an emergency locator transmitter signal at location 51N 15 W and all ships in the area should be requested to report to Valentia. Three other vessels, the *Ali Baba*, *Kongstein*, and *Western Arctic* radioed in with offers of assistance. Within a half an hour, four Sea King choppers were en route to the scene.

It was almost exactly two hours after the aircraft was blown out of the sky that the eighteen thousand-ton cargo vessel *Laurentian Forest* reported sighting what appeared to be life rafts about two miles from its position. Within minutes, the ship's crew spotted more wreckage from the downed airliner and reported that the rafts were not inflated. At 9:37 a.m. (GMT), they found the first bodies: three corpses floating in the cold waters of the Atlantic. They were naked, their limbs twisted hideously like rag dolls.

By 9:45 a.m. (GMT), one of the largest search and rescue operations in history was underway. For operational and security reasons, MRCC Shannon had decided Cork would be the base for the search mission and air traffic control at Cork airport was informed of the decision. An hour later, a prohibited zone for aircraft was established within a radius of forty miles from the scene of the disaster. Valentia Radio then assigned specific quarters for each ship to search, with all bodies and wreckage found to be taken aboard and a report filed with the *L. E. Aisling*, which was established as the

command ship for the recovery operation. Lieutenant Commander
Robinson was appointed the on-scene commander and coordinated
the efforts of the ships assisting in the search. In all, nineteen ships,
both naval and merchant vessels, took part, combing hundreds of
square kilometers of the Atlantic. Most were commercial ships like
the *Laurentian Forest*; others included oil-rig support vessels, fishing
boats and a volunteer lifeboat from the Royal National Lifeboat
Institution in Valentia, Ireland. Many aircraft, including search and
rescue units from the RAF, joined the surface vessels.

Four hours after the explosion, the crash area was being combed
by aircraft, helicopters and more ships, including eight Spanish
trawlers that had volunteered their services. The *Star Orion* had also
arrived and offered to refuel any vessel in the search area.

Robinson, commander of the eighty-metre-long Irish helicopter
patrol vessel *L. E. Aisling* would later recount the grim scene that
greeted him and his crew on June 23, 1985 in the waters where
much of Air India Flight 182 had rained down:

"Over the next thirty minutes or so, as we moved into the area
of the major search, more helicopters came on the scene, more
ships began calling in," said Robinson. "The situation on the bridge
of my ship was, as you can imagine, somewhat tense. The area was
full of smoke from the searching aircraft. And I must admit, I got a
little bit concerned myself. I thought, this is what you've been
trained for; now go ahead and do it. And at 12:32 we found our-
selves at what we reckoned to be the datum and we were
surrounded by wreckage and just bodies everywhere."

To Robinson and other searchers, it was soon apparent there
would be no rescue operation. The task now was to recover as many
bodies of the victims as possible. Despite the near-certainty that there
would be no survivors, those involved in the search risked their lives
as they combed the debris field. As the weather grew worse, the task
of recovering bodies from the heaving green waters became more
treacherous. Aboard the *L. E. Aisling*, Robinson watched through his
binoculars as a tiny Gemini inflatable carrying three of his own men
bobbed up and down in the swells. They'd fished five corpses out of
the sea, with room aboard their craft for one more. One of the crew
jumped into the freezing water to get the sixth body out, hoping

against hope that somehow, this one might be a survivor. Robinson had caught sight of the tell-tale fin before the men on the Gemini did. He'd opened his mouth to holler, but a pair of burly arms had hauled the crew member out of the sea just in time. As if there wasn't enough death strewn about them, the sharks had arrived.

Robinson's brave men were getting help from above from the Royal Air Force (RAF). The crews of the three RAF Sea King helicopters from the search and rescue detachment in South Wales also risked their lives during the operation. Squad Leader John Brooks and Air Load Master Mark Tait worked feverishly in the increasingly foul weather, plucking bodies from the sea. Brooks operated the huge helicopter's winch, lowering Tait into the frigid Atlantic to recover corpses and wreckage from *Kanishka*.

The deck of the *Laurentian Forest* soon resembled a morgue, with sixty-six bodies laid side by side. The *L. E. Aisling* had also picked more corpses. The body count would rise to 130 by nightfall as the search wound down and the alert was downgraded. The rest of the victims would stay with the scattered, ghostly remains of the flight at a depth of six thousand feet, entombed in a silent grave.

By that evening, the bodies of sixty-four victims had arrived at Cork airport. Five pathologists had been summoned to Cork Regional Hospital to perform the autopsies. Wreckage was also being brought in, among the flotsam was a child's Cabbage Patch doll, found floating amidst the scene of disaster and death. It foreshadowed what Cork could expect for months to come. Investigators from India, the United States, Britain, and Canada, as well as grim-faced relatives hoping to provide a decent burial for their kin, would begin to swamp the town the next day as the search for more victims and debris continued. A steady stream of planes and helicopters were landing and taking off from the airport.

When the search was finally over and the statistics had been tallied, the Air India tragedy had become the fourth worst aviation disaster in history and the worst ever for Canada: 165 of the 329 victims were Canadians. It was the bloodiest act of bombing of a civilian aircraft in history: a record that stands today. And the attack had been launched from Vancouver.

THE NEWS HITS HOME

In Vancouver and Montreal, people were still asleep when television and radio stations first began broadcasting the news of the Air India disaster. It was 5:30 a.m. when the telephone rang at the Ottawa home of Yogesh Paliwal. Was it Mukul calling from London to tell him he had arrived safely on the first leg of his journey? Who else, Paliwal asked himself, would call so early in the morning? But it wasn't Mukul. It was a friend who had been listening to the radio. He broke the news of the flight's disappearance. Paliwal got out of bed and woke his wife. She began to cry. Paliwal, his hands shaking, grabbed Mukul's favourite short-wave radio and tried to tune in the BBC from London. His son's radio confirmed the worst.

There appeared to be no survivors. The child who had respectfully kissed his feet in the traditional Indian way less than eight hours earlier was dead.

Just about the time Paliwal was tuning in the radio in Montreal, the telephone was ringing at the Vancouver home of Air India's western region manager, Jehangir Parakh. He'd been out late the previous evening, partying with friends. He was in a deep sleep when the telephone rang at around 2:30 a.m. (PDT). His wife answered. It was Air India sales representative Derek Menzes from Montreal calling.

What Menzes was saying about the disaster did not register with Parakh. He hung up, thinking there was a routine technical problem of some sort. At 6:30 a.m., Parakh's son shook him awake.

"Dad, something has happened to the Air India flight—it's hit a radar station or something."

Parakh soon learned what had really happened to Air India flight 182 on the morning television news and headed straight for his office at Air India's downtown Vancouver headquarters on West Broadway. A telex was waiting for him.

"On behalf of Air India, I regret to have to advise you that one of our aircraft, VT-EFO Flight 182 of 22 June from Toronto and Montreal to Delhi and Bombay via London, was reported lost at sea off the coast of Ireland in the early hours of the morning. The 747 aircraft lost contact at approximately 7:15 a.m. (GMT), 180 miles from Cork, Ireland. The total number of passengers on board was

307, plus twenty-two crew. The latest information available is that the wreckage has been sighted and several bodies have been picked up. There are no reports of survivors as yet. The passenger list will be released once next of kin have been informed. We have further been advised that some more bodies have been sighted.

"The last contact with the aircraft was 7:10 a.m. (GMT) when the aircraft was cruising at thirty-one thousand feet. Conditions at that time were reported as normal. The control tower lost contact with the aircraft at approximately 7:15 a.m. (GMT). The commander of the aircraft was Capt. Narendra. He joined Air India in the year 1951 and has been a senior commander since 1964."

Parakh put the communiqué down, shaken.

"God, 329 people!" he thought. "Sam Madon was on that flight. I could have been on that flight."

In Mumbai, at approximately 3 p.m. on June 23, someone knocked on Amarjit Bhinder's door. The man, a family friend, appeared anxious. Slowly, he began asking her where *paji* was. That's what Capt. Satwinder Bhinder and the friend called each other. It means "brother" in Punjabi. He asked her if he had come back from his flight. Amarjit's heart skipped a beat.

"Oh, he is about to land in London, or he must have landed in London by now," she replied.

"What flight was he on?" the friend asked.

"He was on 182."

"Are you sure?"

"I am sure because he asked me to call him in London," she replied.

"There has been an accident," said the friend.

"What kind of an accident?"

Her world had come to an end. She began crying endlessly. She banged her head against the wall. In July, she would fly to Cork. She took with her a set of Satwinder's clothes, thinking he would need them when he came ashore. His body sank to the bottom of the ocean and was never found. But Amarjit stood by the water in Ireland. She carried his clothes with her for two years.

"He was so strong," she thought. "He will come back."

Later, she sent me an e-mail. It broke my heart.

"I worship him, next only to God. That was my husband. I love him even today as much as I loved him then. Imagine my loss."

Crying relatives and anxious friends began pouring into the Air India offices in Vancouver, Toronto, and cities across the world. In Bombay a crowd gathered outside the Air India office near the scenic Marine Drive. Sheila Narendra, wife of the commander of the aircraft, was among them. She knew then that her husband had died. Earlier, Air India representatives had come to her house, saying only that the flight had gone missing. Special telephone lines were set up by Air India in several major cities to relay news of the tragedy to families. A telephone call from London to Bombay told Perviz Madon that Sam wouldn't be with her for his birthday or for Eddie's *navjote*. As Sam's younger brother Cyrus left Vancouver for London, Perviz was also making her way to England from the other side of the world. Three days later, Major Sidhu was on his way to identify the battered body of his sister Sukhwinder and little Parminder. Their bodies had been fished out of the Atlantic with 129 others found floating among the debris of Kanishka. In total, sixty children under the age of ten had perished aboard Air India Flight 182. Seven of the children had flown unaccompanied. An Air Canada agent who had assured their parents they would be safe had seated them in their seats and handed them into the care of flight hostesses. Some 165 passengers were citizens of Canada, more than one hundred were Indian nationals and twenty-two were American citizens.

"Something big" had happened. The largest criminal investigation in Canadian history was about to begin.

SIX

THE DOCTOR AND THE RUPEE MAN

"It has to be Parmar, I am telling you. Parmar did it."

Province assistant city editor Damian Inwood was on the other end of the phone, having awakened me early Sunday morning. My normal shift did not start until noon. What he told me had struck me like a bolt of lightning. Instantly my mind raced back several months to a conversation I had had with a highly placed Sikh militant.

"They are going to do something really big," he had warned.

And now, it had happened.

Inwood was reading me a portion of a wire story. An Air India plane en route to London from Toronto had dropped from the sky like a stone. Early reports speculated it was a bomb. At the New Tokyo International Airport in Narita, some sixty kilometres northeast of Tokyo, a bag off-loaded from a CP Airlines flight originating in Vancouver had also exploded and two baggage handlers had died.

"We need to get some families," he said. "We should get some reaction."

I was out of bed and dressed within minutes and made my way to the Air India office on West Broadway where I thought perhaps there was a chance of catching relatives who might come looking for information. As I drove, I flashed back to that first meeting I had had with Gill and his Sikh militants at the Khalistan "consulate" at 45 Kingsway. I recalled also Parmar's ominous promise–in the aftermath of the Golden Temple massacre–that "the government of India will pay a price for this!"

Is this was what he had meant, I wondered. Had he really blown up a plane with 329 innocent passengers on board? Was this why rumours had been spreading throughout temples in Ontario and British Columbia that it would be dangerous to travel by Air India?

It was inevitable, I had worried, that the intense, pent-up emotions that the Sikh community had experienced and which I had reported on in the wake of the Temple massacre might at some point erupt into violent retaliation. I had no doubts about it now.

I was sickened by the tragic loss of innocent life. However, the reporter in me smelled what would undoubtedly be the biggest story of my career. I parked my car and hustled over to the Air India offices on West Broadway. When I walked in, I noticed only two people sitting there. One was a turbaned Sikh sitting at a chair. The other was Air India assistant manager Chani Sachdeva. Sachdeva and I had met at some of the functions held by Consul-General Jagdish Sharma.

"You just missed Gurinder Singh," said Sachdeva. He was referring to India's vice-consul and the R&AW spy in Vancouver. "He was here a few minutes ago."

"You got any word about what happened?" I asked.

Sachdeva said they were still waiting for passenger lists and more information, but a grim message had already arrived from Air India headquarters. It had said the aircraft had crashed. Bodies had been sighted in the water. Air India manager Jehangir Parakh was in another room as I spoke with Sachdeva. I was told he was still in shock because his friend Sam Madon had been on board. In his hand, Sachdeva clutched the bulletin from Air India announcing the grim news: Air India Flight 182 had crashed and there appeared to be no survivors.

I looked at him and said, "329 people." Then I turned to the turbaned man who was still sitting there.

"Did you have family on the aircraft," I asked.

"No, just some people I knew," he said.

He said he was a travel agent. His name was Amarjit Singh Pawa. It struck me then that this man was a ticket agent for Parmar. Two months earlier, I had heard he had booked tickets for Parmar's wife and sister to visit Pakistan to lend moral support to the hijackers during their trial.

What the hell was this man doing here today?

"Friendly Travels, right?" I asked him as he sat on a chair in the Air India office. He nodded.

"Well, maybe we can talk later, eh? May be this afternoon I can call you up," I offered.

Pawa wrote down his name and his phone number on an Air India office business card. I pocketed it and left. Later I tried to call the number on the back of the card. I got a recording that said it was a wrong number. I checked the phone book for the Friendly Travel Agency. The number Pawa had given me was different from the one listed in the directory. The number Pawa wrote out on the back of the card was only one digit different from the correct one. He sure knew how to manipulate phone numbers. And I knew he also manipulated Parmar's name often to allow him to travel incognito.

I left the office not much further ahead than when I'd arrived. It was intriguing that Gurinder Singh had already been there, but I couldn't use that in a news story. Pawa was a complete cipher. My instincts told me these two incidents—one in the air southwest of Ireland and the explosion at New Tokyo International Airport had to be connected. I had to find that thread.

Luckily, I had no shortage of sources inside the Sikh community, not to mention those whose task it was to keep an eye on them. I decided to start with the Indian spies since in my opinion, they were always the best informed about what was going on in the community. In between trying to find out if anyone had heard of any families from Vancouver being on the Air India aircraft, I called India's vice-consul in Vancouver, Gurinder Singh, and Maloy Krishna Dhar in Ottawa. Dhar was a senior member of the Indian spy agency IB, who had been seconded to the Ottawa High Commission of India as a security officer.

Since the crew had no chance to relay a mayday message and the aircraft had fallen from the sky like a stone, Gurinder Singh and Dhar were convinced that the Air Indian plane had been sabotaged. Dhar went further. He suggested I look at the two Sikhs who had gone through explosive training in Frank Camper's mercenary school in early 1985 in Alabama and then escaped an FBI dragnet following the discovery of an assassination plot against an Indian cabinet minister who was in New Orleans for eye-surgery. FBI fugitives Lal Singh and Amand Singh had still not been located. Dhar suggested these could be the guys who could have done it, since they were known to Indian intelligence to have contacts in the Vancouver area and both were wanted terror suspects.

What was most intriguing to Indian intelligence at that time was the fact that the bag that exploded at Tokyo Airport in Narita killing baggage handlers Ideharu Koda and Hideo Asano had flown from Vancouver on a direct trans–Pacific flight. There was an Air India flight waiting to take off from Tokyo. The two agents said they believed the bag that exploded was destined to connect with that flight. The Indian agents, Gurinder Singh and Dhar, already had a telex from Air India's office in Tokyo that added fuel to their suspicions.

"Good morning. Kindly investigate details of following two passengers supposed to travel CP 003 22 June Vancouver/Narita and Air India 301 23 June Narita/Bangkok, who no-showed Air India 301. Singh/A Mr. PNR H6269 original CP/Vancouver booking reference YVRCP/QG4JIBA301XF of 16 June and Singh/L Mr. PNR H639R original CP/Vancouver booking reference YVRCP/UZCJPSA301XF of 20 June 85. Most grateful your urgent reply due above required by manager Japan in connection with Narita Airport baggage explosion. Regards."

Clearly, the two agents knew what they were talking about. The missing passenger whose ticket identified him as L. Singh was to fly to Bangkok via Air India Flight 301 after arriving in Tokyo. All other passengers had been accounted for. It had to be L. Singh's bag and the man's initial matched that of Lal Singh.

Gurinder Singh and Dhar had good arguments, but they also had an axe to grind. I had to find out what Canadian law enforcement was saying. I called Richmond RCMP's general investigation section and was surprised to find that Inspector Bruce Giesbrecht was at work on a Sunday. And so was my good friend Staff-Sergeant John Kovalick. Both officers had been called in to work on their days off. I was starting to put two and two together very fast. The fact that they had been called in to duty at Richmond RCMP detachment where Vancouver International Airport was located was significant. Both agreed they had been called in to work on the bombing in Tokyo and the suspicion of a bomb on Air India Flight 182. They told me that when CP Air Flight 003 took off from Vancouver all the bags had originated here. No bags had arrived from other airlines.

The fact that the bag bomb that exploded in Tokyo came from Vancouver, and that there was a missing Mr. Singh on the flight that took that bomb to Tokyo, raised further suspicions that the other incident in the air southwest of Ireland was possibly linked to it. After all, B.C. was the epicentre of Sikh militancy, outside of India. The investigators also confirmed they were looking at the possibility that a bomb downed Air India Flight 182.

I had the spies, I had the police, and now I needed to track down the suspects. Early in the afternoon I began looking for Parmar to see if he would make a comment on the Air India disaster. It would be interesting to see what he had to say about this tragedy. A couple of calls to his home went unanswered, so I called Surjan Singh Gill. I told him I was looking for Parmar and I would appreciate it if he could relay a message to call me. And of course, I asked for his reaction to the disaster. He was quite composed as he told me he regretted the loss of life and voiced his opposition to violence. From the man who had categorically supported hijackings to achieve his political ends, this declaration was a complete about-face. I thought his remarks were disingenuous, to say the least.

I was unaware at the time that my calls to Surjan Singh Gill and then a later conversation with Parmar would be picked up on CSIS intercepts until many months later when a RCMP Air India Task Force member showed me an intercept. The first call referencing my attempt to contact Parmar was recorded by CSIS when Surjan Singh Gill left a message for Parmar on June 23, 1985, the day of the tragedy. "Call Salim Jiwa about Air India," was the message he left for Parmar. It was probably the first time the spies had picked up a reference to Air India on Parmar's phone.

I tracked down one of the relatives of the victims. It was Air India Captain Bhinder's cousin, Harinder Mahal, who was still in shock over the co-pilot's death. She spoke of Bhinder's call to her just a couple of days previously.

"It was his first trip to Canada and he was really happy," she said.

The Mahals would be the first of many, many victims I would talk to covering the Air India tragedy. Every victim of crime leaves a mark on you, an emotional scar. Interviewing victims of tragedy or crime is one of the most gruelling tasks a crime reporter faces. My colleagues always said to me I was "zero Celsius" inside my core. They thought I was never affected by emotion. But that was only because the pain was camouflaged at work. I took it home with me. Often lying awake, I would think about the tears that I had seen on faces, or choked up voices on the phone describing the agony of losing loved ones. These things always haunted me at night, while I was alone with my thoughts. In the Air India bombing case the scope of the tragedy was so overwhelming it would not be possible ever to recover from it completely

On Sunday, June 23, 1985, I was ready to write my story, raising the spectre that two bombs had been checked in from Vancouver, most likely by Sikh militants. I also wrote an analysis of rising Sikh militancy, with a special mention of Parmar and Canada's failure to extradite him to India in 1982. But I knew that the work that had been done in a day was only part of a process, a long search for answers that had just begun.

The connections I was able to make between the downing of Air India off the coast of Ireland and the other bag explosion in Tokyo landed on the front page of next days' newspaper. In the days that followed, the contacts that I had made within the Sikh community in the past four years would put me way ahead of other reporters in Canada in the Air India case. My understanding of the culture, my list of contacts, my ability to talk to militants, moderates, the RCMP, Indian government agents would afford me a deep and panoramic view of complex and entrenched world of Sikh militancy. It wasn't until the next day that I got a call back from Parmar and again the call was captured by CSIS. It seemed the pressure Surjan Singh Gill had put on Parmar to talk to me had worked.

"On the 24th of June, 1985, at an unknown time, CSIS monitors intercepted a telephone conversation from Surjan Singh Gill to Talwinder Singh Parmar. Mr. Gill told Mr. Parmar to return Salim Jiwa's call. Mr. Gill advised that Babbar Khalsa was getting the blame for the crash and that Mr. Parmar should clarify the view and give his statement about the crash incident. Mr. Gill advised that he could not come over to Mr. Parmar's as there were people at his residence for inquiries and the like."

Parmar phoned me back to deny his organization had any role in the disaster. Once again, that conversation was also captured by CSIS. It is sometimes disconcerting talking to suspects in crimes. I had often been warned by police officers while working on other cases. "Be careful what you say, we have wires running all over the place."

"On the 24th of June, 1985, at an unknown time, CSIS monitors intercepted a telephone conversation from Talwinder Singh Parmar to Salim Jiwa, a reporter. Mr. Jiwa mentioned to Mr. Parmar that someone had called Bombay Air in India and said that a Babbar Khalsa member was responsible for the bomb. When Mr. Jiwa asked if Mr. Parmar's association had had a hand in the bombing, Mr. Parmar denied any involvement."

Knowledge about the intercepts by CSIS of my own conversation made it clear to me that Canada's spy agency had been listening to Parmar during the days leading up to the bombing. I found it ironic that CSIS had been tracking Parmar for the wrong reasons. Canada was trying to prevent an attack on Rajiv Gandhi during a visit to Washington, D.C. That preoccupation with Gandhi's safety seemed fuelled by the FBI arrests in the U.S. of Lal Singh's terror partners. That FBI investigation had sent CSIS and the RCMP down the wrong road. When Parmar was visited by the RCMP and U.S. Secret Service on June 12, just eleven days before the Air India disaster he must have thought, "They know nothing."

The law enforcement agencies had made sure that Parmar knew both Canada and the U.S. were taking the security of Gandhi very seriously. But it was not something that had ruffled him or diverted him off the track he was on. The police were thinking one thing; Parmar another. If anything, the visit probably made Parmar even more cautious and secretive about his own plan.

Meanwhile, anguished relatives of the victims were heading to Ireland in droves. Most of those flying out were hoping against hope of finding loved ones. Bodies were being held in a makeshift morgue at Cork Regional Hospital. Relatives faced a gruesome task of identifying grotesquely disfigured bodies. One of those who flew in from Vancouver was Major Singh Sidhu. He had lost his sister Sukhwinder Kaur Uppal, her daughter Parminder and son Kuldip. The two children had taken leave from school early to fly to India. Sidhu told me he was shocked by what he saw.

As a first step toward identification he was shown pictures of Sukhwinder and Parminder. They didn't look anything like they did when he had seen them on June 22 when he had said goodbye. Sidhu said he would never forget the missing eye, the broken nose and a huge stitched-up cut on Parminder's face.

"I couldn't be positive it was them. I was only 50 per cent sure. Then we had to use dental records for positive identification," he said.

The body of his nephew, Kuldip, was not among the 131 bodies picked up within two days of the disaster. When I went to the family's home, I saw the seventy-year-old Mehnga Singh Sidhu sitting in one corner of his home. He was gazing at the ceiling with a blank look in his eyes. There were tears still streaming down. I sat in one corner and looked at his face. The pain etched on it was unbearable. I could not even begin to fathom how deep his pain must have been to have lost his daughter and his two grandchildren. So many years later I still remember the pain on his face. I also remember that the room had looked quite misty for a while, until I wiped my eyes. This was the kind of pain you suffered when you came face-to-face with tragedy. But it was not something you told your editor, nor your family. Would they ever think of you as a tough reporter if you told them of these tears?

In Canada, there appeared to be a lack of empathy for the victims, although a majority, 165 of the 329 on board, were Canadians. Prime Minister Brian Mulroney did not go on national television or radio to offer his sympathies for the loss of Canadian lives. Never before had Canada lost so many people in a single disaster in peacetime, and yet, there was no mourning or a church mass inside the country. At first, Mulroney sent his condolences to India. Later, he offered his sympathies through a statement: "I would like to convey my deepest personal condolences and those of the Canadian government to all members of the bereaved families on the occasion of the terrible loss of Air India Flight 182."

Victims of the tragedy complained they felt abandoned by their nation in their hour of need. There was no move to mobilize any form of victim assistance as relatives arrived in Ireland. It was all left to the Irish. Many in villages near the shores where the bodies were first brought took relatives into their homes, offering a little warmth at a time of terrible tragedy.

It was quite clear to the government of Canada though intelligence reports filed by CSIS and the RCMP that this was not simply an accident, but all reason suggested it was a terrorist attack. Every newspaper in the country was running the news of suspicion that a bomb had destroyed the aircraft, yet there was no sign of Canada's collective sorrow as a nation. Families felt a strange alienation. They felt like second-class citizens in their own country. Lata Pada, an Ontario-based internationally renowned dance choreographer, who lost her husband and her two daughters, called this lack of empathy a "blight" on Canada, a national shame. It would take twenty years for a Canadian prime minister to even visit Ireland to pay his respects at the site of a memorial built near the shore facing the scene of disaster.

For many years, the government of Canada would be virtually silent on the topic of the tragedy. In fact, what was set in motion that awful day was a campaign of official silence, which included vigorous efforts to frustrate even a suggestion that a bomb had, in fact, been the cause of the disaster—even as CSIS and the RCMP began piling up evidence to the contrary.

Why? I believe the reason was the government's assumption of liability in the event the families of the victims filed a lawsuit.

After all, when an inquest into the disaster was convened in Cork, Ireland, in September 1985, the lawyer representing the Canadian government, Ivan Whitehall, aggressively attempted to impose limitations on how far coroner Cornelius Riordan could go with his inquest. To observers, it was hard not to conclude from his presentation that the government of Canada was interested less in truth and justice and more in limiting its exposure to future lawsuits. The last thing they needed to have revealed, for instance, was that the government had been less than comprehensive dealing with the threat of terrorists in their own country.

September 17, 1985

Coroner Riordan was to hear some gruesome, gory testimony. It was the kind of stuff that made me suggest to the RCMP at one time that they should mail the results of the pathologist's examination of bodies to each of the Air India suspects. Riordan's job was to establish where, when, and how the victims died as accurately as possible; to make some sense out of this tragedy.

"It is my very sad duty today to open an inquest into the deaths of the victims of the Air India disaster," he began. "You are all aware of the grim tragedy which overtook the flight on the morning of the twenty-third of June. As it left Montreal for London Heathrow on what turned out to be its last and fateful journey it had, I understand, 307 passengers and twenty-two crew members. Early on that June Sunday morning it encountered a fatal catastrophe over the Atlantic Ocean off the south coast of Ireland."

Riordan's first witness was Air India passenger agent Divyang Yodh, who was the man in charge when Air India Flight 182 left Toronto. He had travelled with it to Montreal. He had seen the passengers and crew off. But all Yodh could tell the court was the seating arrangements in the aircraft and the number of passengers in each of its sections.

Thomas Lane, the air traffic controller who was monitoring the radarscope when *Kanishka* vanished from his screen, then took the stand to describe the events in the control room at Shannon.

"I was at radar control at Shannon when I took up position at the radar screen. We had three aircraft in position [on the screen]," he said. "There was between six and twenty miles between the first and last. I was in contact with the jumbo jet and it was one of three aircraft approaching Shannon Control Zone about the same time. The three aircraft identified themselves and were given coded identifications by Shannon Control. These would enable Shannon Control to lock onto them, using computers in all subsequent transmissions. Air India was the first. There is a transponder code and we gave them their transponder code, which they acknowledged and were immediately identified by the radar controller. He would punch his number in and we would receive that then on our radarscope. That should then record what the altitude readout was and where the aircraft was."

Lane testified that once the aircraft's transponder tunes in to the Shannon Control radar, the aircraft's position would show up as a diamond with five dots.

"At 8:13 a.m. local time, (7:13 A.M. GMT, 12:13 a.m. PST) I observed that the AI-182 signal deleted itself from the screen. It did not respond. He was not answering then. The three planes were on the screen for approximately eight to ten minutes when the Air India jet disappeared," said Lane. "The position was now serious and they did not reply and I called the aircraft that were behind and that was the TWA and *Empress* Flight (CP Air Flight 282)."

Then when all efforts to reach the Air India plane had failed, Lane said, he realized something deadly had happened. He declared a full-scale emergency. Desmond Eglington, chief controller at Shannon, testified that the last contact with the aircraft was at approximately 8:09:58 a.m. local time (7:09:58 GMT). Less than four minutes later the plane disappeared from radar, he said.

"The only other significant thing was that at approximately 7:14 a.m. (GMT) a carrier came up frequently and it lasted for approximately five or six seconds. A carrier wave. In other words, it is a [radio] wave, which was not modulated—a carrier with indecipherable modulation—it was like a shout or a noise of some description."

Eglington concluded that someone had let out a screech that the cockpit microphone had transmitted as the aircraft began to disintegrate.

"One would think the microphone was turned on," he continued. "At the end of that wave a noise—there was something there. Other people say it was a screech or a voice."

Eglington said any number of scenarios could be put together on how that last transmission occurred from the aircraft. It could mean that the pilot was desperately trying to convey a message or that the microphone button could have been pressed inadvertently.

Thomas O'Connor, a plastic surgeon and deputy medical director of Cork Regional Hospital related the grim events that transpired subsequently as a major search effort was launched and bodies began arriving in Cork.

"It was something we had not experienced in the past in any of the previous major disasters," he reported grimly. "Our mortuary facilities were insufficient and the gymnasium had to be used."

Army trucks had begun ferrying the bodies of the victims to hospital. The bodies had been labelled with numbers.

"We, in fact, did use the same numbers as the numbers given by police to prevent confusion. We forced teams of a doctor, a nurse and a clerical officer to make sure we had a record in relation to each body. Each victim was medically examined and relevant information was entered on charts."

O'Connor said arrangements had to be made for shelving in refrigeration units to accommodate the 131 bodies which had been recovered. Post-mortems were performed by seven teams of doctors. All the bodies were X-rayed. The scope of the disaster was massive, and yet the normal functions of Cork hospital had to be carried on too.

The bishop had already offered the church for religious ceremonies of all kinds for relatives who were arriving. In fact, several inter-denominational services were arranged. Sikhs and Hindus, Muslims, and Christians, were praying together in one church. Sadly, though, it was religious strife that had brought them here together in the first place.

Professor Cuimin Doyle, head of the histopathology department at Cork Hospital, was the first witness to testify about the post-mortems, which began on the afternoon of Monday, June 24 and continued until late Thursday evening. He performed examinations on twenty-three bodies in that period.

"My information is…no evidence of an explosion was found," Doyle stated. "There was no evidence of burning on any of the bodies. There was no evidence of which I know of fire and no obnoxious sign in so far as explosive substances were found."

"What you are really saying is that if there was an explosive substance activated on the plane it did not touch the areas where these people were sitting?" asked Riordan.

"Yes, that's correct."

Doyle agreed with Riordan's observation that if a bomb had exploded in the baggage compartment in the front of the aircraft, underneath the area where passengers were sitting, no evidence of the explosion would necessarily be found on the bodies of the victims—bearing in mind that a majority of those recovered had been sitting in the back of the aircraft.

Doyle was excused for the moment. Next called to the witness stand was police officer Con McGrath, who was in charge of the laborious process of identification of the bodies.

"Each body was fingerprinted by members of the Garda (Irish police) and each body was photographed," McGrath told the inquest. "Physical features such as age, sex, clothing, jewellery, or any other matter for record was put on forms. The items of clothing on each body were removed and placed in a bag. That bag was numbered with the number of the body from which the clothing was removed and there was one bag per body. Likewise, items of jewellery were removed from each body and placed in plastic bag and numbered. Each body was again photographed, this time in the nude. There was a dental examination of each body."

When the relatives arrived, they were shown pictures, items of familiar clothing, jewellery, and distinctive scars. The grim process enabled police to identify all 131 bodies that had been found.

Doyle came back to the stand and described the standard medical procedure employed in post-mortems: examination of body tissue, internal organs and brain tissue, and microscopic examination of small samples of flesh taken from bodies. One of the bodies he examined was one labelled "body number four:"

"This body was that of a young girl," he said, "an Indian girl of about ten years. She was of average build and partly clothed. There was no evidence of burning. There was some evidence of the body having been in the water. The external examination showed there was laceration of the scalp and there were fractures of the facial bones and of the left leg, and there were other bruises and abrasions on the surface of the skin. Internally, there were multiple fragmented fractures of the nose and the skull with tearing of the membrane and of the brain itself. The lungs were damaged and there was hemorrhage."

If the testimony sounded unnecessarily cruel in its precision and detail, the court was to hear of worse. This child's body was one which was in relatively good condition. Another body, that of a girl only nine years old who had been sitting in the tail end of the aircraft, showed extensive dislocation of bones. In this child's case, shoulders were broken, the right leg was broken above the ankle, the skull was fractured and the spinal column destroyed. She had suffered what was described as flail injury, caused by wild rotation of the limbs consistent with being thrown clear from the aircraft at high altitude. From this it could be deduced that the tail section of the aircraft had suddenly been blown wide open.

"My understanding is that flail injury occurs when the body is thrown out of the plane. My understanding is that as the body descends it flutters like a leaf and the limbs are thrown about and clothing torn by the air," said Doyle.

Doyle also shed light on one of the more interesting findings of the inquest. Lower portions of the bodies of many of the victims showed penetration by tiny fragments of plastic and, in some cases, metal. Many of these fragments had struck the bodies as though the fragments had shot upward from somewhere below the bodies. There were also flakes of paint which had penetrated the bodies of some of the victims, indicating to Coroner Riordan that the particles had been propelled by a high velocity stream of air. That too would indicate break-up of the plane or opening of its pressurized cabin while in flight.

Dr. John Hogan reported a nearly incredible finding he made while examining a woman who had been five-months pregnant. Unbelievably, she was alive at the time of hitting the water. She had fallen from the sky and survived, only to die of drowning.

Referring to this victim, he said, "Significant findings were large amounts of frothy fluid in her mouth and nostrils, and all of the air passages and the lungs were waterlogged and extremely heavy," said the doctor about this victim of drowning. "There was water in the stomach and the uterine. The uterus contained a normal male foetus of approximately five months. The foetus was not traumatized and in my opinion death was due to drowning."

The topic of fragments of metal embedded in bodies came up again during the course of the doctor's testimony. Again the coroner was advised that Canadian authorities had asked for forensic evidence to be kept secret.

Barry Galvin, state solicitor for Cork, stated that "there is a murder investigation going on arising out of this incident–certainly not [originating] on our shore–[to determine if] there was an explosion and as a result of the explosion…these people were murdered. So far as forensic reports are very relevant to the murder investigation it is privileged. At the request of Canadian authorities the Attorney General has been asked to keep the documents in this regard privileged."

The key witness at the inquest was Dr. Ian Hill of the U.K. Accident Investigation Branch. Since 1975 he has probed numerous air crashes of all kinds and is a specialist in aviation pathology. Hill had analyzed the severity of injuries suffered by the victims whose bodies had been recovered, a majority of them women and children–there were some eighty children aboard Air India 182–and come to the conclusion that the most severe injuries had been suffered by people in the rear of the aircraft.

"It suggests to me that something went very wrong in the tail section because a lot of the force was transmitted to those individuals sitting there," said Hill. "If we look at pelvic injuries, there appears to be a concentration of them in the rear portion of the aircraft, particularly on the right-hand side. These people sustained a severe vertical loading passing up through their seats, not necessarily aircraft seats, but through their seats."

Air India maintenance engineer Parasnuram Kaule was then called to testify about the structure of a 747, including its passenger cabins, luggage holds, and electronic equipment and their locations. Kaule said the forward luggage hold, which begins right behind the vital electronics bay of the aircraft, is about forty-two feet long, ten feet high, and twelve feet wide. The aft hold is sixty-two feet long and shares the same dimensions of width and height, he said.

"The main equipment centre of the aircraft is situated forward of the cargo/baggage hold and aft of the nose undercarriage bay,"

Kaule continued. "The main electronic centre contains much of the aircraft's electronic equipment, including two transponder sets, three VHF radio sets and the flight data acquisition unit. The two-transponder antennae are located immediately below the main equipment centre. AC power for the aircraft's electronic equipment is provided by four engine-driven generators.

"There are also batteries adjacent to the flight engineer's section in the cockpit, providing emergency DC power to the captain's essential flight instruments and one FHF radio set. Emergency battery power is not available for the two transponders, nor for the flight data acquisition unit. The digital flight data recorder is located adjacent to the cockpit voice recorder and it is fed from the flight data acquisition unit in the main equipment centre. It monitors some seventy parameters of airframe, engine, and systems behaviour and performance."

Further, Kaule pointed out that from the electronics bay, data obtained by the flight data acquisition centre is fed through a cable below the floor level to the black boxes in the rear of the aircraft. He said that if the cable were severed recording would stop.

"Everything is gone if the main equipment centre is gone?" asked Riordan.

"Yes," replied Kaule.

"If an event occurred which would have physically knocked out all the electric power, including the communications system in the pilot's cockpit, such an event would have to occur in an area towards the front of the plane? There is nowhere else from where it could have produced such a catastrophic effect?" Riordan asked.

"No," replied the London-based maintenance engineer.

By the end of the inquest, there was more than enough evidence to suggest a bomb had brought down Air India Flight 182. The aircraft had dropped like a rock from the sky without warning, scattering bodies and baggage over a nine-mile path. But the Cork coroner would receive a lecture from the Canadian government lawyer about what he could and could not do at the inquest. Whitehall presented a long argument to Riordan about the restrictions he was under in terms of his jurisdiction. Whitehall's argument against reaching any conclusion about the cause of the destruction was completely at odds with the evidence that was turning up in Vancouver in both the RCMP investigation and revelations I had made in my stories.

The coroner protested that he was being advised to play a merely administrative role of being a registrar of the deaths. He was being told just to "fill in a form". Whitehall then said he didn't even see how the jury was in any position to make any recommendations in this case.

Riordan knew he was being squeezed so that he wouldn't say what was on his mind. He replied that he could see nothing wrong with narrowing down the possible causes of the accident to either structural failure or an explosive device.

"There are others but they are a bit far-fetched and remote possibilities," Riordan pointed out.

"Only when you examine the facts in detail," argued Whitehall. "With respect, you had no facts to examine."

"I had the fact that it is almost certain, I think there is sufficient evidence there to be very suggestive that there was a major violent issue up there, near the nerve centre of the plane, there was a violent incident up there," Riordan retorted.

"With respect, sir, you don't have that evidence," said the Canadian lawyer.

"Well, it is very suggestive, I have evidence that both transponders failed, I have very strong evidence that the pilots were rendered incapable at the same time and I have very strong evidence that the navigational systems failed all at once," Riordan shot back.

Whitehall then concluded the evidence of system failures had come from a mechanic, not an expert. The coroner reminded him that the Air India witness was a mechanical engineer.

Despite all the objections, the coroner was determined to speak his mind.

"I am satisfied that Section 30 [in connection with the legal powers of a coroner] is not as restrictive as Mr. Whitehall has submitted. I feel the section provides authority to go behind the immediate cause of death. If it didn't I feel that the role of the corner would merely be that of completing an administrative document for the purpose of registering the deaths."

However, the coroner agreed that it would be premature for him to make a ruling over security at Canadian airports, or to conclusively point his finger at an explosive device. He had pulled his punch, despite the fact that he knew he was on the right track.

"There in the loneliness of the Atlantic Ocean lay lifeless wreckage and human bodies floating on the water," he said. "This was 51.03 degrees north and 12.44 west. That was about five miles away from where the airliner was when it went off the screen. One of the wonders of modern technology had been reduced to a pitiful sight."

Regarding the technical information he had heard, the coroner continued, it appeared that all the electrical systems had failed simultaneously and without a moment's warning. He came to this conclusion:

"In short, if the nerve centre should fail the plane has had a serious stroke, call it what you like. The plane was almost certainly in autopilot and it was travelling at about six hundred miles per hour at the time of the incident and it was in the sea five miles ahead so it must have lost altitude very, very quickly. It would do five miles in half a minute. This suggests that the first violent incident put the nerve centre completely out of order and the pilot and co-pilot were rendered incapable."

Riordan, nevertheless, asked the jury to make no positive finding, and not to make a recommendation.

Shortly after the inquest, I called Riordan up and offered him a chance to unload and to say what was on his mind.

"You know I didn't get much cooperation in terms of calling the witnesses. Only a bomb explains everything," he told me.

Lawyer Whitehall's strenuous objections notwithstanding, Riordan was right: anything less than a bomb was inconceivable as a cause of the disaster.

The official silence in Canada, however, was deafening. I could hear it. And I understood why. Blame for the tragedy lay, with csis, the rcmp, and aircraft security. Everyone bore some responsibility, a share of the blame, a share of the shame.

The effect of the Air India tragedy on the Indo-Canadian community was mixed. One militant in particular (a close confidante of fundamentalist Sikh Hardial Singh Johal) went around the Ross

Street Sikh Temple the day of the bombings saying, with some glee "We warned you not to fly Air India." When I talked to him about what he'd been saying, the militant asked me a question in return: "How many people died in the Golden Temple assault?"

But most people were close-mouthed. Many had been harassed and intimidated by the ruthless fundamentalist militants who had taken over the temples. The Air India bombing was a strong message: don't mess with us. We mean business.

Fear and suspicion ruled the Sikh community. I felt it at my front door a few months later. There was an unexpected knock that made me jump. It was evening, my wife and kids were out and I was alone. I opened the door and there was Surjan Singh Gill; a man I had seen lustily dismember a blazing effigy of Indira Gandhi with a sword. He was nervous and edgy. My heart was thumping a little as I asked him to come inside and offered him some tea.

"I was not involved," he said to me. "I swear I was not involved. When you come to know all the facts you will know it was not me."

Gill did not have to come to my home to tell me this. We had met a number of times for lunch at Raga Restaurant. And each time our conversation had turned to Air India. He had already told me he was not involved. So the visit was a bit of a surprise and a little unnerving. However, we chatted for a bit before he stood up.

Then, he turned and said, "I am good friend, Salim. But I can be a bad enemy."

The meaning of what he said was clear. It was a warning. It was unambiguous. "You know Surjan, there is one thing you will find out about me. I am not afraid. I am glad you say you were not involved, but I will keep working on this," I replied.

After Gill left, I wondered about his denial of involvement. He was an intelligent man, and in my mind never appeared overly religious. He was more of a politician than a religious zealot like Parmar. Later, it would be established that Gill had resigned from the Babbar Khalsa organization on Friday, June 21, 1985. The CSIS observation post outside Parmar's home observed Gill delivering a manila envelope to the "Living Martyr." Gill would also write the B.C. Registrar of Societies declaring he was no longer a director of the BK. But all this I would find out later.

In the aftermath of the Air India tragedy, at least some Sikhs loyal to India were not shy about weaving theories around the bombings. Indian spy Gurinder Singh and I sat down for lunch at a fast food corner at the Sinclair Centre opposite the Indian consulate on Howe Street. He told me he had already checked out a group of Sikhs who worked at Vancouver Airport to see if the terrorists had received inside help. He'd discovered that a brother of BK lieutenant Bagri worked there as a janitor and other friends as well as a nephew had access to many areas of the airport as employees. He was looking at every possibility; he was doing his job as an agent.

"I can tell you the RCMP suspects Parmar. They have told our people that they think he did it," he said.

I agreed everything was pointing to Parmar.

A few days later, I phoned Sachdeva at the Air India office in Vancouver to see if he could lay his hands on the tickets of L. Singh and M. Singh, if he could provide me a copy.

"It is in Parakh's desk," said Sachdeva. "You take it out of his desk."

"Well, Jesus, you're kidding, I can't do that," I replied. "Ask Parakh and get me a copy."

On August 18, 1985, Sachdeva had quietly handed me a copy of the tickets. They were consecutively numbered and had been paid for in cash. Someone had coughed up more than $3,000 for two tickets to fly in different directions from Vancouver. In both cases, the passengers were to connect with Air India flights. These passengers had not boarded their aircraft after checking in their bags. This was evidence of a conspiracy. Damn good evidence, I thought. And it certainly was worth putting this on the front page, or so I thought.

Sometimes, reporters puzzle over decisions made by their news editors. Today, armed with the tickets of the two men, I pushed my boss to headline the story. Steve Carlman, one of the ex-patriot Brits who ran the *Province*, gave me his typical, quizzical look through his coke-bottle glasses.

"Well, where does it take us?" he said.

"What do you mean where does it take us?" I said. "We have the tickets of the two terrorists and it proves what we have said: that two men boarded bags, but did not board the planes. This is proof, in black and white."

"Well we will give it a masthead, but it is not a line story," he replied.

He was offering me a headline above the newspaper's logo, but not the main headline story of the day. It was time to play a little hardball with Carlman.

"If I send this to the *Toronto Star*, they will line it," I said to him.

"Well, show me," Carlman replied.

I phoned Haroon Siddique, the national editor at the *Toronto Star*. The next day's *Star* had the story on the top of the front page and I made sure I took a copy and tossed it onto Carlman's desk as he sat there with my other boss, city editor Neil Graham.

"There," I said, tapping a finger on the front page.

"Fuck off, Salim," said Carlman, smiling.

Graham and I burst out laughing. It might not have been the line story, but *The Province* piece had run with the tickets and pictures of Lal Singh and Amand Singh since we still felt these two FBI-hunted terrorists had something to do with the bombings. I'd hoped the story would have an impact, make somebody nervous. Indeed, the very next day, I would get a strange call.

"My name is Hardial Singh Johal," said the man on the other end of the line. "You don't know me, but I know you."

I remained silent. I knew him well. He had a reputation as a hard core Sikh fundamentalist, one who had led a campaign at the Ross Street Temple to make the covering of the head mandatory. But I had never heard his name mentioned in connection with the struggle for Khalistan or the BK.

"The two people who you had in your paper did a very bad thing. They left my telephone number behind when they booked the tickets," Johal said. (If our thinking was incorrect that it was Lal Singh and Amand Singh who owned those tickets, then clearly it was in the interest of Johal to reinforce our mistaken belief.)

I asked Johal why any terrorist would be so careless as to leave behind his telephone number when booking tickets.

"Only an enemy would do that, not friends," Johal replied.

Was he asking me to believe that he had somehow been set up?

Johal went on at some length about how he was a peaceful man who supported reconciliation between Sikhs and India. He was a supporter of Longowal, the leader of the Akali Dal party who had by now begun to negotiate with Rajiv Gandhi in a bid to resolve the impasse in the Punjab. He said Longowal had stayed at his place when he visited Canada some years back. Looking back at this call later I would realize that Johal had begun taking counter-measures to deflect any suspicion that he was involved in the Air India bombing. Subsequent investigation would prove he was the chief executor of the plot. All trails from Parmar's house led to him. I didn't know at the time that he'd been spotted at the airport by Raghbir Grewal on the morning the bags were being checked in.

As Johal talked to me on the phone during his surprise call, I asked him if an enemy had left behind his phone number when booking the fatal tickets, I needed to know who that enemy was.

"The International Sikh Youth Federation," Johal insisted. "Don't tell anyone I told you, but they also left behind a telephone number for Sodhi Singh Sodhi (the assailant at the Indian consulate and ISYF executive member) and they left behind the telephone number of the Ross Street Sikh Temple."

Sodhi confirmed that his telephone had also turned up on the tickets. He also agreed that when he emigrated from India, his name was Lambhar Singh: "L. Singh."

Sodhi countered that Johal knew his name was Lambhar Singh because they had a telephone number that was one digit different from one another's: Johal's phone number was xxx–3216 and Sodhi's was xxx-3215. The first three digits of their telephone numbers were also identical. When friends called him, said Sodhi, they would amuse themselves by asking for the old name, and sometimes they would dial Johal's home by mistake asking for Lambhar Singh.

I was now confronted with a fascinating but perplexing puzzle. Had Johal booked the tickets? Had he left his telephone number because he had no time to think when asked by the ticket agents for a contact number? The numbers mystery merely added to the evidence that a plot had been hatched in Vancouver: genuine travellers don't leave behind phoney phone numbers when they book tickets. But sometimes, even clever terrorists make mistakes. It would not

ABOVE: Bowing to their leader are a group of sympathizers of Babbar Khalsa chief Talwinder Singh Parmar upon his return from Germany on July 7, 1984.
The Province photo by David Clark.

LEFT: Fundamentalist Sikh Sodhi Singh Sodhi raises his fist in defiance after being released by police outside the Indian consulate on June 6, 1984.
Photo by *The Province*.

RIGHT: Smoke rises from the surface of the Atlantic as rescue ships and helicopters arrive at the scene where debris from the Air India Flight 182 explosion had rained down over a nine-mile path.
Photo by Thomas Smyth.

ABOVE: A large chunk of the fuselage of the Air India Boeing 747 floats near the surface of the ocean.
Photo by Thomas Smyth.

LEFT: A rescue helicopter and a crew member pluck a lifeless body out of the stormy North Atlantic following the downing of Air India Flight 182.
Photo by Thomas Smyth.

ABOVE: A reconstructed segment of the destroyed Air India Boeing 747.
The Province photo by Arlen Redekop.

TOP LEFT: Irish sailors bring to shore the body of a victim of the Air India bombing on June 23, 1985. The picture was taken at Cork, Ireland where authorities had set up a makeshift morgue to deal with the calamity.
Photo by Thomas Smyth.

BOTTOM LEFT: The grim scene at Cork, Ireland, as army trucks waited to carry the dead to morgue.
Photo by Thomas Smyth.

TOP: Talwinder Singh Parmar (white turban) turns to talk with his deputy Ajaib Singh Bagri in this photo captured in July 1985 by a Canadian Security Intelligence Service surveillance team. Parmar's home was regarded by CSIS as the headquarters of the violent Babbar Khalsa group.
Photo by CSIS.

BOTTOM: Fundamentalist Sikh Hardial Singh Johal walks towards the front of Talwinder Singh Parmar's home while a Canadian Security Intelligence Service surveillance team was taking pictures.
Photo by CSIS.

LEFT: RCMP composite drawing of M. Singh. He was the well-dressed man who, on June 22, 1985, checked in the fatal bag at Vancouver Airport that exploded aboard Air India Flight 182. The man has never been identified.
Composite drawing by RCMP.

ABOVE: Terrorist Inderjit Singh Reyat emerges from a Duncan courtroom on November 14, 1985, after being ordered to pay a fine of $2,000 for possession of dynamite.
The Province photo by Gerry Kahrmann.

ABOVE: On January 11, 1997 four people were injured while trying to bring tables into the Guru Nanak Sikh Temple in Surrey, B.C. Three were stabbed with ceremonial daggers and one suffered a broken arm. Picture shows two bloodied men on the ground with one receiving help from a relative.
The Province photo by Arlen Redekop.

BELOW: July 25, 1987 photo shows Babbar Khalsa chief Talwinder Singh Parmar, centre, with his lieutenant Ajaib Singh Bagri, left, at a press conference at the Ross Street Sikh temple discussing the future of the Sikh separatist movement.
The Province photo by Wayne Leidenfrost.

TOP: March 2000 photo shows businessman Ripudaman Singh Malik, head of Khalsa School & Bank, joining Sikhs and Muslims in a protest at the killing of thirty-five Sikhs in India's Kashmir State.
The Province photo by Colin Price.

BELOW: Talwinder Singh Parmar's daughter, Rajinder Kaur, cries at a press conference while demanding answers from the Canadian government about the truth behind her father's October 1992 death at the hands of Indian authorities. She accompanied by then Burnaby MP Svend Robinson.
Vancouver Province Photo by Gerry Kahrmann.

RIGHT: Air India Flight 182 Co-pilot Satwinder Singh Bhinder poses with his wife Amarjit Kaur during happier times.
Photo courtesy of Amarjit Bhinder.

BELOW: Indian Airlines Captain Ashamdip Singh Bhinder, the son of Air India Flight 182 co-pilot Satwinder Singh Bhinder poses with mother Amarjit Kaur Bhinder shortly after his engagement in India in 2005.
Photo courtesy of Amarjit Bhinder.

take many months to figure out that Johal had simply screwed up while booking the tickets and was now trying to divert attention by claiming he was a moderate; planting suggestions someone had tried to frame him.

The next day's story was headlined: "Police Check City Phones in Jet Probe." It wasn't the best headline in the world, but it told the story. And it was another exclusive.

I was miles ahead of other media, an advantage I had gained by being in the community for so long. I was determined to pursue this further, every day, from every possible angle. I next called the Japanese police in Tokyo to see what forensics they had uncovered from the Narita blast. A Japanese investigator told me the bomb that had exploded was contained inside the outer casing of a Sanyo Tuner model FMT 611K that had been bought in the Vancouver area (The Japanese cop's geography was a little poor. The place where the tuner was bought was across the water from Vancouver–on Vancouver Island.) The actual purchase location was a Woolworths store in Duncan, the hometown of Inderjit Singh Reyat. He, Parmar, and the mystery third man–the so-called Mr. X–had performed the bush explosive experiment there just days before the Air India bombing and the stereo tuner had been bought one day later, on June 5, 1985. That story about the Japanese identification of the tuner as the device that had contained the bomb made headlines around the world.

For the first few days after the worst case of aviation bombing in history, Staff-Sergeant Kovalick's Richmond RCMP detachment had handled the investigation. The ride had lasted a whole five days, Kovalick would muse later. His detachment was too small and did not have the capacity to probe an international incident, he said he was told. But before his foray into a terrorism investigation ended, his men had interviewed Jeanne Adams about the man who had checked in the bag and not boarded. In fact, it was Adams who had also boarded the second bag that had flown to Tokyo. Kovalick's other men had interviewed Martine Donahue at CP Air who had taken the telephoned bookings on June 19, 1985. She said the Mr. Singh who called appeared to have a polished voice and spoke like Rajiv Gandhi (she had heard Gandhi's voice on TV). She had asked the caller if they had a deadline of some kind because he insisted on connecting with particular Air India flights in Toronto and Tokyo.

"You seem to have a deadline, what is it?" Donahue said she asked the man, and the reply was: "It's to connect with the Air India flight."

Every airline ticket has its own biography. The time it was booked, the time it was picked up and paid for, the telephone numbers of patrons or their place of contact—even previous route selections and cancellations are kept on a computerized file called a Passenger Name Record (PNR). The clerk who could give the police those crucial answers was Donahue.

Donahue was interviewed by RCMP officers John Schneider and Bobby Sellinger. Schneider would later become the chief of the Air India Task Force and the two of us would lunch together often. We also enjoyed chicken tikka at the home of Sodhi Singh Sodhi, both of us having been invited separately by Sodhi.

Schneider and Sellinger would go over Donahue's story of the ticket bookings over and over. It was an amazing story. One interview started with Schneider asking her about the crucial call.

"The gentleman who eventually called himself Mr. Singh called (in) these reservations for two other people," recalled Donahue. "Other than himself that is, one was to Bangkok and one was to Toronto; both had to link up with Air India."

She finally managed to find the right connection for one of the passengers who would fly from Vancouver to Tokyo and connect with an Air India flight to Bangkok. She said the caller did not argue about the fare even though it was a little high.

She had more trouble making connections with for the passenger who was to fly Vancouver to Toronto and then connect with Air India Flight 182 in Toronto. So she booked the passenger to fly to Dorval Airport in Montreal which would mean the passenger would have to then make his way to Mirabel Airport from where Air India Flight 182 would pick up more passengers en route to London and Delhi.

Schneider: Were there any particular phrases or words spoken by the caller that seemed unique?

Donahue: No, nothing outstanding; he spoke good
English.

Schneider: Do you think you could possibly describe his
laughter?

Donahue: Oh! Quiet. Like the rest of the conversation, it's
not a peal of laughter. Um…very pleasant voice, mature,
er, poised voice with good command of English, a good
choice of words, simple but precise.

She said the caller told her he would arrange to pick up the tickets from the CP Air office and did not want them delivered to him.

CP agent Gerald Duncan would provide more answers during an interview with RCMP officer Al Armstrong, another of Kovalick's Richmond Mounties.

"Could you please view the photocopies of airline tickets issued to L. and M. Singh on 20 June 1985 by yourself at the CP Air ticket office and tell me what you recall about these transactions?" asked Armstrong.

"I was working from 10 a.m. to 6 p.m. on June 20, 1985," Duncan recalled. "We can be sure it was early afternoon because it was only two hours till noon and I'm sure it was not right off the bat (that the man came into his office)."

"As far as I am concerned it was not one of the passengers that picked up the tickets. I got that impression because I thought he was an agent. I suppose I thought, I thought that because the tickets were going both ways," Duncan added. "He kept referring to the people travelling as 'they,' so I presumed the tickets were for two other people.

"The man was as tall or taller than I am and I'm five-foot-eleven-and-a-half. He was in by himself–I'd describe him as 210 to 220 pounds, wearing a light gold-yellow or mustard color turban. He spoke good English. He didn't have to repeat anything. Mind you, there is always a trace of an accent. He wore more casual Canadian-type clothes, nothing radical or no Nehru-type suit."

"Do you recall any particulars on the dress?" asked the Mountie.

"No, it was just ordinary."

"Do you recall anything else distinctive about his appearance, such as jewellery, scars, birthmarks?"

"No. He was not an ancient man. He wasn't grey—I'd say late thirties."

"Do you recall him associating with anyone else in your office—employees or customers?" Armstrong prodded.

"No, because he kept referring to the people who were destined to use the tickets as 'they.' I was sure he was by himself, usually if there was more than one, they'd both be at the counter."

"Do you recall how he produced the money—from a wallet or in a roll, pre-counted?"

"When I got it, I think it was in a wad, folded in half. He may have known how much it was going to cost, because he had this information written on a piece of paper. He knew the flight numbers and routes," Duncan replied.

"Did he keep that piece of paper?"

"Yes."

"How long did the transaction take?"

"It must have been ten to fifteen minutes."

"Do you recall why the first ticket was marked void?" asked Armstrong, referring to the mark put after the final destination, Bangkok, on L. Singh's ticket.

"See, the booking was already on the machine—I think. I don't remember making it (the booking). That would mean someone phoned it in. See, the first ticket was booked 'open return.' I'm sure he knew what he wanted. It seems to me they were planning to come back, but they were planning on staying more than a year or they didn't know when they were returning so he changed it to a one-way ticket."

"Was he concerned about the method in which the original flight had been booked?"

"Since the bookings were made, the people didn't know when they were coming back and that was it," said Duncan, clarifying the change from a return ticket to a one-way ticket. "The guy was quite well-versed."

"Did he comment about the short notice for booking or buying the tickets and the wait-list from Toronto?"

"No—probably because he looked to me like he knew what he was doing. He looked like an (travel) agent to me. There was never any discussion about alternative bookings."

"Do you recall if he introduced himself when he approached your counter or identified himself at all?" Armstrong asked.

"No, he did not," Duncan responded. "Again, because he didn't do something like that, I presumed he was not one of the people travelling."

The ticket agent added that he didn't recall seeing any ride waiting for the man outside the office. He then described the turbaned man in great detail as Armstrong continued to tape the conversation.

"This guy had a reasonably full face. Most of them look skinny and this guy was a big man. He seemed to have more meat on him than most of them do. Because I see so many I can't be positive about the description. He may have hair from his beard braided beneath his chin—it looked like cloth."

"Could we just do a complete description, then?"

"Six feet, 210 to 220 pounds, full face, mustard turban, beard—possibly braided, casual Western-type clothes, spoke good English, no distinctive jewellery, carried list of flights, flight numbers and times, and spoke as if tickets were for someone else. I'd say he was in his late thirties. Polite and maybe even soft-spoken."

While his memory was fresh, Duncan would say he saw no distinctive jewellery on the man's hand. But later under hypnosis he would remember seeing a large diamond ring on the man's finger.

After less than a week on the case, Kovalick received a message from headquarters that his tenure as an investigator of international terrorism was over, but his men had done a valuable job. They had proof beyond reasonable doubt that those who booked the tangled tickets and the man who had picked them up were no ordinary travellers.

Now, there was a new man heading the Air India Task Force, and the publication of my stories about a trail of phone numbers, about the tickets of the terrorists and the fact that the stereo that exploded in Tokyo was bought here in B.C. made his team nervous.

Province managing editor Don MacLachlan soon received a phone call from the new boss: RCMP Inspector John Hoadley, who was concerned about the paper's coverage and wanted a meeting.

When he arrived at the *Province* reception desk at the Granville Street offices in Vancouver, MacLachlan was faced with an imposing, six-foot tall, blue-eyed Mountie who spoke in a deep, gruff voice. Forty-nine-years old at the time, Hoadley already had thirty years of police work behind him. Fourteen of those years had been spent in intelligence work with the RCMP Security Service. The impressive CV made him the natural choice to head the largest task force in RCMP history. Hoadley coordinated an investigative team of well over two hundred members in Vancouver, Toronto, and Montreal.

Behind the closed, frosted-glass door of the *Province* boardroom, Hoadley came straight to the point: he was worried the newspaper was about to name Jeanne Adams as the CP ticket agent who had allowed the bomb bag aboard the Vancouver connecting flight with Air India in Toronto. He said Adams was frightened. She was the only one who could identify the man who boarded the bag and it would be appreciated if the *Province* did not name her. He was also concerned with the stories about the stereo used in the Narita bombing having come from the Vancouver area.

"Your reporter is sometimes one step ahead of us, and sometimes one step behind us," Hoadley told MacLachlan.

MachLach told me about the Mounties' concerns and I decided to ask Hoadley for a meeting. We met for the first time at the Moghul Garden restaurant on Beach Avenue in Vancouver. I thought it was appropriate we lunched here, since the restaurant was owned by my friend Surinder Cheema, who had lost a brother in the bombing. I introduced Cheema to Hoadley and told him of his loss. Hoadley stood up and shook hands. It was probably the first time he had met a victim's family member.

"I am sorry to hear that," Hoadley told Cheema.

Hoadley outlined his concerns, but appeared more interested in tapping into my thoughts on events and who I thought the RCMP should focus on. Following that meeting, Hoadley and I met regularly, often at Cheema's restaurant and other times at the Raga Restaurant, located underneath the CSIS offices. Meeting at the Raga gave Hoadley a bit of a nostalgic thrill.

"Well, Doctor, we might as well go dance on some old tombstones eh?" Hoadley, the former RCMP spy, would say about meeting for lunch at Raga which was located under the civilian spy agency's Vancouver regional headquarters.

Later, Hoadley would introduce me to other top investigators who were working with him: Don Brost, Staff-Sergeant Bob Wall, and Howie Walden. And as I talked to them, it became evident to me that they were finding it difficult to bridge the culture gap and it would take some time before they became familiar with Sikh names and cultural practices which were different from their own Western backgrounds. I found some officers would shorten the names of suspects to make it easy to pronounce them. Wall would call Inderjit Singh Reyat "Indy." Talwinder Singh Parmar would be named "the Big T."

Hoadley and I often met to puzzle over some of the information that simply would not click for a while. One of the puzzles we tried to sort out was the trail of telephone numbers left behind at the time the tickets were booked on the phone and then picked up and paid for in cash the next day. Why did the telephone contact number change? Both of us reasoned that when a person is unexpectedly asked for a phone number, the person is likely to tell the truth. We also reasoned that the ticket booker had realized it was a mistake to leave behind a phone number that would lead back to him. Therefore, the caller had then made sure the ally who picked up the tickets changed the telephone number by one digit. To the two of us, that meant it was Johal who had initially called in to book the tickets. When the phone number was changed, the telephone number of an activist for the ISYF member, Sodhi, was left behind.

That made Sodhi a suspect. But he would swear he did not pick up the tickets. He explained to me that Johal knew his phone number and had deliberately planted it. Much later, Sodhi would take a lie detector test administered by the RCMP and pass.

Hoadley and I developed a camaraderie based on our common interest in the investigation. We often sat in restaurants just to conjure up scenarios of who had done some of the jobs in the Air India bombing. We would think of Parmar as the centre of the hub of terror, with radiating spokes leading to other associates. We needed to know who built the bombs, who timed them (logically the bomb-maker), who put them in the bag, who booked the tickets, who picked them up, who took the bags to the airport. There were many questions that were elusive at that time but we were rapidly developing some logical scenarios based on available facts or in some cases, even speculation. Our knowledge base would change over the years and we would discard some of our earlier theories, or modify others.

On one occasion, while we were eating at the Moghul Restaurant, Hoadley wiped his fingers with a serviette and leaned forward.

"Doctor, where is the money coming from?" he asked. "Who is financing Parmar?"

Hoadley kept referring to me as "Doctor;" it was just his style and there was no particular reason for it.

I told him the word in the Sikh community was that a local Sikh businessman was a substantial donor of funds to Parmar's Babbar Khalsa Society. The man's name was Ripudaman Singh Malik. There were also thousands coming in to Parmar from various other donors as well as fundraising events, such as the martyr's fund.

"How the hell do you spell that name, eh?" he asked.

As I spelled it out, Hoadley slowly wrote it down on a piece of paper towel, with some difficulty, making me repeat it several times, then looked up and said, "Why don't we just call him the 'Rupee Man', Doctor, huh?"

That stuck and the Mounties would often call Malik the Rupee Man just as they referred to Inderjit Singh Reyat as "Indy" and Parmar as "the Big T." In the newsroom, someone coined a different name for Parmar: "Sidewinder," a play on his first name, Talwinder.

Hoadley's initial visit to the *Province* newsroom and his first meeting with me had been dictated by concerns based on a series of stories that I had written, all scoops that put a lot of information in the public domain. The RCMP were concerned that some of the information that I had would tip off terrorists that the Mounties were on to them.

Just how worried the police were about the stories I wrote and the possibility they would jeopardize the police investigation became apparent in an RCMP affidavit to obtain wiretap on various suspects. I would see that affidavit many years later.

On September 19, 1985, the RCMP Air India Task Force presented a sealed affidavit to the courts to seek authorization to wiretap the conversations of Reyat, Parmar, Surjan Singh Gill, Lal Singh, Johal, Gurcharan Singh Reyat (the father of Inderjit Singh Reyat), and Pawa (the man I had seen at the Air India office on June 23, 1985). Lal Singh was included for good measure, just in case he surfaced somewhere or his conversations were intercepted, although the RCMP were unaware of his whereabouts at that time. Reyat's father was included because of an erroneous conclusion on the part of the RCMP. CSIS intercepts that the RCMP had now been authorized to use in their affidavit had shown a conversation between Surjan Singh Gill and Reyat's father about "bows and arrows," which the dad had in his possession. Gill had asked Reyat's father if he could keep them ready for pickup since he was going to see Reyat in Duncan. The "bows and arrows" had been construed as being code-words for the bombs. It would take CSIS many months to obtain receipts for the purchase of real bows and arrows. Apparently Reyat was an avid archer, and those "bows and arrows" were real, not code words. That was the peril the cops faced in trying to decipher the nuances in the conversations of Parmar and his friends.

Hoadley's concerns about *The Province*'s coverage were echoed in RCMP officer Howard Walden's affidavit for the wiretap application made to the courts. It said:

"I am informed by Sgt. Michael Roth of the Royal Canadian Mounted Police that he was contacted by a person named Salim Jiwa, reporter for the Vancouver *Province* newspaper, on the tenth day of September, 1985 and that Jiwa informed Sgt. Roth that he was aware that a Sanyo stereo tuner model FMT 611K was described as having housed the explosive device which detonated at the Narita Airport in Japan, and that Jiwa knew the identity and the address of the individual who purchased the Sanyo tuner which had housed the explosive device which detonated at the said Narita Airport."

Walden further stated, "Copies of articles written by Jiwa appearing in the *Province* newspaper on the nineteenth and twentieth days of August, 1985 and the nineth and eleventh days of September 1985 are affixed as appendices, to this my affidavit.

"As a result of Mr. Jiwa's stories and as a result of his conversation with Sgt. Roth, I am concerned about the effect of his printing the name or names of persons who have purchased Sanyo stereo tuners model FMT 611K, as the publishing of those names may enable those responsible for the explosion to escape detection or enable those responsible for the explosion to flee or destroy evidence."

The warrant to intercept conversations of key suspects in the Air India bombing was approved.

Hoadley, who was from the old spy world of the RCMP Security Service, was well acquainted with Ken Osborne, deputy director general of CSIS for B.C. region. Hoadley's boss, RCMP commissioner Robert Simmonds and CSIS director Ted Finn had just recently met in Ottawa to hammer out how the two agencies could collaborate on matters of national security and criminal investigations. It was clear from Finn's memo to his men on July 8, 1985, that Simmonds and he had agreed to work together on matters pertaining to the Air India bombing and the other major counter-terrorism issue, the Armenians. Finn, one year into the formation of CSIS, was still trying to negotiate with Simmonds on making police computer records (CPIC) and motor vehicle plate information available to CSIS. That Canada's spy agency had no access to CPIC as late as one year into its founding says a lot about how ad hoc and hasty the agency's creation had been. Basic policies were still being formulated after twelve months of operations.

Hoadley and Osborne were old chums, but now Hoadley was running into problems. He was a police officer and Osborne was a spy. There was bound to be a clash of cultures. A meeting of senior Air India investigators and top CSIS officers, including Osborne and regional director Randil Claxton, had occurred shortly after the Air India bombing. CSIS told the RCMP they had been intercepting Parmar's conversations during the critical period of May to June and beyond. But they had kept only transcripts of most of the tapes: many of them not verbatim. When Hoadley and his investigators saw the transcripts, they wanted the tapes. But CSIS had erased them based on policy that all intercept tapes must be destroyed within ten days of being heard or a maximum of thirty days when "significant subversive activity" was not evident on the recordings. While the conversations clearly meant nothing to CSIS, when combined with the RCMP's investigation, the relevance of the tapes had become clear.

Memos written by csis brass at the time both at agency head-quarters in Ottawa and the B.C. region made it clear csis was willing to collaborate completely with the rcmp. csis had offered all other help, including allowing rcmp officers rides in their vehicles while agents worked on Sikhs.

However, the tapes were a major sticking point. Tape erasure had continued even after the bombing. In the end, only fifty-four tapes survived, but they were from April and May. The critical conversations—although coded—occurred in June. And the rcmp believed the conversations, when collated with evidence, would incriminate Parmar, Johal, Pawa, Reyat, and others.

Both Claxton and Osborne later testified they saw nothing on the tapes that would have tended to incriminate anyone. That was not a wrong assertion. Most of the conversations the rcmp later felt were nuanced references to ticket bookings and bomb check-ins would not have meant much without context. There was nothing there that would have significantly alarmed anyone or alerted anyone about Air India. But now the picture had changed. csis had only seen what appeared to be a meaningless half of a picture. The rcmp investigation had found the other piece of the broken photograph. When the two broken pictures were put together, they told a tantalizing story, but one that would still need some deciphering since csis had maintained few written records from the massive numbers of phone conversations they had intercepted.

Osborne had gone out of his way to accommodate Hoadley. He even "indoctrinated" him—a process whereby a person under oath is able to have a hands-on ability to handle csis material. csis still had serious concerns about the security of their sources, methods of operation (which no spy agency would want revealed), and issues concerning how federal judges who issued csis warrants for interception for intelligence purposes only would react to future applications if they saw this lower threshold as a means of bypassing the higher criminal code requirements for collection of evidence by the rcmp. There was merit in all these arguments, but it would take time to hammer out an understanding between two completely different cultures, both working for the people of Canada.

By November of 1985, CSIS authorized the RCMP to use their transcribed information from the tapes to obtain search warrants at the homes and offices of suspects in the Air India disaster. The RCMP complied with a CSIS requirement that the agency's intercepts be paraphrased, that CSIS sources be protected and its methodology not compromised.

On November 6, 1985, the telephone rang at my desk at *The Province*.

"Doctor, how are you?" Hoadley's voice rang out over the phone.

"What's happening, Doctor?" I asked.

"Find out where your friends are."

"Are you making arrests?" I asked.

"Why don't you phone them and find out, and listen, I will be on the Island tonight," he said.

"Thanks," I said. "We will be in touch."

My first call was to the home of Surjan Singh Gill. He said he had been forced to sit on a sofa and the police were going through all his belongings as we spoke. He said they had given him a copy of a search warrant and it listed the bombing of Air India Flight 182 and the Narita investigation as reasons.

The fat lady was singing finally and I loved the tune. I ran over to the city desk.

"The cops are raiding suspects in Air India."

There were no arguments this time. Photographers set out to take pictures and I hit the phone.

Hoadley's troops were all over the place. They had raided the offices of Pawa, the travel agent from Friendly Travels I had met at the Air India office on June 23. They also raided the home of fundamentalist Johal's home. They went to Parmar and Surjan Singh Gill, Bagri of Kamloops, who was out of town that day. Most crucially RCMP raided Reyat's place of work at Auto Marine Electric as well as his home in the city of Duncan.

Police were in for a surprise when they searched Johal's house, even though at this time they were not aware he had been at the airport the morning the bags were checked in. Police found no evidence relating to Air India, but there were hundreds of dollars worth of supplies he had taken illegally from the school where he worked.

Peter Leask, a school board security officer and a former Vancouver police officer, was later called to RCMP headquarters to examine the school board property. There were several boxes containing stationery items. Leask wanted charges laid, but the school board decided to simply suspend Johal for a few days. It seemed God's soldier had no problem with the morality of theft.

Manmohan Singh, a spokesman for the ISYF, was also raided, but the warrant had come from Vancouver police as opposed to RCMP. The VPD wanted to check out reports of illegal guns. The RCMP had more than Manmohan Singh's vitriolic words favouring Sikh militancy. They also had the benefit of intelligence from Vancouver police that indicated he had been asking a suspected terrorist, Pushpinder Singh (a refugee applicant in Vancouver who later went to Pakistan and then into India on a terrorist mission where he was arrested), why "no consuls have been killed, no ambassadors have been killed, what are you doing? Nothing!" At that time, two weeks before the Air India disaster, Pushpinder had responded, "Wait for two weeks and see what happens." (This conversation was outlined in an RCMP affidavit filed in court.)

Vancouver police officer Don McLean was photographed by *The Province* bearing both an armful of weapons and a broad grin as he emerged from the Punjab Restaurant, where Manmohan Singh lived upstairs. A furious Manmohan would lash out at the police and me later that night.

Massive amounts of documents were seized at Pawa's travel agency. He was suspected of providing timetables and helping with the ticket bookings. He had been a ticket booker for Parmar for a long time, often falsifying Parmar's name on tickets to allow him to travel incognito.

Parmar's wife confirmed that her husband had been taken away by police. She had no idea where they took him.

As I started writing my story of the raids, the phone rang again. It was Indian intelligence agent Gurinder Singh, officially India's vice-consul in Vancouver.

"Who are they taking away, Salim?" he asked.

I listed the names for him. Then he asked me something extraordinary.

"Why Johal? He is not involved in this. Rule him out, *yaar* (friend)," he said.

That request would puzzle me for years. Why did Gurinder, an Indian government agent, want to rule out a particular suspect in the Air India bombing? Some answers would come later. Right now, I was on deadline and too busy to give it much thought. I had not asked him why he wanted to rule the man out. Later, I figured Gurinder Singh had bought into Johal's attempt to bolster himself as a moderate who was unlikely to be involved in a terrorist bombing.

The threats against my life began that night at home.

The first caller was Manmohan Singh, outraged over the police raids.

"Since you wanted this to happen to Sikhs it happened," he said. "The Indian government agents succeeded in doing this to us. Now we have information that Indian government agents are going to assassinate you and blame the Sikhs!"

I was getting angry and nervous at the same time. In fact, I was fuming.

"Manmohan, if you have that information you better be careful. And if you have that information someone is going to kill me then take it to the cops, don't call me at home to tell me about it," I said. "You are indirectly threatening me."

"We would be willing to put sixty Sikhs in front of your door to protect you," he retorted.

"I don't need Sikhs to protect me," I said, then hung up on him.

The second threat came at midnight. The caller wouldn't identify himself. He supplied the same information as Manmohan and I told him to go to the police, but not to call me. The third call was more brief, but more sinister.

"You bastard, we are going to burn your house down!" said the voice on the phone.

"Listen you asshole, I am going to burn your ass if you call me again!" I hung up.

I would not sleep the rest of the night. I was rattled badly. They liked me while I was writing stories that suited them about the treatment of Sikhs in India and the growth of militancy. Now they had turned against me because they feared I had more information on Air India than the police did.

The danger would persist for many years to come, changing my life forever. Many more threats would come, by letter, by phone. I would look over my shoulder to see if I was being followed, I would keep parting the drapes at my home to look outside to see if anyone was parked there. I would keep track of any car that was behind me for more than a few blocks of driving. I would take different routes to work. Hoadley advised me to drive the wrong way up a one-way street if I felt in serious danger or even cause a minor collision with another car to draw attention to the danger. *The Province* hired security specialist Ozzie Kaban to provide security for my home. Big lights were installed in my backyard and an alarm system installed at my house directly monitored by Kaban's company. Each person in my home had a portable panic button.

At *The Province*, management decided it was prudent to beef up security. The reception desk was put behind thick, bullet-proof glass after Manmohan came into the office and told city editor Neil Graham, "Now Salim is caught in the crossfire between Sikhs and India."

Police cruisers circled my home every thirty minutes. My friend and colleague Don Hauka would many times accompany me to the parking lot. I even let him open my car door sometimes. I told Hauka it was better if I lived since someone has to be around "to tell the whole story."

It was remarkable we could even laugh considering the terror had taken hold.

SEVEN

THE DUNCAN PROJECT

The November 1985 round-up of suspects was the result of the RCMP being able to put the big picture together with the help of material provided by CSIS. It took months of haggling over the protection of CSIS sources and methodology before the spy agency parted with transcripts of key telephone intercepts. Combined with the physical surveillance of Parmar carried out by CSIS, notes from the stationery observation post outside the rebel's home; and with pictures taken through a telephoto lens from a rented house next to the "Living Martyr's" residence, investigators were able to develop a detailed timeline. It was a vital guide to who, where, and what. Who was going to and who was coming from Parmar's house. What were their car license plate numbers? Who Parmar was talking to, and at what time of day, what people were carrying with them, when they went to his home. During the period between May and June, and later in July, CSIS had intercepted hundreds of calls on Parmar's phone. Some were routine conversations but some seemed to carry overtones of conspiracy and the nuance of language being used indicated something had been afoot. Put together, it was like a Rosetta stone to the bombings.

In a crime of this magnitude, and with so much critical evidence in the Air India Flight 182 case buried six thousand feet under the sea, the RCMP most certainly would have been almost at a loss. CSIS had provided the RCMP a valuable roadmap, a pathway to success. But the haggling over erased tapes of Parmar's conversations continued endlessly. RCMP suspected CSIS was deliberately not providing those tapes and even possibly withholding pictures that they may have taken during the surveillance carried out on

Vancouver Island of Parmar, Reyat and Mr. X. CSIS was exasperated as its officers gave one interview after another to the RCMP about what happened to the tapes and why the tapes were erased. RCMP kept asking questions. What was the procedure for retaining tapes? Who made the decision to keep the tapes? Who had the authority to order erasure? I felt the RCMP should have been satisfied with the honesty with which its men recounted the sequence of events that had led to the tapes being erased. In my opinion, CSIS had also told the cops the truth that the surveillance team which followed Parmar to Vancouver Island on June 4, 1985 did not take any pictures. I thought there was a case here for the RCMP to show some gratitude to their sister agency for handing them suspects on a platter, having told them about the bush trip carried out just days before the bombing by Parmar and his cohorts. But I heard officers from the RCMP making comments about how CSIS probably followed the bombers all the way to the airport and then covered up the surveillance to save face because they realized men they had under surveillance had checked in a bag under their nose. I felt that was a ridiculous suggestion to make.

In the end, a combination of the composite picture provided by CSIS and a lot of legwork by teams of investigators would come tantalizingly close to breaking the case just fourteen weeks after the bombings.

The key element of the RCMP strategy was to go after the man they felt was the weak link: Inderjit Singh Reyat. The case against Reyat had begun with the CSIS report of the June 4 explosion in the woods incident. Agent Larry Lowe, an avid hunter, had interpreted the "loud report" as a gun having been fired. In an extremely brief and cursory sweep immediately after the two suspects drove off, however, Lowe was unable to locate evidence, like shell casings. For him it was like looking for the proverbial needle in a hay stack in a moment of dashing through thick woods. More important, the RCMP had conducted *no* search of the woods to determine exactly what had caused the "bang." No officer at any time confronted either Reyat or Parmar for fear of blowing CSIS surveillance. CSIS also never initiated an interview nor was there any meaningful follow-up conducted into the strange trip to the woods. Protocol aside, one must wonder about their lack of basic curiosity. Even were it something as simple as a gun having been fired off in the woods, as CSIS apparently believed, would that not have been enough to arouse their suspicions? After all, Parmar was the man they believed capable of orchestrating an assassination of Rajiv Gandhi on his trip back in June to Washington, D.C.

At some point, should he not have been asked what he was doing in the woods? Why was no CSIS agent sent back to Duncan to take another look at Mr. X who had stayed on Vancouver Island with Reyat? Part of the reason for this lack of curiosity, I was told by sources, was the assumption that Mr. X was Parmar's son—Jaswinder. RCMP would prove that wrong later, after checking school records and discovering that Jaswinder was in school all day on June 4. CSIS also made a faulty analysis of the event in the woods. It was assumed it was a gun that one of the Sikhs had fired. And if it was a gun that went off, then like some of their Sikh counterparts in the U.S.A., Parmar was likely learning to shoot a weapon. It was mistaken as a weapons training session, not as a bomb experiment. CSIS had then recalled a small team of surveillance specialists who had spent the night in Duncan and the next day in a roadside ditch outside Reyat's home. But no pictures were taken by this team that had stayed overnight in Duncan and they had already begun to verify with Duncan RCMP the identity of the man who drove the car with the plate number: "I-Reyat." This issue of why no pictures were taken by the surveillance team and why RCMP was not formally informed through normal liaison channels about the bush blast would remain a sore point between the agencies for more than twenty-years. Both sides are still talking about this incident on what actions should or should not have been taken by CSIS.

It was only the destruction of Air India Flight 182–a full nineteen days after the suspicious explosion in the woods–that investigators returned to check out the woods for clues as to what might have caused the blast that CSIS had heard. Also, CSIS agent Larry Lowe was taken to an isolated area by the RCMP and told to listen to sounds they made. Lowe decided the sound he heard in the woods was closer to the sound of exploding dynamite than a gun going off.

On June 28, five days after the disaster, Special Constable Tom Townsend of the RCMP explosive disposal unit accompanied an explosives-sniffing dog and a handler into the bush where CSIS had reported seeing the parked car bearing the plate "I-Reyat". They searched for three to four hours and found nothing. On July 2, Townsend and his team returned and searched from 9 a.m. until almost until 4:30 p.m. They finally hit the jackpot–a blasting cap shunt and a paper wrapper were found on the side of the road near the spot where Reyat's car had been parked. Townsend determined the scene bore the signature of a rudimentary explosive experiment, a test of a timer device possibly. It looked like the bomber had used a small amount of gun powder triggered by a blasting cap. Another search two days later turned up another blasting cap shunt in the vicinity where the first one was found. The recovery of a second blasting cap suggested that more than one test had been conducted. This discovery would add to later evidence that showed Reyat had gone to great lengths to learn to make a bomb.

About the same time, blasting expert Edward Robertson reported to Duncan RCMP that while he was visiting Auto Marine Electric sometime in 1983, he casually mentioned to clerks at the store that he was going to be doing some blasting at a quarry in nearby Cowichan Lake. Robertson claimed a car mechanic–a Sikh man–working at the store overheard the conversation, and a short time later turned up at the blast site on Mountain Road, near Duncan. Robertson identified the man as Reyat. According to Robertson, Reyat watched the expert blaster set off an explosion. He wanted to know everything about it.

"He was interested in how we set it off," Robertson told police. "He'd seen me set the wires. He told me he could make a remote control device to set it off. I didn't have any need for that. I think he asked me where he could get dynamite. He mentioned he had a lot of stumps to blow. I gave him a blaster's handbook."

Over the next two years, even as late as May 1985, Reyat persisted in his attempts to get dynamite and fuses from Robertson. In summer 1984, for instance, he went so far as to offer two or three times the going price for several cases of dynamite. Refusing, Robertson asked Reyat what he wanted so much explosive for.

Reyat was shockingly forthcoming. He confessed, said Robertson, that there was trouble in the Punjab and he wanted to help his countrymen by sending the dynamite to India via Pakistan. Despite this starling admission, Robertson did not go to the police, nor did he in May 1985, when the persistent Sikh phoned at night, again asking for dynamite. Robertson said he put him off.

News of the Air India bombing, Robertson testified, compelled him to go to the police with his information. He had come to believe, he told police, that Reyat was a fundamentalist Sikh, having heard him talk of helping his countrymen in their fight against India and having seen pictures of quotes from Sikh scriptures framed on the walls of his home.

In Canada, the sale and possession of explosives such as dynamite is regulated. Only government-licensed persons may possess explosive materials. Unlawful possession of explosives is a criminal code offence punishable by jail time and stiff fines.

Reyat had failed in his repeated attempt to buy dynamite form Robertson. But there were other sources he could trap into giving him explosives.

Kenneth Slade ran a drilling business on Vancouver Island. He would later tell me he made a big mistake trusting Reyat.

"I thought I was doing him a favour," admitted Slade who had befriended Reyat. To Slade, his Sikh friend appeared to be a mild-mannered and pleasant person who had developed a reputation of being one of the best auto-mechanics in Duncan. After many friendly conversations, Slade let his guard down. Against his better judgment, he relented and gave Reyat ten sticks of dynamite. Slade told me he still feels deeply betrayed by a man who he thought was a nice fellow. "He took advantage of me. It doesn't leave a good feeling."

The dynamite was 75 per cent Forcite, a form of gelatine dynamite. It was pretty powerful stuff, Slade said. When I interviewed Slade after the police had, he was extremely bitter and was near tears as he related how Reyat had conned him into giving him dynamite. That had been just a few days before the Air India bombing. Slade said that Reyat had insisted the dynamite was being used to blow stumps at the construction site of a new temple.

The next key piece of evidence implicating Reyat came via the Tokyo police forensics experts who had sealed off and thoroughly searched the explosion area at Narita Airport. Each of 1,600 pieces from the explosion had been carefully gathered and analyzed and catalogued. They were working with a jigsaw puzzle of massive proportions.

A bomb requires a triggering device, most often from an electrical source of some kind, like a battery; it has to have a timer of some sort and, of course, the explosive substance. Last, a container of some sort. Signs of just what kind of container had been used at Narita started to emerge as the forensic wizards painstakingly pieced together hundreds and hundreds of fragments.

Fragments of detonated material had been recovered from the bodies of the two baggage handlers who had died as well as from the four others who were injured. Out of this jumble of detritus emerged a startlingly clear picture of the bomb. It had been placed in a grey vinyl suitcase and concealed within the aluminium shell of an AM/FM stereo tuner. The experts could even read some of the numbers on the shell and by comparing the numbers with various makes of stereos produced in the Orient; they discovered it was a Sanyo tuner. The terrorists had even placed the tuner in the original box it had been packed in at its production factory. Traces of a particular color of adhesive tape that had been used to fasten the various components of the bomb: the explosive, the detonator, the timer device, even a lantern-type battery were recovered.

But the details didn't stop there. Japanese authorities determined it was a model FMT 611K stereo tuner, which they believed had been part of a batch of stereos that had been shipped to Canada. Inspector John Hoadley told me he went and spent several days at Sanyo's warehouse in the Vancouver suburb of Richmond and figured out that several of these stereo units had been sent for sale to a Woolworths store in Duncan where Reyat had lived.

Then, the RCMP discovered that a Sanyo tuner had been purchased from the Duncan Woolworths store on June 5, 1985—one day after Parmar and Mr. X visited Reyat. The receipt was made out to Reyat.

The Duncan store clerk, however, could not identify Reyat as the person who came in to buy it. The clerk remembered that two men had picked up the stereo, but claimed neither had worn a turban. The person CSIS saw with Parmar–the man who had remained behind when Parmar returned home–had been described as wearing a turban. It would be exceptional–unheard of–for a devout Sikh like Reyat to remove his turban. That would lead to a theory that Reyat was receiving help from two other Sikhs who did not wear turbans in making his explosive devices.

A picture was taking shape. Reyat had purchased a stereo tuner exactly the same as one believed to have contained a bomb in Narita. CSIS surveillance linked him to a mysterious experiment in some woods in which agents testified they heard an explosion. CSIS transcripts also confirmed that sometime in May–about a month prior to the blast in the bush–Parmar and Surjan Singh Gill had made an earlier trip to Vancouver Island to visit Reyat,

The RCMP made elaborate preparations and a game plan was laid out to snare Reyat and–they hoped–nab Parmar in the bargain. The blueprint for action was called the Duncan Project–a classic "good cop, bad cop" strategy that involved extensive pre-arrest interviews and assorted mind games designed to confuse and disorient the suspect.

Over several weeks, Corporal Doug Henderson visited Reyat at his home and at Auto Marine Electric. Henderson had known Reyat for some time. He had his car fixed by Reyat even before Henderson got a call from Raymond Kobzey of CSIS on June 5, 1985 that spies who had Parmar under surveillance had heard a "loud report" in the bush. Kobzey had also informed him that the man with Parmar was a man who drove a car with the plate "I-Reyat." Now the job of luring Reyat into a sense of security and well-being in the presence of a cop was given to Henderson by Hoadley's team working out of Vancouver RCMP headquarters. Henderson, a lanky Mountie with a deep voice and friendly blue eyes would even get invited to have a meal at Reyat's home as he put his strategy into action.

Henderson liked to drop bits and pieces of information on the bombing plot on Reyat. And then he examined him with his keen eyes for any signs of a reaction. During one visit, Henderson even told Reyat that a Sanyo tuner was playing a big role in the police probe of the Air India disaster. Henderson was shaking the tree a little. The purpose behind Henderson's visits was to make Reyat believe that Henderson was an honest, straight-shooting man he could trust–the "good cop". The "bad cop," Corporal Rocky Rockwell, was the tough, beefy Mountie from headquarters who was not going to be so sympathetic when an arrest was finally made.

Part of the post-arrest interrogation scheme was to belittle the Air India bombing in the context of what had happened to Sikhs in India. Further, the two investigators would suggest to Reyat the whole plan had gone wrong when the Air India plane took off late and exploded in the air as a result. Another ploy was to show some sympathy for the plight of Sikhs in India. A large aerial picture of the site where the bush experiment had occurred would be laid out in an interview room where it would be plainly visible to Reyat. It would suggest to him that the two people who he had gone there with had likely talked. Reyat would be isolated and convinced the game was up.

The plan also hinged on arresting Parmar and flying him by helicopter to Duncan. The Mounties were hoping the shock value of taking Parmar back to the scene of the bush experiment would raise questions in his mind about whether someone had talked: possibly even Reyat.

RCMP's Special "O" surveillance unit kept an eye on Reyat the entire time, even as police started searching homes in Vancouver and Kamloops. With Inspector Hoadley supervising on Vancouver Island and Superintendent Les Holmes taking care of raids on the Mainland, all was set to go. On the evening of November 6, 1985, Henderson walked into Auto Marine Electric and arrested Reyat. The flabbergasted mechanic was read his rights and told he was being taken into custody for conspiracy to commit murder and conspiring to endanger the safety of aircraft and possession of explosives. At the same time as the arrest was made a team of cops descended on Reyat's home and handed a search warrant to his wife. The search resulted in the seizure of a receipt for a Sanyo tuner model FMT 611K purchased from the Duncan Woolworths store on June 5, 1985, gelatine dynamite contained in a plastic bag, some black gunpowder and two guns. One was a .357 Magnum revolver and another was a Ruger revolver with a four-inch barrel from which someone had filed off the serial numbers. Inspector Hoadley was notified by the officers conducting the search that a Sanyo stereo receiver had been found along with dynamite and gunpowder. One of the guns would have a fascinating story to tell later.

Meanwhile, the stunned Reyat was driving his own car to the Duncan police station as instructed by Henderson who had taken the passenger seat. It was just another touch of kindness Henderson had demonstrated to Reyat. But Reyat was still in shock and panicky. He was placed in a room which had been wired for sound. In the first two hours or so Reyat played a cat-and-mouse game with Henderson and Rockwell, at first denying he knew Parmar, then confirming it, denying he went into any bush area, then confirming it. It came out slowly but surely, in bits and pieces. He was questioned for more than five hours in total. He was given a two-hour break in a cold cell. He was hungry but refused to eat Western food. He opted for coffee. He looked deflated. As his inter-rogation continued, Reyat started to make a few admissions—and they involved Parmar.

> **Henderson:** Okay, well, I, okay, I'll try to, I'll try to not confuse you, so we'll just switch back to you're in Vancouver and you're talking to Parmar. Okay. Just take your time and try and recollect the best you can what, what he, what he said to ya in that conversation....
>
> **Reyat:** Nothing. I mean he just, you know, he wanted something to use in India, somewhere around…you know…
>
> **Henderson:** Yeah, okay but what's something? Like what did he say he wanted?
>
> **Reyat:** Oh, that's, you know, like, an explosion, you know.
>
> **Henderson:** Yeah.
>
> **Reyat:** I think, you know, make, have a heavy explosion, you know, I don't know how he put it.
>
> **Henderson:** What did he mean by heavy explosion? What do you take for heavy? What do you mean by heavy like? Heavy is big or…

Reyat: No, ah, just heavy like, you know, anything you
   want, ah, car, something or a bridge or something you
   wanta blow, you know.
Henderson: Yeah. Bridge?
Reyat: Or something. I dunno. Why, anything, okay?

After admitting Parmar wanted him to make an explosive for a "big"
job, Reyat seemed slowly to regain his composure. He admitted he
had experimented with explosives, but was insistent that he never
able to make what Parmar wanted. He told Parmar he was sorry, but
he could not make the explosive device.

What about the identity of the third man?

Reyat said he could not remember the man's name: it may have
been Surjit Singh—he was some kind of a teacher from Toronto.
Henderson pressed Reyat further. The man had stayed with him in
his home, showered in his bathroom, eaten meals with his family.
But Reyat said Sikhs just call each other *paji*, or brother. Reyat was
very reluctant to say anything more about the man.

Henderson also questioned Reyat about telephone calls originating from his home to the Vancouver home of fundamentalist Sikh
Hardial Singh Johal (Johal's telephone number had appeared on the
telephoned ticket bookings. Johal—a master manipulator, I was coming to discover—had called me in an effort, I believed, to deflect
suspicion away from himself to his "enemies" in Canada.) The calls,
to and from Reyat's home to Johal, had been made on two crucial
days, June 21 and June 22 (the significance of which I would later
take up with Johal and succeed in making him angry because of the
interpretation I put on those calls).

It was another case of all trails leading to Johal.

If in his post-arrest panic Reyat had let slip some crucial information, Parmar would live up to his reputation as cool and
unflappable. The "Tiger of True Faith" would remain defiant to the
end, conceding nothing as Hoadley and Sergeant Peter Eakins questioned him. Hoadley told me later he sat in front of Parmar, faced
him squarely and asked, "Mr. Parmar, are you an agent of the government of India?"

Parmar fumed.

"Are you going to charge me?" he snapped.

Hoadley admitted that he was not quite ready to charge Parmar—not yet. Parmar then demanded his blanket. He was ready to go to sleep in his cell. It was clear he was resilient, this "Tiger of True Faith".

Following the arrests, I called Hoadley at his hotel room on Vancouver Island for details.

"We found gold, Doctor," he said. "We are making progress."

Progress, yes, but not much. Parmar was recalcitrant and Reyat had still not broken completely. The mechanic was saved by the arrival at the police station of his wife, who demanded her husband be allowed to see a lawyer. A few hours more, and Reyat might have confessed. But Hoadley's crew had set up a "plan B" in case the interrogation failed to provide substantial details. And there was also "plan C."

I have not made this information public before. Hoadley often told me details about his investigation that he did not wish me to print until a more opportune time, perhaps after he retired. Sadly, with Inspector Hoadley having died, it is now possible for me to make full disclosure.

Hoadley and his officers had decided to put Reyat and Parmar inside the back of a police car that had been wired for sound. This would be the first time the two suspects had come face-to-face after their separate interrogations. Hoadley reasoned that Parmar would be anxious to know what—if anything—Reyat had told police. It would most likely be the only time the two would be in each other's presence. Once they arrived at the jail for lockup their activities would be strictly monitored.

The listening device would transmit wirelessly to another vehicle driving a little distance behind the unmarked sedan.

Sergeant Peter Eakins was driving the trailing car. Eakins' car was equipped with the radios picking up sounds from the backseat of the car carrying the two Sikhs and tape recorders were running.

But something went wrong. For some reason the police car carrying the suspects speeded up. A gap opened up between the two cars and the conversation being recorded suddenly dissolved into a garbled hiss.

It was a cock-up of almost unfathomable proportions.

"The marked car was driving too fast and we tried to slow him down a little, but much of the conversation had become undecipherable," complained an officer in the trailing vehicle who I interviewed later.

There are several versions of what was heard. Or whether, it was even recorded in time. According to Hoadley, one thing came in loud and clear.

"What did you tell them?" asked Parmar at one point.

"Not much, not much," replied a very scared-sounding Reyat.

But since the rest of the conversation became distorted, the whole discussion was wasted and could not be produced in court. Officers were heartbroken about the failure. One officer I interviewed thought the bug must have malfunctioned.

"It should have been tested and retested."

The bug failed, Henderson answered when asked about it later.

Eakins said he believed that a Sikh officer and he were just getting into the car to follow the vehicle carrying Parmar and Reyat when they heard something. The Sikh officer with him said Parmar had asked Reyat what happened. According to Eakins, Reyat had pointed at Henderson, who at that point was standing near the car and said, "He thinks I did it."

Hoadley had told me that Prosecutor Jim Jardine had fumed that planting a bug in a car went beyond the authority to wiretap Parmar and Reyat's conversations and the conversation could not be used for legal reasons. But other cops who were there said there was no issue with the legality of the bug in the police car.

Henderson said plan C was to put the two together in Reyat's car if no charges were laid.

"If they were released at the same time and Parmar and Reyat were in Reyat's car then it could have produced some interesting conversations," said Henderson. However, that plan was never implemented since Reyat was charged with possession of explosives which Henderson called "Mickey-Mouse charges."

Despite the RCMP's careful planning and best efforts, the Duncan Project had fallen a little short of gaining enough evidence to press conspiracy charges directly related to the Air India Flight 182 bombing or the Narita Airport explosion.

After nine days of deliberation between RCMP officers and Crown prosecutor Jim Jardine, Reyat was finally charged only with possession of explosives and the illegal possession of a gun. Charges against Parmar were stayed. Reyat, looking relieved, walked out of the courtroom with only a $2,000 fine. That fine was at the lower level of the sentencing scale for possessing explosives.

For the police, much more work needed to be done to convince the hard-nosed Jardine there was enough evidence to lay serious charges against Reyat, and possibly against Parmar since Reyat had admitted Parmar had asked him to make a bomb. The RCMP was confident it was only a matter of time before forensic evidence from Japan would make its way to Vancouver. Then they would have the evidence they needed to go after Reyat , Parmar, and others like Johal. In the mean time, they continued to pound the pavement and wait for a break.

The arrests of Parmar and Reyat, however, had sent shockwaves through the Canadian Sikh community, especially at its epicentre: Vancouver.

The RCMP's top investigators continued their community interviews, talking to every potential source, banging on many doors, but the persistent answer they got from those who knew much more than they were admitting was that this was the work of Indian government agents. The incident was seen as blight on Sikhs living in Canada and each headline in the newspaper provided more fodder for racism. One separatist came to me with a story indicative of the racism that surfaced in the wake of the terrorist bombing.

"Someone asked my son at school today, do you guys put bombs on airplanes?" he said. Fear that Sikhs would be tarnished as a group, it would seem, led the community to coalesce around the theme that no Sikh true to his faith would have harmed innocent people.

Tara Singh Hayer was one of those who continued to maintain in his newspaper editorials that Indian government agents had carried out the bombings. And he had managed to get on the wrong side of some key militants who he had sided with earlier. Most of his problems stemmed from the way he ran his Punjabi gossip rag. The paper was full of innuendo, malice, rumours, and mud-slinging. Hayer cared little for accuracy or objectivity or fair journalistic practices. He was a chameleon when it came to loyalty.

Sergeant Ralph Miller was one of three officers from the Air India investigation–dubbed Project Nightmare–to pay a visit to Hayer at his home in Surrey on Oct. 10, 1985, just prior to the November arrests. Hayer would try to bamboozle them about whether there was anyone here in the Sikh community who would even know how to make a bomb. Miller's report filed at RCMP headquarters is a bit of an eye-opener in the context of the double-talk that Hayer did then and would continue until the unfortunate end of his life several years later.

"Hayer stated his personal views are that he supports the cause of Khalistan but views that objective through political means rather than through violent means," Miller stated in his report. "Hayer does not believe a Sikh is responsible for the Air India disaster. He states that, 'A Sikh would not kill other Sikhs for the cause of Khalistan and second there are no Sikhs locally who have sufficient knowledge in explosives and the making of time bombs.'"

Hayer also told Miller he felt the BK led by Parmar had hired someone to kill him for $10,000 because of what he had written and that threats against his life had escalated.

What Hayer was telling Miller about his own support for a peaceful political struggle to get Khalistan was completely contrary to his speech at a Seattle Sikh temple on June 10, 1985, just thirteen days before the bombing, as militant Sikhs were on the move all over the world looking for revenge to mark the first anniversary of the Golden Temple attack. The gist of the speech at the Sikh temple in Burien, a Seattle suburb, was reported in his paper and penned by his own hand. Hayer declared Sikhs would fight India in the trenches, in wards, in the streets. His support for this armed struggle was clear, yet a few months later he was saying he was opposed to violence to achieve Khalistan. The statement to the police also belied his past involvement with the BK and the Khalistan National Council led by Dr. Jagjit Singh Chauhan of London, England.

The Air India bombings marked the beginning of a year of extraordinary terrorist activity in Canada, and yet this wave of beatings, shootings, and explosive plots barely caused a ripple in the mainstream media. Almost as incredible, there were still gaping holes in the security net that was supposed to be protecting Indian diplomatic personnel in this country.

In mid–May 1986, I met Indian consul-general Jagdish Sharma for lunch. Two Mounties sat conspicuously a few tables away. He was under protection and it was quite evident he was being driven around by the RCMP. During the luncheon meeting, Sharma mentioned that he was concerned about the safety of Punjab cabinet minister Malkiat Singh Sidhu who was on a private visit to the Vancouver area to attend a wedding. I asked about security arrangements and Sharma replied he did not know if any had been made.

On the afternoon of May 25, 1986, Maloy Dhar, security officer with the Indian high commission in Ottawa, called me out of the blue with some startling news: I should check out a report he'd received that Sidhu had been shot on an isolated logging road on northwest Vancouver Island by a group of Sikhs. It took several calls to confirm this with Canadian authorities. Sidhu had been driving with his sister, Gurdell Gill, and her husband, Nachatar, when their car had been forced off the road near the village of Tahsis. While the assailants were striking the car with chains, ISYF militant Jaspal Singh Atwal, a tall, hefty Sikh with one glass eye, pulled out a handgun and started firing. Sidhu was shot four times, with one bullet lodging in his chest. The assailants panicked and drove off.

Sidhu would survive the attack at the hands of his brother Sikhs. A few days later, as he sipped tea with me at his cousin's home in Richmond, preparing to go back to India, he told me, "Wherever we stay, we should live in peace." Sidhu could not escape the wrath of his fellow Sikhs who did not believe in this golden rule. In April 1991, while campaigning for re-election in the Punjab state legislature, Sidhu was shot and killed in his own doorway by a gang of armed men. Militants had finished in the Punjab, the job they had started in B.C.

While Dhar knew of the Sunday attack on Sidhu within minutes, it took CSIS until after news of the attack had become public to check their surveillance tapes, only to discover that part of the plot to hit the Indian politician had been discussed almost twenty-four hours beforehand and captured by a bug planted in a warehouse.

CSIS handed the intercepts to the RCMP and subsequently, nine militants belonging to the ISYF were charged with attempted murder and conspiracy.

But in yet another embarrassment for CSIS, the organization discovered that the source who had been quoted to obtain the warrant for the wiretap had fed them misinformation. They were forced to withdraw the affidavit in the middle of the court case, and the Crown's conspiracy charges collapsed. It forced CSIS director Ted Finn to resign. But the four direct assailants, including Atwal, who had been caught virtually red-handed on Vancouver Island, were convicted and sentenced to twenty years each by B.C. Supreme Court Justice Howard Callaghan, who called their crime "an act of terrorism."

Just a month before this incident, I went for coffee with the gunman, Atwal. He lived a few doors from the Ross Street Sikh Temple in Vancouver and I had earlier visited his home. He was a known factor in the picture of Sikh militancy in Vancouver and had been tied to the iron-bar beating two years earlier of Ujjal Dosanjh, who later became Canada's Health Minister.

"You know, Jaspal, I know the leadership of the ISYF and I know what they are going to do with you one of these days," I said to him. "Violence is not the answer. The Canadian public will not stand for it and you guys are going to lose any sympathy you had that poured out of the Golden Temple attack."

Jaspal was unimpressed, so I kept at him.

"One day, your group leaders are going to send you to do something. You will go to jail. And when you come out, your kids will be grown up," I told him.

He took a sip of coffee and then replied, "For religion, one has to do some things."

"Yes, you do. You can pray."

"That is not enough. Look how many innocent people died during the attack on the temple," he said.

Following his conviction in the Sidhu attack, he called me from prison, choking up, nearly crying.

"You were right, Salim. These people didn't do anything for my family," he said.

By now, my first book on the Air India bombing, *The Death of Air India Flight 182*, had been published by W. H. Allen in London, England. In it I had included witness's statements given to the RCMP. The verbatim witness statements of CP Air check-in agent Jeanne Adams, ticket agent Gerald Duncan, reservations agent Martine Donahue, and a host of other witnesses were part of a series of facts included to tell a sceptical world that only a bomb explained the destruction of Air India Flight 182. The book had made headlines around the world; from the *Oman Observer* to a brief mention in *Time* magazine. *The London Sunday Times* had carried excerpts. The publication coincided with the end of the Justice Kirpal Commission Inquiry into the downing of Air India Flight 182 which had been held in New Delhi. With the help of evidence supplied by the RCMP, Justice Kirpal had ruled the aircraft was brought down by a bomb boarded by a person in Vancouver. The book provided conclusive evidence of a bomb aboard the flight. It also made a strong case that Sikh militants were behind both the Narita and Air India bombings. My hope was the publication of the facts would shake something loose—make someone significant talk.

Instead, the silence in the Sikh community deepened—save for the constant threats against my life. They would come by telephone or mail. I was now considered an enemy of the Sikh freedom movement because I was the only reporter who was saying on national television and in newspapers around the world that Sikh militants had blown up the aircraft. Hoadley was concerned. He suggested I should make sure I was not followed.

"Go the wrong way up a one-way street, if you think you are in danger," he said. "Cause an accident if you have to."

Later, Corporal Don Brost came to my home and told me the RCMP had some evidence that a conversation had occurred between Bagri and a member of Parmar's household. The conversation related to my safety and the RCMP wanted me to keep my head down until the possibilities were assessed. I stayed home for two days. Those days of threats were agonizing. There were sleepless nights. I was constantly looking out of the window of my home every time a car drove by. Changing lanes five or six times while driving when I thought I was being followed. And when you're looking for threatening situations a lot of innocent things can look dangerous. Fear can drive the imagination wild.

Despite the threats and intimidation, I refused to let the story go. I kept tabs on all the suspects, working every day either at the office or at home. I talked with Parmar and Bagri on the phone several times during this period. Parmar denied the BK had anything to do with the explosions and on one occasion tried to suggest there was no evidence a bomb had brought the plane down. He pointed to the crash of a Japan Airlines Boeing 747 that crashed near Mount Ogura on August 12, 1985. The aircraft had suffered a catastrophic decompression and all input controls had failed. The plane went down, killing all fifteen crew members and 505 passengers. Parmar argued something similar could have happened to the Air India Boeing 747 he was being accused of bringing down.

I also interviewed Johal on several occasions. He told me that as a young activist agitating for Sikh rights, he had been to jail three times in India. The first time was in 1960. He was barely fourteen years old. At that time, Sikhs throughout the country were demanding changes in the way New Delhi appointed representatives to the temples. Johal spent seven days in custody for his role in the agitation. The struggle against government appointees was still going on in 1971 when Johal landed in jail a second time while working as an engineer with the Shromani Gurudwara Parbandhak Committee, the supreme authority in Amritsar that manages Sikh temples, including the Golden Temple. This stay in jail in support of the cause and his faith would also be brief, but it cemented his attachment to the sacred Golden Temple on a visceral level.

In 1972, Johal moved to Canada. Extremely bright, he was also highly manipulative; the kind of guy who could sell the proverbial ice to an Inuit. The civil engineer was looking forward to a new life in Canada, but he was still stuck in the politics of Sikh parties in India. In August 1982, Johal returned to his birthplace to show his solidarity with Harchand Singh Longowal, the moderate Sikh leader of the popular Shromani Akali Dal party of Punjab. Longowal had stayed in Johal's house in Vancouver during a two-week visit in 1979 and now he was in the middle of his dharam *yudh* (literally, religious war) against the Gandhi government.

Johal was a man of two countries. While in Punjab in February 1985, mourning the death of his father, he was honoured by the presence of the head priest of the Golden Temple, Giani Kirpal Singh, who had come to show his grief at the funeral services. But shortly after the priest left Johal's house in Amritsar, unknown assailants shot Giani Kirpal Singh. Fortunately, Singh survived the attempt on his life. Johal's father, Sardar Joginder Singh, had been a senior member of the fundamentalist prayer group known as Akhand Kirtani Jatha. In India, at the outset of militancy, it was this group that had linked up with the BK to avenge the death of AKJ leader Fauja Singh during a demonstration against the Nirankaris who had riled the traditionalist with their suggestion that a living guru was necessary to sustain the Sikh faith. The idea of a living guru went contrary to Sikh belief because the words of the gurus in the *Guru Granth Sahib* are immortal. The holy book is given the same respect accorded to a living guru.

During our conversations, I asked Johal why he thought militants had bombed the Air India flight. Militants may have thought the attacks would bolster Longowal's hand at the negotiating table, he explained. He felt Sikhs would have been negotiating from a position of weakness if they showed no ability to hurt India. This was an alternative to his earlier hypothesis that the downing was vengeance for the Golden Temple attack. Perhaps, I thought, his own participation had been motivated by the same dual motives: help the Sikhs to negotiate from a position of strength with Gandhi and get even for the attack on the temple.

Shortly after the Air India bombing, Longowal and Gandhi announced a peace accord. Johal welcomed it publicly. But Longowal was seen by the militants as a traitor and on August 20, 1985, he was assassinated. Those who did not understand the real motivation behind his public support for the Longowal accord would see Johal as a traitor. I am convinced that Johal was portraying himself as a moderate because he had been one of the key architects of the Air India bombing. His call to my office giving me the clues about the trail of phone numbers left behind at the time the fatal tickets were purchased was part of this campaign to prove he was not an extremist, but a victim of extremists. He was a master of diversion, deception, and double-talk.

His telephone number, he had argued both to me and the RCMP, was available to anyone. After all, he said, he was very active in the Sikh community in Vancouver and had served as temple treasurer from 1980 to 1982.

"Every criminal tries to protect himself," said Johal. "My number was used by an enemy, not a friend."

That was the explanation Johal had offered to both myself and the RCMP after his telephone number had turned up on the ticket bookings.

It was not inconceivable that Johal could have made some nasty enemies among the Sikh faithful. That was because Johal had set out to promote himself as a moderate to counter any suggestion he was the hub of the Air India terror plot. Those who were unaware of why he was promoting himself in this way began to believe he was an Indian government agent. They began to wonder if Johal was talking out of both sides of his mouth. His history though was one of a man bent on defending extreme fundamentalism. He had been active in the back-to-basics movement that was the trademark of the AKJ group; its creed basically an unflinching adherence to traditions of the Sikh faith. In 1979 he had played a major role in wresting control of the Ross Street Temple from men he felt were diluting the tenets of the Sikh faith. At that time, people were entering the temple without covering their heads. That had offended Johal greatly. Under his guidance, it became mandatory to cover the head upon entry into the temple.

Now he was supporting the Longowal-Gandhi accord on the Punjab. And that was a disgrace as far as the terror groups were concerned. Those riled by his support for the Longowal–Gandhi accord attacked him with iron bars a few months after he publicly endorsed the agreement. He was about to hoist a flag at the school where he worked when three Sikhs accosted him, saying they had a little "*prasad*" (present) for him for supporting the accord. The first blow glanced off his turbaned head. The second bruised his foot. Johal managed to run indoors and wrest a fire extinguisher off the wall. He turned it on his attackers while flipping the fire alarm switch. His assailants fled before they could inflict serious harm to him. *The Province* took a picture of a wounded Johal and I wrote a story about it. It served Johal's purpose. I know the man who attacked him. He was a senior thug for the ISYF organization. But Johal told police he could not identify the attacker.

To further my investigation, I had telephoned Johal to ask him why—on those two crucial days in late June when the bombs would have been checked in—there had been a flurry of back-and-forth phone calls between Johal's home in Vancouver and Reyat's home in Duncan. Nothing at all suspicious about that, he assured me. He was talking to Reyat, he explained, simply because Reyat had some video tapes of his father and he wanted them back. (Johal's father had died earlier in the year.)

I pointed out that Reyat could *not* have made a late night call from Duncan on Friday, June 21. Reyat was *not* in Duncan on those two days, but in Vancouver. I reminded him that the first bomb was checked in early in the morning on Saturday and that preparations had begun as early as 4 a.m. I said Reyat had to have come to Vancouver at the very latest with the last ferry on Friday, June 21, since he would have to arm the bombs and time them. I said to him that the call that came from Reyat's home at around 11:30 p.m. could not have been made by Reyat, but most likely by a family member back home wondering if he had made it safely with his load of dynamite and blasting caps. In fact, I pressed, Reyat's family knew where they should contact him while he was in Vancouver—at Johal's home. So the calls were coming from family members to Reyat, and not from Reyat to Johal. I also asked about two calls made from Johal's home to Reyat's home on Saturday, one in the morning and one in the afternoon. I suggested Reyat had been seen in Vancouver on Saturday, and after the second bag was checked in he was probably calling his own home to say he was on his way back to Duncan.

"You're investigating me!" he shouted. Then he hung up.

A few days later Johal called to ask if my son was a student in the same elementary school where he worked as a janitor.

"I see his name on the notice board and I thought that must be your son," he mentioned in what I determined was a deliberately casual tone.

I fumed. "Listen Hardial, now that you have phoned me about this you be careful," I said.

"No, no, I was just curious."

This was blatant intimidation. I wasn't fooled by his sheepish manner for a second and I was angry as hell. There was no way I was going to take this crap.

Soon after the call, I phoned the elementary school. I informed the principal who I was and that according to reliable sources I knew that Johal was a suspect in the Air India disaster and that he had called me about my son. I wanted him moved from the school. A few days later, Johal was transferred.

Parmar, meanwhile, continued to travel the country raising money and organizing mayhem in his campaign against India. But the RCMP was watching him closely, and on June 13, 1986, police arrested Parmar in Hamilton, Ontario, on charges that he and others were involved in a Guy Fawkes–style plot to blow up the Indian Parliament buildings and kidnap the children of Indian MPs. Also arrested were Bagri, Parmar's deputy in B.C., and several members of the Ontario BK. Among those taken into custody were Tejinder Singh Kaloe, Daljit Singh Deol, Surmukh Singh Lakhain, and Sadhu Singh Thiara, all of Hamilton. Also arrested was Rampal Singh Dhillon of Brampton.

On December 12, 1986, after a twelve-day preliminary hearing on charges of possession of explosives, conspiracy to cause damage to property (namely, the Indian Parliament buildings) and kidnapping of the children of Indian MPs, an Ontario Provincial Court judge decided to send five of the seven, including Parmar, to trial. But Judge Morris Perozak decided the evidence against Bagri and Dhillon was too speculative and they were released. RCMP had believed they had intervened just in time to stop the plot and before members of the BK could leave for India to unleash a wave of terror. The Mounties had in their possession incriminating conversations caught on wiretap. I read these sinister conversations between Parmar and his alleged cohorts line-by-line. There were around one hundred conversations that had been taped both in B.C. and in Ontario, in homes and in cars, and by police officers who sat directly behind Parmar while he flew from Vancouver to Toronto.

Despite the amazing evidence contained in those wiretaps, the RCMP's case collapsed a few months later. On April 14, 1987, a judge ruled that the crown must reveal the full extent of the affidavit used to obtain wiretap authorization. The crown had blacked out some portions of the affidavit and did not want to tell the defence teams who their informants were to protect them from potential harm. The Crown withdrew their affidavit rather than compromise the safety of sources. The judge ruled the five men were not guilty and released them.

The chief Tiger, Parmar, and his friends walked out of court free men.

The three years beginning in 1985 had been startling times in the history of terrorism from Canadian soil. The Air India case was still not solved. BK members including Parmar had been freed on serious charges during the Ontario trial on the plot to blow up the Indian parliament and a Punjabi cabinet minister had been shot in B.C. But one more case, involving the BK in Montreal, was slowly making it way through the courts and this one had sinister overtones because it involved a plot to blow up a loaded Air India Boeing 747 flying out of New York's JFK Airport.

This case had begun just days before Parmar was arrested in the Ontario plot in June 1986. On May 30, 1986, RCMP acting on the information of a source and a sting operation conducted with the help of an undercover FBI agent arrested five BK members from Montreal. It seemed from the charges that the BK was bent on forcing Air India out of North America, since the airline had ceased operations in Canada following the Flight 182 bombing.

While three of the BK members had their charges stayed for lack of sufficient evidence, Crown lawyers decided to proceed with the prosecution of Santokh Singh Khella and Kashmir Singh Dhillon. The case had begun with information supplied by a mysterious informant identified only as "Billy Joe." Later, the FBI was brought in and worked in collaboration with the RCMP and Quebec police. Now, in developed democracies the accused have a right to face their accuser and have a right to see all the information in possession of the Crown so the defence can assess the strengths and weaknesses of the case against their clients. However, in this case, despite repeated requests by the defence counsel, the Crown refused to produce "Billy Joe" in court. Nevertheless On January 28, 1987, both Khella and Dhillon were convicted and sentenced to life in prison. They appealed, arguing their right to confront the informer "Billy Joe" had been denied. A new trial was ordered and in 1992, the Crown was forced to produce "Billy Joe". In a surreal scene, the Crown's key witness appeared wearing a hood and protected on either side by two large policemen. The defence argued they could not possibly conduct a valid cross-examination with a hooded witness. Ultimately, Khella and Dhillon were ordered released by an appeal court. Another key case against the BK had gone down the judicial drain. Khella, a staunch Parmar supporter, would talk to me later about this in Vancouver, claiming the charges were trumped up by Canada to please India.

Khella and Dhillon weren't the only fundamentalists free to walk.

Some were free to fly. And did—at the first opportunity

Reyat had begun packing his bags as soon as he was released from jail on the explosives charge in Duncan. Born in India on March 11, 1952, Reyat had moved to England at age thirteen. Afterwards, he married Satnam Kaur, whose family had settled in the United Kingdom after emigrating from East Africa. In 1973, the couple came to Canada and eventually became citizens. But Reyat had never given up his British passport and held dual Canadian-British citizenship. Now he was heading back to England. The RCMP could do nothing but watch on helplessly as Reyat exited Canada in July 1986. Reyat was not entirely out of reach in England, however. The RCMP would continue to build a case against him and—they hoped—at some point arrange with British authorities for extradition.

Reyat got his old job back with the Jaguar automobile manufacturing company near Coventry, where he had lived before. His in-laws helped him settle down in the ancient Midlands city. At Jaguar, Reyat would, ironically, assist in the manufacture of anti-theft devices.

Meanwhile, in Punjab, a bloodbath had followed the death of Longowal and negotiations were over. And in the midst of all this, with the BK walking free from courtrooms in Eastern Canada, the Mounties now had a much bigger challenge: protecting Indian prime minister Rajiv Gandhi.

In October of 1987, with Sikh militancy on full-throttle here and in the Punjab, the RCMP and CSIS were on edge as the Commonwealth Heads of Government met in Vancouver at the Pan Pacific Hotel. Present were three of the most protected people in the world: Gandhi, British prime minister Margaret Thatcher, and Queen Elizabeth II. I obtained a chart of security arrangements for all heads of government who were visiting and noticed Gandhi had been allocated the highest security threat, ranking ahead of Thatcher and even the Queen.

The security charts showed the extraordinary measures the police had taken to protect Gandhi, the target of Sikh militants who wanted to wipe out the dynasty that had ruled India for much of the time since 1947. CSIS and the RCMP monitored the movements of virtually every known militant. Gandhi's food was tested. Some portions of what he ate were then refrigerated for later testing in case he suffered poisoning. Canada also borrowed British technology used in Northern Ireland to neutralize certain short-range frequencies to protect Gandhi's motorcade from remote-controlled bombs along motorcade routes. Sewer grates were sealed and RCMP divers took turns in the water, patrolling under the pylons on which the waterfront hotel is built. Decoy motorcades roared away and choppers took off and landed almost nonstop to confuse terrorists. It was the most extraordinary security arrangement I had seen.

During a break in the conference proceedings, a few reporters were invited to meet privately with several heads of government. We were not allowed to bring tape recorders or notebooks into the room. In the high-security ballroom in the elegant hotel, chit-chat flowed as freely as the champagne. I met Thatcher, the president of Tanzania, and then I saw Gandhi arrive, escorted by RCMP Inspector George Foulon, who was his security point man. Foulon nodded as I approached the smiling Gandhi, who was looking radiant and unruffled. Flanked by legendary journalist Jack Webster, I asked the prime minister of India, "Mr. Gandhi, what are your thoughts about Khalistan?"

Gandhi, known for his quick wit, fired back without hesitation, "Tell them to take it in Canada."

Webster and I burst out laughing at this suggestion that Khalistan should be created in Canada, and it was clear the most protected man in the world was amused as well.

"Seriously, why don't you negotiate with Sikhs?" I asked.

"There is really no one in leadership that one can negotiate with," he said.

After a few more moments of chatting, Gandhi moved on.

Next day what he had said made a great headline story.

The truth was, while Gandhi may have appeared at his ease and even able to joke about the Sikh threat, other Indian government officials were nervous. Earlier, I had met with Maloy Dhar, who was back in Canada as part of Gandhi's security team. Dhar said he was prepared to pay a million dollars to anyone who could provide information about a real threat to Gandhi. As I drove with him from his hotel where we had coffee to the convention site, he bluntly asked, "Is CSIS any good?"

I wish I could have told him right then that CSIS and the RCMP had defused at least six plots against Gandhi already. The RCMP had been so apprehensive, in fact, that they had cancelled a function arranged for Gandhi by the Indian consulate in Vancouver. The guest list supplied to the RCMP had included several names authorities had red-flagged as dangerous.

Gandhi was a very likeable, young, and charismatic leader. It had been an experience of a lifetime to be able to exchange a few words with him. It was a terrible shock when years later in a 1991 election campaign a female suicide terrorist detonated a bomb, killing him instantly.

For reaction to his death, I had phoned Inspector Foulon, who expressed his shock and horror. During the days that he had protected him in the October 1987 Commonwealth Heads of Government meeting in Vancouver, Foulon had been charmed by Gandhi's sense of humour and his magnetism. Curiously, there had been no display of wild jubilation among Sikh militants. Perhaps because the assassination had been accomplished not by them but by another terror group; apparently, they had done the job that Sikh militants had failed to do. It was determined that the suicide bomber was a member of the Liberation Tigers of Tamil

Eelam (LTTE) who had been waging war in Sri Lanka for a separate Tamil state.

Ultimately, twenty-six members of the LTTE were tracked down and convicted by India. Four were sentenced to death.

Prior to Gandhi's visit in October 1987, I had wanted to canvas the community for a sense of how the wind might be blowing. My assignment was to write about the security arrangements for the Indian prime minister so it only made sense to visit as many Sikhs as possible, whether they were militant, moderate, or in-between.

I had paid a visit to Ripudaman Singh Malik's office a few days before Rajiv Gandhi arrived in town. I also wanted to talk about word he was giving money to Parmar. Malik was talkative during the chat at his office on Hamilton Street, in Vancouver. He said he contributed money to Parmar's religious work but did not support terrorism. He said he gave about 15 per cent of his income as tithe money. He saw the required 10 per cent as "just a passing mark."

He also told me not to say publicly that he gave 15 per cent because people might think he was boasting about religious donations. Malik said that every night at 10 p.m., he would sit in meditation and give God an accounting of his day. He said he favoured negotiations between Rajiv Gandhi and Simranjit Singh Mann, a Punjab politician who was becoming an emerging power in the wake of the death of Longowal at the hands of militants. It was partly because of what Malik said about the government of India negotiating with Sikhs that I had asked Gandhi my question. But Gandhi ruled out negotiations with Mann, telling me he did not represent the Sikhs.

I asked Malik what would happen if someone attacked Gandhi in Canada. Would that affect the cause of the Sikhs fighting the government of India? Would that be considered negative publicity?

Malik shrugged, "What does negative publicity mean to the cause?"

As usual, Malik's reply was ambiguous and could be interpreted in a number of ways.

Later, he invited me to attend a prayer session at the Khalsa School, which he had founded in Vancouver in 1986. He sat on the floor, appearing comfortable during the hour that we sat there listening to children singing hymns; I must have crossed and uncrossed my legs a hundred times, trying to shake off pins and needles. I put my hand on his shoulder to stand up and my legs felt frozen.

As the vortex of violence in India continued, its spill-over effects on Vancouver's Sikh community turned murderous.

For several months beginning in June 1986, Hayer had been bugging me about a Sikh who had entered Canada from the U.S. and claimed refugee status here. The man's name was Major Santokh Singh Bagga (a.k.a. Dharam), a retired Indian army officer. He had arrived sometime in June 1986 and was among more than a hundred Sikhs who had suddenly turned up at immigration offices in downtown Vancouver, claiming refugee status, insisting they would be persecuted if returned to India.

Hayer had insisted that Bagga was, in fact, an agent of the Indian government. Bagga, he claimed, had been sent to Canada in a clandestine effort to infiltrated and disrupt the Sikh militant movement. I wrote a brief story about the sudden appearance of the Sikh refugees for *The Province*. But I could find no corroborating evidence to link Bagga to the Indian government.

Hayer, however, neglecting to share with me any proof whatsoever, was possessed by the conviction Bagga was an Indian government agent who had been sent to Canada purely for the purpose of discrediting the cause of Sikh independence. Hayer though was in the habit of using that label for a lot on other Sikhs. For example, when Ujjal Dosanjh, (former B.C. premier and later Canada's Health Minister) was beaten with an iron bar in the early '80s for speaking out against Sikh militant violence, Hayer ran a tirade against him. Instead of chastising the attackers, Hayer labelled Dosanjh "a lackey of Mrs. Indira Gandhi" and "anti-Sikh." Privately Hayer labelled him an Indian government agent too. Dosanjh was just one of many Sikhs who had sued Hayer for running wild with his pen–which was a destructive weapon in the hands of a maverick. Writers working for mainstream media could not possibly understand the way Hayer ran his newspaper. Checks and balances, accuracy, dispassionate coverage of real news were all alien to Hayer. His newspaper was his political tool.

I had no doubt that there were Indian government agents based in Canada, and that they routinely paid informants to collect and disseminate information aimed at discrediting Sikhs they had determined constituted a security threat. But I interviewed Bagga at a residence in Ontario and at no point did I get an impression that he was an agent of the government of India. Besides, my sources also informed me this was not credible information. Why Hayer was so intent on destroying Bagga's reputation was not entirely clear, but Hayer's motives in his writings and information he supplied to me often remained unclear. This disinformation Hayer spread about Bagga continued well into 1998. In August 1998, Hayer phoned to tell me he had done a story discrediting Bagga. The story was based on his conversations with Bagga's son, Harkirat Singh, who was only seventeen-years-old. Harkirat had been in Pakistan before smuggling himself into Canada. He had been separated from his father and hardened by living with Sikh militants in Pakistan.

"Major Dharam (Bagga's other name) calls himself the preacher of the religion and like Mohandas Karmchand Gandhi, (Mahatma Gandhi) he keeps (one to two) young women with him to sing religious hymns as well," wrote Hayer, implying that there was something insidious about Mahatma Gandhi's and Bagga's association with young women. "My Father Santokh Singh Bagga Is Involved with Lajwanti, Alias Jasbir Kaur," shrieked Hayer's headline.

Hayer also told me that he had proof that the Harkirat had told him about his father, and the story was based on the youngster talking about his own dad. He urged me to pick up a tape at a store in the Punjabi market. He had sent it there so people doubting the written version of what he said about the senior Bagga, could verify it by listening to what the Harkirat had said.

There were several conversations between the young man and Hayer on that tape which I obtained. In one, the youth was spreading rumours about his father. In another conversation, recorded after the story ran, Harkirat could be heard pleading with "Uncle Hayer" to retract the story as it had done great harm and brought great shame on his family. (Hayer was no relation to Harkirat but younger Indians refer to those men who are older than themselves as uncle as a sign of respect.)

Hayer was oblivious to the youth's plight. Hayer might have gloated that he had succeeded in discrediting the elder Bagga, but the story certainly did not end there as Hayer, regrettably, was soon to discover.

On August 26, 1988, a distraught Harkirat stormed into Hayer's office and shot him six times with a .357 Magnum. Three bullets hit Hayer. He did not die, but he was left a paraplegic. A heroic employee of Hayer's chased after the shooter and held him down until police arrived.

Because of the severity of the crime, Harkirat was raised to adult court. There he decided to defend himself and in short order pleaded guilty. Confusion reigned about whether the attempt on Hayer's life was based purely on personal motive: namely the shame that Hayer had put the youth to by quoting him about his father's alleged improprieties. Prosecutor Sean Madigan, with whom I talked a great deal, painted the shooter as a well trained militant who had spent time in Pakistan with terrorists. Madigan said Harkirat had been in contact with several senior militants. In fact, in his first interviews with RCMP, Harkirat told them he got the gun from members of the ISYF in Toronto. Later he said he got it from senior BK member Ajaib Singh Bagri, who was Parmar's deputy. Then he changed his story and said he bought it from a black man in Seattle.

Acting as his own lawyer Harkirat told the trial judge he lied to cops about where the gun had come from but declined to say now where he got it. Harkirat also said he shot Hayer because of emotional trauma that he suffered when Hayer wrote about his father. The truth of who put him up to it, if anyone, had now become so hopelessly obfuscated. And Hayer's bad mouthing of the youth's father loomed large as a motive.

On December 16, 1988, Judge Patrick Hyde rejected the notion pushed by crown counsel of an international terrorist plot aimed at Hayer. However, he conceded Harkirat was likely "subtly induced by others" for political reasons.

The penalty phase was even more bizarre. The youth told the judge he deserved the death penalty for what he had done. Mindful of his youth though, the judge gave him fourteen years in jail. A few months later, I reported that Harkirat had tried to kill himself on his eighteenth birthday. He was despondent over being in jail. He was found unconscious in his cell but revived by prison doctors.

I believed based on all my research in the community and my sources that Harkirat was a highly unstable young man. His behaviour at trial, his decision to represent himself and his insistence he should be put to death, led me to question whether the youngster was completely sane. Some Sikhs who knew him actually doubted if he was. He was easily manipulated, as was proven by the way Hayer obtained such personal details about his family from him. Nevertheless, there were other factors that still left a lingering suspicion that terrorists too had taken advantage of the young man's instability. While no one could prove who gave him the gun, a number of clues surfaced that raised tantalizing possibilities that at least, the gun, if not instructions on what to do with it, came from militants.

At that time, several Sikh militants were in some serious gun-smuggling business, including a few on Vancouver Island who were personal friends of Inderjit Singh Reyat. They transported weapons out of California and brought them into B.C., and among their key customers were some powerful Sikh militants.

What was most confounding though was a discovery made by police after Harkirat was convicted.

One of two weapons found in Reyat's home during the November 1985 search had its serial numbers filed off. But police were able to use "acid etching" to reveal the indented numbers under the scratches. The gun was tracked to a man in Sutter County, next to Yuba City, California. Amazingly, the gun used by Harkirat was also tracked to the same person.

While doing research for this book I almost fell off my chair when I found out that the cops had actually gone and interviewed the man who had earlier owned both weapons.

I called the retired sheriff of Sutter County Roy Whiteaker, who owns a gun store called The Ammo Outlet. He confirmed he got a call first and then a visit from the RCMP and the FBI. At the time, in the '80s, he was the sheriff of Sutter County, which has a large population of Sikhs.

Whiteaker told me cops from Canada wanted to know how the two guns ended up in the hands of criminals. One found at the home of Air India bomber Reyat and the second found in the lethal hands of would-be assassin, Harkirat, were both in the collection of deputy sheriff Bharpur Takhar, a Sikh unknown to have any militant connections. By the time the cops from Canada arrived, Takhar had been let go from the Sheriff's office because of an unspecified reason that Whiteaker said he was not at liberty to discuss.

Whiteaker said Takhar told authorities he could not recall who bought his gun collection. Whiteaker said he had no idea why an officer of the law would not remember who he sold the guns to. The retired sheriff said some of the weapons sold along with the two guns that turned up in Canada were automatic guns. He said both the FBI and the RCMP investigated but he was unclear on what the outcome was. RCMP sources said they could not connect the dots on how two weapons that were in the same hands in California turned up in Canada.

Takhar, who now lives in Washington State, denied knowing either Reyat or Harkirat, said the source. With the gun tracks vanishing on them, RCMP could not make a case for conspiracy for the moment. But it raised the possibility that an angry youngster who had come to Canada from Sikh militant camps in Pakistan just months before the shooting had been used by someone else who also did not want Hayer around.

I visited Hayer at his home after his release from hospital, where he spent months. I felt sorry for him. He sat in a wheelchair and talked about the constant pain he suffered. He looked like a broken man and I could tell he was depressed. He was also bitter that the cops had been unable to prove that his shooting was motivated by militants in B.C. He was absolutely convinced that the BK had him shot. He pointed to the fact that Harkirat had told police at one point that BK deputy Ajaib Singh Bagri had given him the gun. Hayer, it seemed to me, had a thing for Bagri. He called Bagri a coward often. He said Bagri could not carry out the instructions of his leaders when he was sent on a mission and "shit his pants." Hayer never said what that mission was. I still had my doubts about Hayer's theories. I had yet to see the evidence that Bagri was involved. Yet I listened to Hayer patiently and comforted him, telling him to have faith that justice would happen–that this was Canada and I was sure the cops would keep working on it to get to the bottom of the incident.

After the shooting, Hayer was promoted as a champion of moderation by the media despite the fact that Hayer had been a champion of separatism and, had spoken in favour of violent thugs who ruled the Khalistan terrorist movement. He had described Ujjal Dosanjh a "lackey of Indira Gandhi" following his beating, written a book glorifying Sikh rebel Bhindranwale who started the flames of violence in the Punjab, had praised an earlier attack on the Indian consulate by Sodhi Singh Sodhi who he said had made Indian diplomats run "like dogs." He had even decorated Sodhi by presenting him with a sword for his attack on the Indian mission in Vancouver. Yes, Hayer had his disputes with other separatists, but they were fuelled for personal reasons, or political reasons. For example, he asked the ISYF leadership in Vancouver to buy out his book on Bhindranwale on a wholesale basis with a cash payment. The ISYF said it was willing to sell the book but Hayer would only collect money when the books sold. Hayer was bitter about that and attacked the ISYF for several months after that, using his dreaded weapon, his own newspaper.

A Punjabi writers' group in Vancouver was so puzzled by the fact that the media was calling Hayer a voice for moderation that it put out a communiqué stating, "Mr. Hayer has been portrayed as a moderate Sikh who opposes violent means to achieve Khalistan, the separate Sikh state. The attack on him is seen as an attack on moderation and democracy.

"Mr. Hayer consistently ridiculed the moderate Sikhs and supported extremist actions and glamorized militant activities.

"For example, the title pages of two recent issues of the *Indo-Canadian Times* carried full-page colour portraits of two well-known extremist Sikh leaders killed in India. They were portrayed as martyrs by the paper."

Gurcharan Rampuri, who was a member of the Punjabi writer's group, had earlier been described as a "hermaphrodite" by Hayer. Rampuri was one of some thirty people, including Dosanjh, who had sued Hayer for name-calling, misinformation, and pure malice.

But Hayer, the man who had given Sikh militancy a jump-start and who was an advocate for terrorism, was given the Order of British Columbia in 1995. (The citation said he was a model of tolerance. It said, "Tara Singh Hayer has continued, even when faced with violence, to be a voice of moderation and reason. In August, 1988, he survived an attempt on his life that left him in a wheelchair. Despite this attack, Mr. Hayer has never wavered in his commitment to tolerance, peace and understanding between cultural communities").

As the RCMP worked on the attempt on Hayer's life, they had been making headway on their bigger investigation of the Air India bombing.

Much of the evidence gathered in Japan around the Narita bombing had finally made its way to the RCMP labs in Vancouver. Police were able to use it to match some of the items found in Reyat's home and other personal possessions with the Narita blast. Vancouver prosecutor Jim Jardine decided he now had enough evidence to pluck Reyat from the U.K. Charges were filed against Reyat and the B.C. Supreme Court issued a warrant for his arrest on February 1, 1988.

Several officers, including RCMP Corporals Don Brost and Tom Graham, would make their way to the British Midlands. I knew in advance Reyat was going to be caught soon. I withheld the story until he was safely in custody. But I did call Brost in England to let him know I knew. He was a little ticked off; worried I would break the story before Reyat was picked up.

"Ever seen me screwing up an investigation?" I asked.

I attended the Bow Street Magistrate's Court in London, England, throughout the extradition hearing where compelling Canadian evidence was presented on behalf of Her Majesty by London lawyer Clive Nichols, assisted by Jardine. Once, while we stood around outside making small talk, I asked him the rationale for not charging Reyat and Parmar jointly with conspiracy:

"Tell CSIS to give me the tapes," he snapped. Clearly, the RCMP was not alone harping about the erased CSIS tapes; Jardine also felt it was crucial ammunition that had been destroyed.

As I sat taking notes in the small court room alongside *Vancouver Sun* reporter Larry Still and others journalists from Canadian television outlets, Reyat turned around during a break and said to me, "Wait till you hear my side of the story."

"I look forward to that," I whispered back.

But I never did hear anything from him.

The British High Court ruled it was justified extraditing Reyat to Canada. They described the events leading to his arrest in England like this:

"In July 1986, he (Reyat) and his family left Canada and settled in this country. His intention to do that was well-known to the Royal Canadian Mounted Police who placed no obstacles in his way.

"He made a new home, in or near Coventry and found employment in his trade with the makers of the Jaguar motor cars. He looked forward apparently to living here for the rest of his life. But on February 5, 1988, he had a nasty shock. As he was making his way to work that day, he was confronted by police officers from New Scotland Yard and West Midlands."

On December 13, 1989, Reyat was back in Vancouver, escorted by Mounties who had flown to England to pick him up. Since Reyat was now in the custody of Canadian police and the chances of him returning to England any time soon were slim, his wife and three kids soon followed him back to the Vancouver area. While he awaited trial, his wife went looking for help from members of the Sikh community. Prominent among those willing to help her were Malik and Johal. They considered it their spiritual duty to help her survive while her husband battled charges. Nothing in the law says you can't help an accused man or his family.

Reyat would soon face the music, but his boss, Parmar, by now a millionaire who had built and sold four houses, had taken off to Pakistan, possibly fearing the other shoe was about to fall with Reyat's extradition to Canada being imminent. As the RCMP watched Parmar cross the Canada–U.S. border, they had no idea he would never see Canada again.

EIGHT

REDUCED TO ASHES

One of Parmar's first tasks upon his arrival in Pakistan in 1988 was to appoint himself the commander of BK operations for the New Delhi area. Indian intelligence now had to worry about his capabilities while operating in a hostile nation that was a major base for thousands of other Sikh rebels. Pakistan was not likely to hinder Parmar or care what targets he chose. At least, while Parmar had been in Canada, India could be assured that CSIS and RCMP were watching him. But by fleeing his home in Burnaby, B.C., he had slipped the Canadian law enforcement leash. And those of us in Canada had little idea what Parmar was up to. We knew that his wife and the rest of the family had stayed behind, but reports of his activities became scant for CSIS, the RCMP and for me.

While Canadian authorities were in the dark, Parmar's moves were now being monitored by India's powerful intelligence agency, R&AW. The agency discovered alarming evidence of Parmar's abilities as a terrorist shortly after his arrival in Pakistan. A glimpse of what he was up to is contained in the massive report compiled by Justice Jain's Commission into the assassination of Rajiv Gandhi.

"During this period, information was also received indicating that the Sikh extremists, based in Pakistan, possessed two to six Stinger missiles, which they had possibly procured from the Afghan Mujahideens with funds brought by Talwinder Singh Parmar and Tejinder Singh Kaloe of the Babbar Khalsa, Canada. The possession of these missiles implied that it had become necessary to provide adequate protection to the prime minister's aircraft during its flight from the Stinger missiles in the possession of the Sikh extremists as well as the Afghan Mujahideens," states the Jain commission report, made public in 1997.

The word among Sikh militants in Canada was that Parmar had left the country with a million dollars in his possession. How he made that much money (which, according to Indian intelligence, was being used to buy surplus weapons from the Afghans that the Americans had supplied to Islamic fighters) could possibly be explained by the sizeable amounts of cash Parmar had collected during his Martyr's-Fund campaign and another business that he had begun a few months before he left Canada.

A CSIS intercept of June 19, 1985, two days before the twin explosions showed that Parmar was no longer a mill worker with a minimum salary. The taped conversation with real estate agent Ved Sharma from Parmar's home in Burnaby revealed that the "Living Martyr" didn't wish members of the Sikh community to know that he was now buying and selling homes and building lots. Nor did he wish it to be known that he was dealing with a Hindu real estate agent.

"On the nineteenth of June 1985, between 1007 hours and 1133 hours, CSIS intercepted four telephone conversations between Ved Sharma and Talwinder Singh Parmar. During these conversations, the two discussed real estate transactions that Mr. Parmar was involved in. Mr. Parmar impressed upon Mr. Sharma that he should not tell anyone what Mr. Parmar was buying and selling as several Sikhs had questioned that he was dealing with a Hindu real estate agent. Mr. Parmar also did not want other people to know that he was investing money here and there when he was not working," RCMP reported in one of their affidavits.

I asked Sharma, who enjoyed a loyal "family–type" relationship with Parmar, about his friend's real estate ventures between 1985 and 1988. Sharma said Parmar had bought a duplex lot on Union Street in Vancouver for the "very fair" price of $65,000. He built an enormous house at a cost of approximately $150,000 and then sold the property at a substantial profit. But Sharma would not talk about the value of the sale. Further, Sharma said he showed Parmar two lots on Vancouver's Renfrew Street, which he also purchased at a good price. He subdivided the lots into four parcels and built four homes that were also sold at profit. Given the market value of new homes in 1988, each home would have sold in excess of $300,000, making the total value of sales well over $1 million.

In 1988, as completion of the homes neared, Sharma said Parmar appeared to be in a hurry to sell the houses. Sharma did not find out his client had left Canada until one day he called his home and the family told him he was no longer here.

The RCMP did not know of Parmar's true wealth at the start of their investigation. But it became evident that he was a real estate entrepreneur capable of building homes with investment values in the hundreds of thousands of dollars. Within months of his release from Germany, Parmar had begun accumulating a fortune from donations made to the Martyr's Fund, and by 1985, he had become a well-heeled businessman. He had enough money to act as a banker to Ripudaman Singh Malik. In one telephone conversation intercepted by CSIS, Malik was heard offering Parmar better interest than the bank if Parmar loaned him $100,000.

One of the questions investigators had asked from the beginning was who paid for the Air India bombing operation. When I added up the cost, it turned out the cost of creating havoc in the skies south of Ireland and the explosion in Tokyo was minimal. The notion that an act of terrorism too horrible to contemplate had cost next to nothing was hard to digest. But the numbers didn't lie. The Air India bombings were a relatively simple operation. The two tickets were purchased for around $3,000. Reyat got the dynamite for free, the Micronta twelve-volt timers were bought from Radio Shack in Duncan for around twenty dollars and the relay switches (which allow the current to pass to the blasting cap for the detonation of dynamite) were purchased for a measly few dollars. Reyat had paid $129 on his Visa card to buy a stereo tuner—a tuner of an identical make and model to the one identified as having been used as the outer casing for the bomb.

In the case of Air India, police had found an empty VCR box in Reyat's home, but no VCR. There is no reason to suspect the Air India Flight 182 bomb was any more complex than the Tokyo bomb. The VCR would not have cost much more than $200. In total, the Air India Flight 182 explosion and the Tokyo bomb cost a little over $3,000 to produce. Parmar could easily bear this cost with his newfound prosperity. Terror is inexpensive.

So while India's intelligence worried about the Stinger missiles Parmar had apparently acquired, he added to their woes by vowing to bring down more Air India planes. He was now in Pakistan and free to say what he wanted, and he must have also felt that he was beyond the reach of law enforcement agents from Canada because there was no extradition treaty between Islamabad and Ottawa. The interview he gave in Pakistan to the London-based *Des Pardesh* newspaper was chilling. He told the Punjabi-language journal that those travelling by Air India were "suicidal because their aircraft would burn in the sky and fall to the ground."

A statement like that made so close to Inderjit Singh Reyat's trial in Vancouver following his extradition from London was unwise to say the least.

In September 1990 the scene was set for a major trial in the Supreme Court of British Columbia in front of Justice Raymond Paris, an experienced judge known in judicial circles as an astute, soft-spoken, just, and compassionate man. As a preview, I wrote a story to highlight the enormity and importance of the proceedings. I interviewed Crown Counsel Gordon Matei to lay out for the public the logistics of what promised to be one of the longest trials ever in Canada. Matei estimated it could take eight months and would involve some 190 witnesses, including eighty to be flown in from Japan. One of his key witnesses would be the survivor of the bomb–Masaharu Asakura. Three top prosecutors were assigned to the case: Jim Jardine, Matei, and Richard Cairns. Jardine, a no-nonsense Crown prosecutor, whose disdain for the media I disliked but whose brilliance I had come to admire, was the main architect in getting Reyat extradited from London to stand trial in Canada. Japan's request to have him tried in Tokyo had earlier been rejected by Canada (Japanese police were quite eager to see Reyat on trial in Tokyo. They told some of my police sources they would try to get him hanged upon conviction. Canada, they reminded the RCMP, had no death penalty). It made more sense to try Reyat in Canada rather than Japan because the crime had its origins in Vancouver and Canadian law makes it difficult to send an accused to a country where the death penalty is applied.

Reyat would be defended by famous Vancouver lawyer David Gibbons, who made no secret of the fact that he was no fan of local cops. He would be assisted by Vancouver lawyer Mark Hilford.

When Reyat took his seat in the dock in front of Justice Paris in B.C. Supreme Court in September 1990, he faced two counts of manslaughter and five charges relating to making and possessing explosives, including the making of an explosive device with intent to cause damage to property and making an explosive device with intent to assist others to cause damage. The two charges of manslaughter against Reyat stemmed from the deaths of the two Japanese baggage handlers, Ideharu Koda and Hideo Asano (manslaughter is the lowest form of a murder charge in Canada— first-degree murder is planned and deliberate and constitutes the most serious of three available murder counts). The rest of the charges were related to possession of dynamite.

Jardine, was once again meticulous in providing a step-by-step account of the evidence against Reyat that he said could lead to only one conclusion: Reyat had participated "in an act of terrorism directed at the state of India and in particular at the state-run airline, Air India."

One by one, with witnesses after witness, the prosecution team accumulated a mountain of evidence against Reyat as the manufacturer of the bomb that had killed Koda and Asano. The Crown demonstrated that the accused was a fundamentalist Sikh who was greatly upset by events in India. Although Reyat's interest in dynamite seemed to date to 1983, he began serious efforts to acquire materials for a bomb in the spring of 1985. Witness, Ian McIntyre (a friend of Robertson, the blasting expert who Reyat had pestered for dynamite) testified he overheard Reyat talking on the phone: "He said something about getting even for the sacrilege at Amritsar."

Painstakingly, the prosecutors laid the facts before the court. How on May 8, 1985, following the first visit to Duncan by Parmar and Gill, Reyat went to a Radio Shack outlet and purchased a Micronta car clock. Then on May 28 Reyat obtained six to eight sticks of powerful dynamite from Kenneth Slade along with three blasting caps. On June 4, the same day Parmar and Mr. X were observed in the woods by CSIS, Jardine proved that Reyat had purchased a second Micronta twenty-four-hour alarm clock as well as two relay switches which would allow a current to pass through a bomb-trigger.

The Crown produced the credit card receipt that proved that on June 5, 1985, Reyat had purchased a Sanyo tuner model FMT 611K (although the receipt was made out in the name of Reyat, Woolworths store clerk Karen Smith had told police that it was not Reyat who had picked it up. She said two other men who did not wear turbans picked up the tuner. Who these two men were has never been determined. Police believed the men were his helpers. Many years later, in another trial, Reyat would concede he did buy the tuner. But he did not say who picked it up from the store).

On the same day the tuner was purchased, Reyat also bought a can of smokeless gunpowder. According to witnesses, he exchanged one of the electrical relay switches for a different type. Evidence also showed he had gone to several electronics stores asking store employees to show him how he could make the alarm clock buzzer stay on rather than sound intermittently. It would be necessary to keep the buzzer going to supply constant power from the battery to the trigger to set off the bomb.

On June 19, three days before the bags were to be boarded, Reyat purchased another relay switch. On June 22, Reyat walked into the Auto Marine Electric store in the Vancouver suburb of Burnaby and purchased a twelve-volt battery. An employee testified Reyat brought a plate with him and attempted to fit the battery into the metal bracket. He even asked for an "employee discount" since he worked at a branch of the same store in his hometown of Duncan. It was extremely significant to the prosecutor that the Crown prove Reyat was in Vancouver area on the day the bag bombs were checked in at Vancouver Airport. The bombs exploded several hours later.

Jardine said Reyat had acquired seven items that matched the components of the bomb that exploded in Japan. And he had access to two more that were also part of the deadly configuration. During the search of Reyat's home in November 1985, police had recovered the receipt for the Sanyo tuner, but could not find the device. Reyat had told police earlier he had given the tuner away as a gift to Mr. X, who had visited his home with Parmar. Reyat had played games with the cops when they asked him repeatedly to identify Mr. X, and supplied no information that could lead to the proper identification of the mystery man.

During the trial, Jardine told the court that Reyat had enclosed the tuner in its own box complete with a Styrofoam cover in case the Jet Steam-model suitcase containing it was scanned or opened. To authorities it would look like any other working stereo.

During the same 1985 search of his home, police also recovered a plastic bag in which Reyat had emptied gooey, gelatine-based dynamite, as well as green tape of the type found in Tokyo that he had used to tie the bomb in place

Jardine proved that no one had occupied seat 38H that Jeanne Adams had assigned to L. Singh (whose ticket was connected with that of M. Singh who had earlier checked in the bag that had exploded on Air India Flight 182).

CP Flight 003 Second Officer Kenneth Bews, who sat on top of a highly unstable bomb for almost ten hours, testified that the flight left Vancouver at 20:37 (GMT). The total flying time was nine hours three minutes and ramp-to-ramp time from Vancouver to Tokyo was nine hours and twenty-five minutes. That would have still left two hours and ten minutes for the bag to be transferred to waiting Air India Flight 301.

Masaharu Asakura, a survivor of the bomb blast, was one of several baggage handlers assigned to off-load the flight after it docked. He told the court they first dealt with bags destined for Tokyo and then noticed there were ten bags left over that were to connect with other flights. He turned the container so it could be off-loaded from the side opposite to where he was. He had just become the luckiest man in the world.

According to Asakura, no sooner had the baggage handler Koda put a suitcase onto the conveyer belt than it exploded. He described a painful, chaotic scene in dimming light with pieces from overhead fluorescent lights falling and heavy dust in the air. He testified how a piece of shrapnel penetrated his steel toed boot and how his second toe on the left foot had to be amputated.

Jardine continued to pile on the evidence to show only Reyat could have made that bomb. Liquid Fire, argued Jardine, is commonly used to jump-start cars on cold days. Reyat, he suggested, had wanted to start a fire and the use of Liquid Fire would be familiar substance to an auto mechanic. The use of Liquid Fire—not a routine ingredient of a bomb–constituted Reyat's signature as the maker of the device, he argued.

He reminded the court that Reyat had told Henderson in 1985 that Parmar had asked him to make a bomb to "do a big job," to blow up something big in India. Reyat had claimed he did not know what Parmar's plan was. But Reyat had to have known that the bomb he was making (with only a twenty-four-hour timer) was to be shipped aboard airplanes. As the bomb-maker working in concert with others, he would also know what time his friends wanted it to explode and whether it was meant to blow up aboard the aircraft or after the plane landed in India.

Jardine also pointed out that Reyat, while talking to Henderson, had said the third man, Mr. X, stayed in the car while he and Parmar went into the bush. Reyat further said he and Parmar were watching the explosive closely and they had the man stationed in the car, so nobody could come upon them by accident and get hurt. Jardine submitted that Reyat had perfected a bomb and he was demonstrating that ability to Parmar. The explosion was powerful enough to make him worry someone could be hurt accidentally while he was triggering it, and hence the watchman he had kept in the car.

The slow avalanche of evidence presented methodically by Jardine was compelling. It had taken seven months and two hundred witnesses to bring the trial to a conclusion. Justice Paris said he would give his verdict on May 10, 1991.

On judgment day May 10, Inderjit Singh Reyat–who his lawyer had described as "just an ordinary guy"–would be officially termed a terrorist. Justice Paris would find him guilty of all seven charges against him.

"I should mention at this point," concluded Justice Paris, "that certain statements made to the police by Reyat help confirm conclusively in my mind that the tuner he purchased was the one used in the Narita bomb. His explanation that he bought and for no apparent reason gave it as a present to the person who visited with Parmar, a person whose name he had to be pressed to remember and whose place of residence he did not know, is simply not capable of belief."

Paris said on the strength of the evidence, he was convinced beyond reasonable doubt of "Reyat's participation in the fabrication of the bomb" and that he found Reyat's motive to be his anger at India.

"There is of course abundant evidence of motive on the part of Reyat. From the testimony of various witnesses it is apparent that he was keenly interested in political question related to Sikhs in India," said Paris. "Several witnesses testified that he had expressed hostility towards the Indian authorities, great indignation at the events at the Golden Temple in Amritsar, and even gratification at the assassination of Indira Ghandhi."

He said there was evidence that Reyat was willing to fight and if necessary "to die for his cause."

On June 10, a month after delivering his guilty verdict, Paris sentenced Reyat to what could be considered a lenient sentence of ten years; mystifying, since the judge acknowledged that Reyat was a terrorist.

The price to be paid for the lives of Ideharu Koda and Hideo Asano was just five years each. In denying the prosecution's request for a life sentence, Paris ruled the Crown had failed to prove Reyat had meant to hurt anyone. He pointed to evidence that showed Reyat was previously a person of good character who worked hard and was very religious.

"The accused is apparently a man of remarkably good character. It is profoundly sad that an otherwise decent person should be drawn into such a mad enterprise," he added.

I found Paris's reasoning baffling. To me, there was simply no such thing as a bomb with benign intent: its very purpose is to destroy. That under any circumstances a judge could have concluded that Reyat had not meant serious harm by exploding a bomb struck me as absurd. People of "remarkably good character" don't manufacture bombs! In any case, it was only a stroke of luck for Reyat that the bomb—highly unstable as it was—had not detonated aboard CP Air Flight 003, sparing the lives of the 390 passengers on board who had departed from Vancouver.

Justice Paris had, I thought, missed the point completely by suggesting Reyat was a religious man who had acted uncharacteristically. It was, I knew, precisely his overwhelming religious fundamentalism that had motivated him to commit his crime.

Not surprisingly, the cops I talked to—the foot soldiers who had worked so hard to bring Reyat to justice—were also appalled by the ten-year sentence. They were stunned. They couldn't know it then, but worse was to come. Much worse. Even then, for me, this was the first time justice had been done in the Air India case. I saw no difference in this case of the Narita bombing and the Air India Flight 182 disaster. The two cases were inextricably linked, and justice done in one case was justice done in the other, as far as I was concerned.

Years before Reyat's conviction, I had met with Consul-General Jagdish Sharma at the Indian consulate in Vancouver. We had planned to have lunch at the Pan Pacific Hotel. As we left his office, however, he drew my attention to a man who had come out to stand behind me.

"Look who is here," said Sharma.

I turned.

Johal! This was the very man whose telephone number had so crucially turned up on the ticket-booking forms; the man who had offered me an "alternative" motive for the Air India crime. Having read some of the csis intercepts of the crucial days before the bombing, I felt all roads from Parmar's home led to this man as a central figure in the crime. I considered him to be the brain of the operation, the instigator, and the project chief who enforced Parmar's "executive action."

"Hello, Hardial," I said as he walked towards me.

"They are not giving me a visa," he said.

He seemed more than a bit distressed. I shrugged my shoulders and walked out with Sharma. Safely out of earshot, the consul-general vented his spleen about Johal.

"He is a snake and I am wondering why Gurinder meets with him; I have told him not to trust Johal, but Gurinder keeps meeting with him," said Sharma, referring to his vice-consul's meeting with the Air India bombing suspect.

I was astonished. What was an agent of the R&AW doing meeting with a prime suspect in the Air India bombing case? I asked

Sharma if he would give me Johal's visa application form. Later that day, he handed me the application to view it while I was in his office. I did not make notes. Johal had listed a New Delhi police inspector as a man who would vouch for him: an incredible reference for a Sikh militant. But I now do not recall the name of the police inspector since Sharma would not allow me to make notes. Not long afterwards, Gurinder Singh and I went for lunch at a restaurant on the second floor of a building at Burrard Street and Fourth Avenue in Vancouver. As we talked about the Air India case and Sikh militancy in general, Gurinder himself broached the subject of CSIS.

"CSIS is breathing down my neck, Salim," he said.

It was the first indication I had that CSIS agents were on to Gurinder Singh and were conducting surveillance on him. Counterintelligence was now catching up with Indian spies in Canada, I thought.

"I have a question for you," I said. "When you know CSIS is breathing down your neck, why are you still meeting with a key terrorist suspect, Hardial Singh Johal? I mean, does that not at least create the impression that Indian government agents are meeting extensively with Air India suspects and does that not arouse suspicions about your activities?"

He looked at me sheepishly, not even asking who my source was. Instead, he replied: "You're right. I will not meet with him again."

When Gurinder Singh confirmed Sharma's information, it took me back to the day in 1985 when the RCMP had arrested Johal, Parmar, and Reyat. In the middle of the raids Gurinder Singh had phoned to ask me who was being arrested. When Johal's name came up, Gurinder had asked me to rule him out as a suspect.

Having obtained this confirmation of contacts between an Indian agent and a suspect in the bombing, I asked him how his investigation of the Air India disaster was going. He said he was being hampered by CSIS surveillance. I asked in particular if he knew the names of the two people who checked in the bags.

"Ask Tara Singh Hayer, he knows the answer," he replied.

After the lunch, it didn't take long for me to phone Hayer. I said I understood he had the names of two people we were looking for who might have checked in the bags. His answer almost floored me.

"Yes, I had the names but I think I must have put it in the garbage somewhere, but I can find it again and call you back," Hayer said.

"You threw the names in the garbage?" I asked him in disbelief.

"Don't worry, I will get them back."

"Please call me back, it is really important," I pleaded.

A few minutes later, Hayer phoned with two names.

"Who are these guys?" I asked, curious because these two had never turned up in any of my scenarios or my knowledge base of Sikh militants.

"They are on Ajaib Singh Bagri's team. The information is coming from their camp," said Hayer.

I carried out background checks on the two men. One owned an auto body shop in Vancouver and was known to Bagri. The other was a relative of Bagri's who lived in Richmond. I will call them M. Singh and K. Singh. The RCMP task force chased the information supplied by Hayer for many months. In the end, both men were taken for polygraph tests and both passed. Police dismissed them as suspects based on the polygraph tests. Hayer's information had turned out to be wrong, police felt.

This was not the only incredible information supplied by Hayer. Around 1988 Hayer told me that Ajaib Singh Bagri had made a key admission to his friend in London, England. The man to whom this alleged confession was made was Tarsem Singh Purewal, editor of the *Des Pardesh* newspaper. While having drinks in a London restaurant Bagri had allegedly said that it was he who had driven bomb-laden bags to Vancouver Airport on June 22, 1985.

Two other people were present and heard the conversation, Hayer said. Later, he told the same story to RCMP, but it had changed somewhat. Hayer now said he too was present when Bagri told Purewal in his London office about the bags. The cops were now curious to see if Purewal would repeat that statement about Bagri if he was on the telephone with Hayer and believed no one else was listening. RCMP considered Hayer an informant, so they had assigned a handler to him as well as a informant code number to keep his identity secret. Veteran Mountie Corporal Bob Solvason was put in charge of extracting information from Hayer.

So when Hayer telephoned Purewal in London, Solvason listened in on the conversation. But Purewal made no such admissions even though he was not aware that a cop was listening. Hayer, it became obvious, had not budged an inch from his belief that Bagri had seduced Harkirat Singh Bagga into shooting him. Was he now saying things just to get even with Bagri?

Unfortunately, Vancouver RCMP were so starved for new leads by that time that even gossip was beginning to pass for intelligence. Rumours in the Sikh community about who might have been involved in the Air India bombings had been circulating for years. An inability to distinguish rumour from fact would plague law enforcement. RCMP had been brilliant in investigating Reyat largely because there was something tangible to chase—forensic evidence in the form of bomb parts—something they could hold in their hands and smell. But now leads were drying up and there was no forensic evidence against anyone else.

In early 1992, fresh rumours swept through the Sikh community that Parmar had secretly returned to Vancouver to bless the planned weddings of his daughter Rajinder Kaur and youngest son, Narinder.

As far as I was concerned, Parmar was a "must get" interview: to spar with him at this point would have been fascinating. I looked everywhere for him, calling some of his close friends living in Kamloops, Vancouver Island, and Vancouver itself, but there was no sign of the rebel leader anywhere. It would soon become apparent that Parmar, for his part, was well aware of my quest to find him.

On May 17, 1992, I attended the wedding of Parmar's two children at the Ross Street Sikh Temple. Sitting with my head covered (a requirement at the temple) among the six hundred in attendance; I realized it was a who's who of Parmar's network. Seated in the front on the carpet of the temple hall were BK members from B.C., Ontario, and Quebec (there are no chairs or benches in Sikh temples).

The brides and grooms entered the temple dressed in traditional wedding attire. Following them was Malkit Singh Parhar, the immigration consultant who had earlier been a leader of the Overseas

Congress Party loyal to Indira Gandhi. Parhar was one of the first people to guide me to the Consulate of Khalistan in 1981 and had been snared by an immigration sting by U.S. authorities several years later. Sikhs had been entering the U.S. via a Sikh-owned farm that straddled the U.S.–Canada border. The rebel leader Parmar had not turned up for the nuptials.

At one point during the colourful ceremony, Parmar's voice suddenly rang out over the loud speakers. The crowd hushed to the taped message of the leader to many who were here today. A wedding of one's children was an important occasion, said Parmar, but even a wedding of one's children took the back seat to the task of liberating Khalistan. Many martyrs had given their lives and they would not live to see the weddings of their children, he said.

Then Parmar made a pointed reference to my numerous calls to his friends in the past few days as I tried to find him, thinking he would be in town for the wedding. Parmar said a journalist had been looking for him in the last few days, hoping to interview him. I was stunned to hear him say that. Obviously someone I had phoned had somehow informed him of my search. There were no other print media types around since at this time no one else was chasing after the Air India story as I had done. And there were no members of law enforcement that I saw who could pick up on this. I recorded Parmar's speech on my small tape recorder and later transcribed it at my office. The cops would have to wait until the morning paper came out to pick up on what Parmar had said about the importance of his struggle for Khalistan and the comparative importance of that job when weighed against the marriage of two of his children.

"Tell him to come to the land of Khalistan and all his questions will be answered," roared Parmar's voice over the temple loud speakers.

"I would come and talk to you," I said under my breath. "That is the sole reason I was looking for you, Mr. Parmar."

After the ceremony I asked Parmar's wife, Surinder Kaur, for an exclusive interview. We were guided to a small room at the back of the temple where there are beds for travellers to rest. She sat down on one of the beds and spoke in a low, patient voice. She was a

woman who had endured unbearable loneliness and yet stood res-
olutely by her husband. Surinder Kaur said many would accuse her
husband of being a coward. But he was a brave general who had
stayed with his fight and made the ultimate sacrifice by not attending the wedding.

"If he came here, people would say he has abandoned the cause,"
she said softly. "Because he didn't come, people will say he is afraid."

Her husband had shown no fear, she said, when he was taken
away by the RCMP during the 1985 RCMP Air India raids and the
Duncan Project.

"When they came to take him away, I asked him where they
were taking him and when he'd be back. He told me to have faith
in God and he'd be back in three days."

Clearly, Surinder Kaur's faith was unshakeable. It had to be to
endure the years that her husband had waged war against India. She
said simply, "My husband says those who are fighting for Khalistan
and becoming martyrs have children, too." I asked her if she did not
worry about her husband's high-risk life, if she did not worry there
would be a phone call one night telling her he was gone.

"I take my comfort from praying twenty-four hours a day," she
said. "I chant the names of Sikh martyrs.

"Only God knows how many breaths a person will take during
a lifetime. He (Parmar) took his shroud with him when he left. He
is not afraid to die."

At the wedding in Vancouver, Montreal BK member Santokh
Singh Khella was one of the speakers. He blamed the Canadian government for his legal troubles. He had been charged and convicted,
then acquitted on an accusation he had plotted to blow up an Air
India aircraft flying out of John F. Kennedy Airport in New York. He
claimed that his six-year fight to clear his name was all India's fault—
that India had pressured Canada to accuse him falsely.

Two weeks earlier, on May 2, 1992, Parmar's eldest son
Jaswinder Singh married Dipinderaj Kaur, Bagri's eldest daughter. It
sealed their relationship and they were now family. Why all three of
Parmar's children were married in one month remains a matter of
speculation and no one has been able to confirm the theory that
Parmar was actually in town and eager to get them all married while

he was there. But if he was around, his wife certainly did not boast of this and instead spoke of what people would say about her husband's absence. I firmly reject speculation that Parmar had been in town. I am convinced that had he been around his wife would not have spoken to me the way she had.

By 1992, police in the Punjab had begun gaining an upper hand in dealing with Sikh militancy, thanks to the appointment of tough police chief K.P.S. Gill. His no-nonsense methodology would not endear him to any human rights group in the world. Accusations are still flying around in India today that he was to blame for the Punjab becoming a police state during the fight against insurgency; that Gill had become a law unto himself. The police chief believed that if you cut off the head of the snake then the body would die by itself sooner or later. His writings reflect his opinion that there should be no corner for terrorism to hide and that the state must act decisively. He set out to track the leaders of the militant movements and many of them ended up dead in so-called police encounters. There were many gun battles during which terrorists roaming the Punjab died. But there were also instances of these fake encounters. Police would have a suspect in custody where the suspect would face torture. In a bid to hide the torture marks police would stage an "encounter." Then they would stage elaborate scenes depicting what would look like a death caused in a firefight. He was not out to send flowers to terrorists. He was out to kill the problem.

During the height of the Sikh insurgency that began in earnest after the Golden Temple attack, many hundreds of militants died in battles with police. But a substantial number died while they were in police custody. Some two thousand have been listed as having been cremated under police supervision over a twelve-year period. Relatives trying to retrieve their loved ones were handed ashes to take home. Human rights organizations and former police officers said they were ordered to supervise cremations to hide torture marks and mask murders of people in custody by rogue police officers. The Indian Supreme Court later ordered the national police force to investigate the activities of Punjab police and in early 2005 the National Human Rights Commission of

India recommended compensation to many families of victims of suspected police atrocities. It also released the names of hundreds of people who had been illegally cremated: names which were recently published in Indian newspapers.

In 1992, Gill's tough cops enjoyed unparalleled success in nabbing or killing top Sikh terrorists. In August 1992, Commander Sukhdev Singh Babbar, the founder of the BK in India, died during his "encounter" with police after he entered India on a mission. In the next few days, militants loyal to Babbar Khalsa went on a rampage, killing fifty-seven policemen and their family members in a wave of bloody revenge. Babbar's own family would later migrate to Canada and be given sanctuary in Surrey, B.C.

Barely two months after the death of Babbar, his friend and fellow fighter Parmar entered India from Pakistan, apparently in a bid to consolidate his leadership in the wake of Babbar's death. On October 14, 1992, Parmar's body lay in the dust on a roadside near his home village of Panchta in the Punjab, along with five others. That day, I reached senior superintendent of police Satish Sharma by telephone at his home in Jullundur and he provided vivid details of a "firefight" during which Parmar had been allegedly killed. He said two others with him were Pakistani agents. He also sent me police pictures of Parmar lying dead in the dirt.

"The whole episode lasted for about two hours and the battle spread over a wide area," said Sharma, adding he'd arrived at the incident about forty-five minutes after it began.

Sharma said police had stopped two cars early in the morning at a roadblock following a tip-off that Parmar was in the area. He claimed the militants opened fire on police and some of the occupants of the cars then fled. Parmar had fired off at least two magazines from an AK-47 during the gun battle before being eventually shot dead, riddled by eight police bullets. A search later revealed a rocket launcher in one of the cars. When I asked him if his relatives in Vancouver or the Punjab could have his body, Sharma replied Parmar had already been cremated. How they had identified and cremated Parmar so quickly would later raise serious questions. Relatives who had come to claim the body were given an urn containing Parmar's ashes. That was incredible, I thought. Why would police cremate Parmar's body on the same day when they knew where his relatives lived? What were the cops hiding that would show up if his relatives saw his body?

Ved Sharma said he visited Parmar's home when news reached Vancouver that he had been killed. "There was a lot of anger there," he said.

Parmar's daughter, Rajinder Kaur, appeared at a press conference in the company of MP Svend Robinson to demand answers from India. But Canada did not forcefully pursue Indian authorities to explain in detail how Parmar had died.

Later, a Punjab police officer who attended a wedding in Vancouver would reveal the details of Parmar's death. The officer said the militant had been in police custody for nine days and had been tortured, then killed and cremated, according to information obtained from top Sikh community sources.

Within a few months of Parmar's death, the RCMP and CSIS would receive information from reliable sources that Parmar had been picked up alive by Punjab police. He had been detained and tortured, yet made no admissions. He would blame the ISYF but not his own group the BK for the Air India bombing.

Parmar's death at Panchta village was a devastating blow to the Air India Task Force. In one fell swoop, one half of the RCMP's bombing conspiracy case had literally been reduced to ashes. With the conviction of Reyat, and his admissions that Parmar had asked him to make bombs, there had been hope of eventually building a case against Parmar. But now that hope was gone.

RCMP Inspector Jim Cunningham, the Air India file coordinator until 2004, would later lament to me that throughout the Air India investigation, Indian authorities did little to assist the police in Canada. The killing of Parmar was another example of this lack of consideration: India did not appear to have much interest in helping solve the terror tragedy, he said. This has been echoed by many other officers who had travelled, as Cunningham had, to India to find suspects and answers.

"They had Parmar. They could have called us to interview him. But they did not. We did not get much help from the Indian government on solving Air India," Cunningham told me in June 2005.

That they should have killed Parmar, while one of the alleged chief architects in the Air India plot–Hardial Singh Johal–was free to enter or leave India whenever he pleased, and be able to meet with Indian spies inside Canada too, would raise many eyebrows in Canada.

Johal was known to Indian intelligence as an RCMP suspect. It was the Indian police service that had pointed out to Canadian police earlier that Johal's business card and a diary that showed drawings of improvised explosive devices had been found in the Golden Temple during the June 6, 1984 attack by Indian troops. Now, Johal was not only able to meet with government agents like Gurinder Singh in Vancouver, but he did not seem to have any problem getting permission to visit India at a time when participating in a small demonstration against the New Delhi government would get you blacklisted and barred from securing visas. It was not until almost 1998 that India revoked Johal's visa to restrict his travel, and only after intense pressure from Canada's External Affairs Department that it was desirable that Johal remain in Canada because of pending police action.

I obtained several letters that Johal had written after the refusal by India to grant him a visa following the Canadian government's intervention. One letter showed that Johal had no difficulty getting Indian visas, unlike his fellow militants who had not been able to enter India even to attend funerals of close family members. In one letter, he states that he had invested substantial funds in the Punjab Bank branch in the city of Ludhiana. The letter, written to the Indian consulate in 1998 and obtained through a third party directly from Johal, reads in part:

"I, Hardial Singh Johal have been living in Canada since June 1972. I was born, raised, and have received my education in India. I was employed in India as a sectional officer (civil engineer) before coming to Canada in 1972. At present I am working as a building engineer (Vancouver school board) and I am a Canadian citizen.

"The first time I visited India in 1982 for the duration of four months.

"Second time I visited India in 1985 (January-February) after obtaining my visas for four weeks.

"Third time in 1995 again I visited India and attended the World Sikh *Samelan* (conference) in Amritsar after obtaining my visas.

"Fourth time in 1997 I applied and was granted multiple visas for three years and I visited India and stayed there two months. During this visit I invested a fair amount of funds through Bank of Punjab in Ludhiana."

It was curious that a terrorist planner who had participated in blowing up Air India Flight 182–a plane owned by the government of India–had the freedom to visit India without being touched by its police or intelligence agents. I was amazed when I contrasted that with the treatment given to Parmar who had been tortured and killed. What was India's motive in being so hospitable to Johal? It wasn't as though Johal was unknown to Indian police or intelligence agents. I have puzzled over these issues for a long time and have not yet found an answer–unless I venture into the theory that some Sikhs expressed locally that Johal himself was an Indian government agent. But CSIS had carried out a vast operation to identify Indian government spies posted in consulates and the diplomatic mission in Ottawa. CSIS had also told the Canadian government that it had turned up no evidence to suggest that Indian government agents were involved in blowing up the plane to discredit Sikhs. The only plausible explanation was that India too was looking to use Johal as a source possibly to find out more about the Air India bombing operation, just as RCMP and CSIS were willing to co-opt at least one of the suspects to flush out the rest of them. And they would have gladly recruited Johal as a source if they could have. Perhaps the Indians were better at co-opting people in the Sikh community than the RCMP or CSIS.

While Johal enjoyed the freedom of movement in India, another militant who had hidden in Canada was not so lucky.

In 1992, police in India were having unparalleled success in either killing or capturing the leaders of the violent Sikh uprising; militants who had been operating from bases in Pakistan with impunity. But not every key player in the Sikh militant movement was to die during a "police encounter." Just two months before Parmar was captured, tortured and killed, police in Bombay were going to great lengths to ensure another prized captive was kept alive.

Apparently fearing he would be tortured, Lal Singh–the FBI fugitive from the 1985 New Orleans plot to kill an Indian cabinet minister–had tried to swallow a cyanide capsule after being arrested near a Bombay railway station. During questioning, he bit off his tongue, hoping he would not be tortured if he could not talk, only to have it sewn back on. Police had to pad the metal walls of the elevator that took the man from his cell to the interview room because he would hurl himself against them. In Vancouver, RCMP still considered Lal Singh a suspect in checking in at least one of the two bag bombs that left the city on June 22, 1985.

The hunt for Lal Singh and his partner, Amand Singh, had been one of epic proportions and would have far-reaching repercussions. Tragically, the FBI and the U.S. Secret Services search for the two fugitives had focused Canada's spy service and the RCMP on thwarting a plot against Rajiv Gandhi during his trip to the U.S., scheduled for "Black June" –the first anniversary of the Golden Temple attack. It was the possibility of Sikhs gunning for Gandhi that had prompted CSIS to obtain a wiretap authorization on Parmar's phone, not an inkling of any threat to Air India.

On June 12, 1985, the RCMP–accompanied by members of the U.S. Secret Service (whose job under Title 18, United States Code, Section 3056, is the protect the U.S. president, vice-president, their families along with visiting heads of foreign governments and diplomatic missions) paid a visit to Parmar and his right-hand man, Surjan Singh Gill. The Secret Service and RCMP officers carried with them photographs of Lal Singh and other "wanted" Sikhs they believed resided in the United States. The visit was motivated by the possibility that Lal Singh and his Partner Amand Singh who had escaped an FBI dragnet may attempt to kill Rajiv Gandhi during his U.S. trip. Secret Service and RCMP agents had arrived to make sure, as mentioned earlier, to defuse any potential plot by Lal Singh and company and to warn Parmar and Surjan Singh Gill that authorities were keeping a close eye on militants in preparation for the visit by the Indian leader.

Gill had told me about this visit. He had said that the agents had carried with them pictures of people he could not identify. In his conversation with me, Gill appeared not the least bit worried about having been paid a visit by U.S. and Canadian agents. But upon later reading a transcript of Gill's conversations on the day of the visit (intercepted by CSIS) it became apparent to me that Gill was bothered by this face-to-face meeting with cops and agents.

Parmar, working on a completely different project, remained unruffled. But Gill made several moves after the visit to begin distancing himself from the BK. I never considered Gill committed to the fundamentalist cause—never as committed, for instance, as Parmar—and this visit from the cops must have cut too close to home. It was clear Gill didn't want trouble with cops.

During a conversation with Parmar, Gill wondered anxiously "where this trouble came from." Parmar angrily shut him up. Within nine days, however, Gill submitted his official resignation from the BK. Parmar showed no cracks in his demeanour, though he must have suddenly worried for the first time that he could be under surveillance. In an intercepted message, Parmar warned Gill to stop talking on the phone about sensitive issues such as money transactions. Parmar was now conducting his business with more care.

Lal Singh's arrest in 1992 had not come to light until word began reaching Sikh militants in Vancouver that their operative and Pakistan representative of the Canadian ISYF had finally been arrested in Bombay by Indian police on charges of terrorism. Lal Singh was of interest to both the FBI and the RCMP. With his Alabama mercenary school training in bomb making and assassinations, he'd always remained a viable suspect in the RCMP's search for the two mysterious men who had checked in the two bags at the airport and then not boarded their flights.

Lal Singh was also at the top of my "most wanted" interviews list, especially because of his use of the alias Manjit Singh while living in hiding in the Vancouver area for several years after he escaped the FBI. The Air India tickets had been booked in the names of L. Singh and M. Singh. On the morning of June 22, 1985, a man who called CP Air to ask if his ticket via Air India Flight 182 had been confirmed yet, identified himself as Manjit Singh. So the mystery had kept the RCMP and I seriously interested in locating the fugitive as we kept pounding away at our parallel investigations.

It had been almost a year before his arrest in India that it had become clear to me that Lal Singh had been hiding at a farm near the Vancouver suburb of Aldergrove and that he actually was in town even when those U.S. Secret Service agents and RCMP visited Parmar and Gill in June 1985. The mystery of Lal Singh sojourn in B.C. became clear when I cornered an ISYF spokesman, twenty-one-year-old Hardeep Samra, at the office of the militant newspaper *The Chardikala*. There, sitting on the opposite side of the table from Samra, I put the FBI pictures of Lal Singh in front of him and asked him if he knew this man. Some of the FBI "Wanted" pictures showed Lal Singh with a turban, in some he was without. Samra looked at them for several minutes. Then he said he could not recognize the picture of Lal Singh without his turban, but the same man wearing the turban was known to him as Manjit Singh.

"Do you have any doubt at all that this man identified as Lal Singh is the same man who you knew as Manjit Singh?" I asked.

"I have no doubt in my mind that is Manjit Singh," he said.

Samra also admitted that he had lived with Lal Singh, alias Manjit Singh, on a berry farm owned by his uncle in Aldergrove, some thirty miles east of Vancouver. Samra said he had lived in the trailer on the farm with Lal Singh, alias Manjit Singh, until he was sent to Pakistan by the ISYF in 1988.

Lal Singh's alias was explained by his use of a Canadian passport belonging to another Manjit Singh, a top militant from the ISYF in Surrey, B.C. Lal Singh had also used the passport when he left for Pakistan from B.C. to camouflage his identity during his travel out of Canada. Once in Pakistan, he had continued to use the name Manjit Singh in an attempt to mislead Indian agents working to capture him as he moved between India and Pakistan on terror missions.

Lal Singh's sojourn here intrigued me. It was the first time anyone had confirmed his presence in the Vancouver area. It made a great page three story for *The Province*.

Around the same time as I wrote this article, I visited Seattle, Washington, some 125 miles south of Vancouver. I wanted to talk to King County coroner's investigator Bill Haglund. The reason I was interest in having a chat with him was that shortly after I wrote the story about Lal Singh's stay in B.C., a militant informant told me that his other partner, Amand Singh, who had also escaped the FBI, had died in Seattle. The informant said that he and other Sikh militants had quietly paid a consolation visit to Amand Singh's sister who lived in Burnaby, the Vancouver suburb.

I wanted to make sure that was true, that Amand Singh was indeed dead

Haglund confirmed the story. He said the corpse that arrived at the morgue was identified by his driver's license as a thirty-seven-year-old named Dalbir Singh. Haglund said it wasn't until he compared the corpse's fingerprints with FBI records that it became apparent who the traffic accident victim really was. Dalbir Singh was none other than the infamous Amand Singh who had escaped FBI warrants for his arrest for the plot to kill the visiting Indian cabinet minister in New Orleans. Surprisingly, Amand's younger brother who was in the pickup truck when it crashed killing Amand, provided no help to the coroner to shed light on the real identity of the man who lay dead in the morgue. I also interviewed Amand's younger brother, who was driving the vehicle when it collided, sending a wheelbarrow crashing into the head of his brother who was in the passenger seat of the vehicle the two used in their landscaping business.

"He brought me up like a son He was my eldest brother," the landscaping businessman told me. "If he was a terrorist why didn't they pick him up?"

I pointed out that no one in law enforcement knew his whereabouts until his death. Haglund said Amand Singh's relatives were listed in his report as a brother living in New Zealand and a sister in Burnaby, the same Vancouver suburb that had been home to Parmar.

Following Amand's death on March 24, 1988, Lal Singh alias Manjit Singh began making preparations to leave Canada. I believe Amand's death prompted Lal Singh to leave British Columbia. The FBI was busy digging up the details of Amand Singh's life and Seattle was too close for comfort for Lal Singh. In Lahore, he would become the chief liaison officer between the ISYF militants in Canada and the terror chiefs in Pakistan.

Following the publication of stories relating to Lal Singh's arrest, I received an extraordinary request for a meeting from Ranjit "Ron" Dosanjh, the president of the Vancouver chapter of the ISYF. Dosanjh would later take centre stage in a gang war which would cost him his life and spawn the infamous jury trial of his suspected assassins involving juror Gillian Guess and her affair with an accused killer. For the moment, the gun battles that would rattle Vancouver were still two years away. Dosanjh asked to meet at a safe place where he would not be seen with me publicly. My home sounded like a good place, since many colleagues at work had complained about the types of dangerous people I had brought into the office for inter-views (Dosanjh was Sodhi Singh Sodhi's brother-in-law. Sodhi, was the man who had attacked the Indian consulate in 1984 with swords. Sodhi was also the man whose phone number was left behind when a Sikh paid for and picked up the two tickets for the Air India flights at the CP Air office in Vancouver having paid more than $3,000 in cash).

Dosanjh sat down on the carpet in my living room, leaning his massive frame against the leather sofa. He was shaking.

"I was asked to hide Lal Singh," he said.

I was flabbergasted. "When was this, Ron?"

"After Air India," he replied. "The people at the temple asked me to hide him because he had done something. He was living at the Ross Street Temple at the time."

"Done what, Ron?" I asked.

"Checked in the bags," he said. "I want to meet with the RCMP. Can you arrange it?"

"What if the International Sikh Youth Federation finds out?" I asked, as I watched my wife Mina make her way upstairs and won-dered if she was thinking how dangerously I lived.

"They will not find out as long as you don't tell them, that is why I need to talk to cops you trust," he said.

"I promise not to tell anyone as long as you are alive, Ron," I said jokingly, trying to calm his nerves.

The next day I telephoned Inspector Ron Dicks, who had taken over as head of the Air India Task Force following Hoadley's retire-ment in 1988. He was eager to meet with Ron Dosanjh, and he suggested we meet at a safe, discreet location where others could not hear what was said. If Ron was seen with cops, it was clear to us that he would be killed.

We met at around 8 p.m. at a location on Robson Street, which Dosanjh considered to be sufficiently private. Dicks, a tall, lean, soft-spoken man walked in with Jim Cunningham, who was in over-all charge of the Air India file. Cunningham took off his coat, revealing his gun in a shoulder holster. He did this slowly. I thought the message to Dosanjh was clear.

Then Ron Dosanjh made an extraordinary demand. He would not talk, he said, unless he was sure the investigators were not wearing wires. He demanded to frisk Inspector Dicks.

Cunningham, appearing aghast at the request, leaned forward. I thought to myself, "The cops are not going to like this—they are not going to like this at all."

Dicks too argued that he could not allow it.

"I can assure you, Ron, we are not wearing wires, I am a man of my word."

I could tell from his body language that Dicks was troubled. Dosanjh held on to his position. Unrelenting, he explained he was very worried about being taped. Extraordinarily, Dicks relented.

"I have never allowed anyone to search me, but I will allow you this one time."

I began to breath again and then watched in astonishment as Ron Dosanjh searched RCMP Inspector Ron Dicks, patting him down. Satisfied, he sat back on a chair and told his story. Ron Dosanjh did not ask to check Cunningham whose coat was off, his gun showing, since he was some distance away from Dicks who was quite close to Dosanjh and doing the talking. I had always respected Inspector Dicks as an honourable man. His action tonight was another indication to me about RCMP's commitment to find a solution to the Air India bombing.

Later that night, Dosanjh and I went to a Greek restaurant in Vancouver's West End that was still open at 2 a.m. As I drove home and Dosanjh went his way, I was wondering what reason he would have to confess this. Had he really been asked by a top Sikh traditionalist to hide Lal Singh in the wake of the bombing? Or was he diverting attention from someone he was close to; perhaps someone he knew had actually done it?

A few weeks later, Dicks and Cunningham travelled to India to interview Lal Singh in prison. Accompanying them was Jeanne Adams, the only person alive who could identify the man who had convinced her to check in a bag at Vancouver Airport on June 22, 1985. I wrote a story about the fact that RCMP officers were on their way to talk to Lal Singh. Adams could not identify Lal Singh as the man who checked in the bag with her. Too much time had passed since the incident and Lal Singh continued to insist he was innocent.

During a meeting in June 2005, Cunningham and I reminisced about this 1992 event–the meeting with Ron Dosanjh and the later visit by him to see Lal Singh in prison in India. Cunningham, now an RCMP Inspector, recalled that Lal seemed ready to admit to anything under the sun when he was interviewed by the RCMP in the Indian police cell, but Lal Singh had insisted he was not involved in the Air India bombings.

"He said. 'Look, I live in a dungeon here, my life will probably end here and I would be much better off admitting it and being imprisoned in Canada, but I didn't do it,' " said Cunningham, recalling his conversation with Lal Singh during the visit to India. To Cunningham, it seemed that Lal Singh was not the man who had checked in one of the two bags. The mystery of M. Singh and L. Singh continues to this day and no one has the foggiest idea who those two guys were.

Once again, Cunningham complained of the Indian government's obstructive and unhelpful behaviour throughout the Air India bombing investigation.

"While we were there talking to Lal Singh," he said, "the Indians told us not to ask him anything about what he did in India; we were allowed only to talk about what he did in Canada."

Both Cunningham and I are still puzzling over the information Dosanjh supplied about how he had been asked to hide Lal Singh by a top traditionalist at the Vancouver Ross Street Sikh Temple following the Air India bombing. We wondered what Ron Dosanjh had to gain by giving us this piece of information. Both

Cunningham and I knew that we may never get the answer to what Ron Donsanjh's intentions were in talking to us about Lal Singh.

Dosanjh is no longer around to answer questions about his intent.

On the morning of April 19, 1994, I was awakened by loud gunshots that seemed to be coming from the area of Kingsway and Fraser Street in Vancouver, just two blocks from my house. I phoned my office a few minutes later. The assignment editor said Dosanjh had been shot dead while driving his red pickup truck. Just one week before the killing, I had taken Dosanjh into the newsroom (once again some in the newsroom were glaring at me for bringing him into the office during a gang war) to talk about the shooting death of his younger brother on February 24, 1994.

"I don't think I will survive this," he said to me.

A war of words had erupted between Dosanjh and drug underworld muscle Bindy Johal. It escalated into a shooting war. It was bound to end this way. It had been like this since Parmar's death in 1992. Air India suspects and potential sources were dying on us. And the Air India investigation was moving on a treadmill.

NINE

ON A TRAIL OF SUSPICION:
1992 to 1995

Talwinder Singh Parmar was dead and Inderjit Singh Reyat was dead silent.

Parmar's death in 1992 at the hands of Indian police had effectively pulled the rug from under the RCMP's Air India bombing investigation, which had been built almost entirely on the premise that Reyat had followed Parmar's directions in making the explosives that had downed Air India Flight 182 and that had killed the two Narita baggage handlers. The Mounties were left chasing after shadowy men to keep a sputtering investigation alive. The RCMP had still not identified some of the key players in the conspiracy

The most important–and enigmatic–of the shadowy men came to be known by authorities as Mr. X. He was believed to be the man who had accompanied Parmar to Vancouver Island back in June 1985 when the "test" bomb presumably was detonated in the woods. Mr. X had been described at the time as a younger man who wore a turban, carried an Adidas bag and wore stylish striped pants. Based on an intercepted conversation between Parmar's daughter and Surjan Singh Gill's daughter where a discussion had occurred about picking up "that fellow from Toronto" at Vancouver Airport, police believed Mr. X hailed from Toronto. Hundreds of names were checked and rechecked, but to no avail. The identity of Mr. X would remain a baffling–and extremely frustrating–mystery. It was clear to the RCMP that if CSIS had taken a picture of Mr. X they'd have been in business. As it stood now, we had a vague description of a man and no clue about who he really was.

Also unidentified were the two Sikhs on Vancouver Island who had picked up the stereo tuner that had been used as the bomb casing in the Narita explosion. It had been thought at first that one of them might be Mr. X, but the Woolworths clerk who served them had stated neither wore a turban.

That made it three mystery men.

Finally, there were the suspects who checked in the bags at the airport.

If M. Singh–the same man who had made such a fuss over his luggage bound for Flight 182 that morning–had tried to check in the second bag to Tokyo that afternoon, agent Jeanne Adams surely would have recognized him. But she hadn't. Police concluded they were looking for two men. Jeanne Adams was able to provide a police artist a good description of M. Singh and a composite drawing was made.

Also, there was really no reason why she would remember the second man, L Singh, who checked in the bag that exploded in Tokyo. His ticket was confirmed and he checked in without making any fuss. To this day no one has even come up with a description of what he looked like.

At every opportunity, we looked for sources who could tell us who these two men were who checked in such deadly bags. Were their names really M. Singh and L. Singh? Were they using bogus initials? Were they aware they were checking in bag bombs? Or did they think they were checking in money going to India? Were they paid to do the job? All of these questions remained unanswered. When we talked to community members the answers we got were almost always speculative or incorrect. For example, Ron Dosanjh had told me and the RCMP that he believed that the man captured in India, terrorist Lal Singh, was actually one of the two men who had checked in the bags. But Lal Singh had denied being either M. Singh or L. Singh. And Adams was not able to identify Lal Singh as the man who checked in a bag when she went to India with the cops. The information supplied by editor Tara Singh Hayer about two more suspects in the bag check-ins had also failed to bear fruit. Both men named by Hayer had passed lie detector tests given by the RCMP (There are many scientists who question the validity of polygraph testing. A well-organized group called Antipolygraph.org calls it "voodoo science" and "junk science" on their Web site. Other experts say it is accurate only up to 90 per cent of the time. And in Vancouver some cops wondered if there was a problem with giving polygraphs to people who were not born into English-speaking families. For example, a Sikh who speaks English poorly would have to first interpret the question asked in English then respond. One cop said flatly, "Polygraphs don't work on Sikhs who don't speak fluent English!" Precisely because of its unreliability, Canadian courts reject polygraph tests as evidence. Yet RCMP were using it every opportunity and dismissing suspects who passed or using it to size up the credibility of witnesses who seemed to be pathological liars in some cases.)

As I phoned hundreds of Sikh sources, met them at my home, office or in their own homes, it became apparent that there were three kinds of people around Parmar: those who actively participated and carried out a task in the plot, those who knew about the plot and were kept informed about the progress but said nothing to stop it, and those who were close enough to find out afterwards and also said nothing. Although no one knows for certain how many people were involved in the plot, there were at least five important figures (mentioned above) in the conspiracy whose identities were unknown to police.

Missing also–and perhaps most troubling–was evidence of a credible link between Reyat and whoever had taken the bags to the airport and checked them in.

Police tried to talk to several men whose names had turned up on CSIS transcripts. Reyat maintained a stoic silence and began adjusting to prison life. Visiting fundamentalist Sikh priests gave him spiritual strength. Parmar's associates, like Bagri, Gill, and Johal were approached numerous times but the police failed to convince them to answer even a few questions. They told the Mounties to go talk to their lawyers. And there was absolutely no forensic evidence to point at anyone else. All the bomb parts traced back to only one man–Reyat. So now the investigation was entirely dependent on someone talking. Someone who could tell the cops from the inside how the conspiracy unfolded.

Following Parmar's death in 1992, investigators continued to work on Reyat, now serving his ten-year sentence at the high-security

Matsqui Institution, about forty-five miles east of Vancouver, and approached his brothers Raj and Awatar; his wife, Satnam; as well as their son—with no results. Awatar Reyat told me he was worried his brother wanted to take the fall for others when the other shoe fell, with regards to charges in connection with Air India Flight 182. He wanted me to meet with Reyat, to do an interview in prison, but Reyat would not consent. The devout Reyat had been a drummer with the Akhand Kirtani Jatha prayer group and would perform exhaustive musical rituals lasting three days. As the drummer, Reyat was the centre of these rites and was often accompanied by his wife, Satnam Kaur, who sang the hymns. Satnam Kaur called the tune in other ways: She was perceived by Reyat's family members as even more devout than Reyat himself. The family saw her as a spiritual pillar of support helping Reyat maintain his faith while in prison. A constant stream of fundamentalist friends visited him in prison, boosting his zeal to become a martyr for the cause by maintaining his silence. He appeared unfazed at the prospect of further charges being laid against him. He sat through his annual prison reviews like the Rock of Gibraltar, unshaken by the constant hammering of parole board officials who told him his chances for early release would be jeopardized by his refusal to accept his guilt.

The RCMP tried to coax Surjan Singh Gill into talking several times, but that failed. One RCMP note of a visit to Gill highlights what the cops were willing to offer Gill to talk to them.

Gill had not changed his denial of involvement since the first visit by the cops on October 18, 1985 when Const. Sandy Sandhu and another cops visited him at his home.

"He stated that no Sikhs are responsible for the Air India Disaster, that it is propaganda by the Indian government (that Sikhs were involved)," states the police report of that visit.

Gill bad-mouthed Parmar, telling the two cops that Parmar could not find five Sikhs to follow him and yet called himself the leader of the Sikh nation!

In another interview, he denied knowing Reyat. He denied there was a third man (Mr. X) when he gave Parmar a ride to the ferry terminal on June 4th, 1985. Frustrated, the cops decided to stop him on the sidewalk near his home and tell him a few facts they knew about him. They told him they knew there was a second person with Parmar on the day he gave them a ride to the ferry, they laid out their knowledge of Gill's involvement in the BK.

"Members presented Gill with some facts as (to) his connection with the Babbar Khalsa, the ferry connection on June 4, 1985, the exchange of envelope with Parmar on the twenty-first of June, the threat on his life (Gill had apparently been threatened after he resigned from the BK), involvement in the Air India conspiracy and protection, relocation and payment if he cooperated with the police," said the internal RCMP document entitled "Surjan Singh Gill–Contacts with police."

The offers of protection, large sums of money and relocation failed to move Gill.

Similar offers of cash were made to others, including Parmar's brother Kulwaran. In each case, they ran into a frustrating brick wall of silence and solidarity.

It got so frustrating the cops started venting their frustration on lawyers. Mountie Doug Henderson said his hopes that Reyat or Gill would talk to him were crushed by their lawyers.

"'No client of mine will talk to the police, it is bad for business:' those were his exact words to me," said Henderson, recalling a stern message from Surjan Singh Gill's lawyer, David Gibbons.

What the RCMP needed to do to get evidence against perpetrators was to penetrate the periphery of Parmar's tight-knit circle of associates where knowledge of what happened also existed. But the RCMP had no way of introducing white men as agents to carry out a covert operation, and there were precious few Sikh officers in the force who could be injected into the group.

The RCMP had had little experience dealing with crimes committed by religious extremists. The Air India bombing had happened after Parmar's blunt promise that the government of India would pay a price for the attack on the Golden Temple of the Sikhs. The attack on the heart of the Sikh faith had fired up fundamentalism and religious extremism. Now the Sikhs were answering back with acts of sabotage and murder. It was divine retribution carried out by men who believed that they were doing God a favour by hitting out at those who had committed a sacrilege by attacking a place of worship.

In Islam and in Sikhism—the two areas where I had done extensive work on extremist violence—it was apparent that crimes committed in the name of God were hard to solve with offers of money or other worldly inducements. Betrayal of a fellow Sikh soldier was not considered just a betrayal of another man, but a betrayal of God. And who wants the wrath of God? Parmar's group was called the Babbar Khalsa, which meant Tigers of True Faith and it was a religio-political organization. Parmar was only one of some two hundred baptized Sikhs in Vancouver. They were the elite of the believers, who had committed to following the strict code of conduct imposed on them by their baptism by *amrit* (holy water). But equally motivated it seemed to me were those who did not even wear a turban on their heads. I recalled what Jaspal Atwal had said to me about the duty to act on behalf of religion when I lectured him a few months prior to the time when he went and shot the visiting Punjabi cabinet minister on Vancouver Island.

These holy crimes form a different ball game for investigators used to dealing with more worldly things like greed, or passion induced by betrayal of love. This was *dharam yudh*, the Sikh version of *jihad*. Martyrdom was the ultimate achievement in what the Sikh Guru had called "this love play" of religion; in it, a man's head needed to be on the palm of his hand, he had said. It was about sacrifice, glorification of those willing to give their lives for their faith or to take lives for their faith. Parmar's wife had told me he was undaunted by the possibility of death, and he carried his shroud with him. Such is the tragedy of crime induced by religious fervour. Even today, Sikh militants pay homage to Parmar as a *shaheed* (martyr), and his family is revered in some circles as the family of a martyr. Many people donate money to the Parmar family because he had made the ultimate sacrifice for his religion. I have seen Parmar's picture hanging in temples from Surrey, B.C. to Freemont, California.

Islamic Mujahideen strap explosives around their bellies in Iraq and in Israel, and fly aircraft into buildings, not for worldly gain, but in the mistaken belief that it is their religious duty to fight the perceived enemy of their faith. Similarly, in Sikhism, tales of heroism of Sikhs invariably are about martyrdom—self sacrifice in the protection of faith, or self-sacrifice as a demonstration of faith. In police torture chambers in the Punjab, Sikhs who had been forced to stand in bare feet on heated frying pans by Indian police and those who had marks of hot irons on their chests exhibited the same strength and single-minded commitment. Some junior police officers who guarded the torture chambers were so aghast at what they saw they defected to Pakistan with pictures of these atrocities.

In my experience, religiously motivated terrorists tended not to walk away from their mission, nor were they inclined to "flip" a brother for cash. Despite this, the RCMP resorted to using money in an attempt to lure suspects to talk. That action was bound to fail, as it became evident when the police dangled a million bucks in front of Reyat. They literally walked around with brief cases loaded with a million dollars in the hopes of cracking the code of silence. No amount of money was going to buy men who had carried out a divine order of vengeance. These were people who faced certain hell if they opened their mouths for a paltry sum of earthly cash– the rewards of paradise were richer and permanent. No baptized Sikh was going to sell his soul, and some of the attempts I saw by the RCMP had a reverse effect, reinforcing in the minds of Air India conspirators that the Mounties had no concrete information if they were willing to trash so much money.

All that this tactic bought the RCMP was rumour. Most of it was worthless chatter and gossip, but it crystallized the roles in the Air India bombing of some well-known people in the community. There was speculation about Surjan Singh Gill and why he quit the BK one day before the bags were checked in; about Ajaib Singh Bagri and businessman Ripudaman Singh Malik, about Daljit Sandhu just because the community leader had gone and recruited a lawyer to defend Reyat and Hardial Singh Johal. But there were no facts. People in the Sikh community said, "We know who did this." But when you asked them what their evidence was, the response was silence–it seemed that this "we know who did it" sense permeated the intelligence community as well as the RCMP.

And often intelligence is just that–crystallized rumours. The gossip soon became the gospel. The rumours about Daljit Sandhu, the former president of the Ross Street Temple, were based on the published fact that a man wearing a net on his beard and a yellow turban had picked up the tickets, and as mentioned earlier, his attempt to secure David Gibbons as a lawyer for Reyat. But linking Sandhu to Air India was pure speculation because he wore a yellow turban and covered his beard in a net—and there was not a shred of evidence to back this up—zero collaborative evidence abounded in this case. Sikhs I talked to asked, "If Sandhu was not involved why would he run off to get Reyat a lawyer?" Later, Sandhu would defend himself vehemently in court, not as an accused but as a witness. There were many other associates of Parmar who wore nets on their beards, including some who went to get passport photos taken wearing the net to disguise their long flowing beards so they could travel incognito. Religious symbols such as turbans and beards were not beyond manipulation for the purpose of disguise.

That is the kind of a wall the RCMP found itself confronting.

"What is different between a motorcycle gang member who takes an oath and goes through an initiation and these guys? Why should it be any different?" Henderson asked me one day in sheer frustration at his inability to reach out to people like Reyat with promises of cash and security.

"Listen Doug," I answered, "these guys have no allegiance to the courts or earthly oaths, they will not tell the truth on the witness stand. You asked if they have no conscience; sure they do, but it is nullified by the allegiance to a higher authority and a belief that even those who died during the attack (on Air India) were pre-ordained to meet their fate this way."

Usually a powerful tool in the investigative arsenal, most of the CSIS telephone intercepts would produce nothing useable in court. Police also acquired telephone bills from B.C. Tel to see if they produced any kind of a trail. One police affidavit filed in court showed the lengths they were prepared to go to find a thread. They went after their usual suspects, of course: Parmar, Gill, Bagri, Reyat, and Johal. But they also pored over the phone bills of a woman believed to be Bagri's girlfriend and those of her workplace. Others targeted for electronic surveillance were Hamilton-based Sikhs Harbhajan Sangha and Tejinder Singh Kaloe; BK members Avtar Singh Narwal and Gurmit Singh Gill, both of Kamloops; Avtar Singh Toor, the former Indian army tank driver; travel agent Amarjit Singh Pawa;

and Daljit Singh Sandhu, who was listed as an associate of Parmar and Bagri (I think the word "associate" always produces a slightly sinister connotation when used in the context of a criminal investigation. It lends a tinge of criminality in most people's minds; in truth, some of these people were simply acquaintances, friends, family, or clan members of some of the suspects). In surveillance terms, this was the equivalent of fishing in a vast ocean with a drift net.

While the RCMP wiretaps proved useless in the final analysis (not a single RCMP wiretap transcript proved useful even though they bugged numerous Sikhs) because of the fact they were put in place after the crime and no one was now talking on the phone, a further study of CSIS intercepts might have yielded vital clues, showing the personal, political and economic ties, and dynamics within Parmar's inner circle. One conversation that intrigued investigators occurred fairly early in 1985. Parmar's wife and sister had run into difficulties going to Pakistan to meet with the hijackers of an Indian Airlines plane who were facing trial in Lahore. Parmar had earlier accused his ticket agent, Amarjit Pawa, of leaking the information that had led them to being stopped at an airport in Pakistan. Parmar turned to Malik, the man who was often his comfort when in trouble. In May, he phoned him about his wife and sister's troubles. Malik reassured him and agreed to Parmar's request to pay half the cost of their tickets.

But much more important were telephone intercepts from the crucial month of June 1985, when reconciled with physical surveillance. Together they raised some tantalizing possibilities. Some conversations contained vital clues, but only fifty-six of the tapes recorded by CSIS had survived erasure and none of the surviving tapes was from the crucial month of June, when Parmar's plan to bomb Air India had moved into the final phase. The fifty-six that survived were from a batch of eighty-one that had not even been translated until September 1985, and these taped conversations dated from April and May. It seemed unconscionable that tapes had been stored for five months without anyone even listening to them.

Most phone calls intercepted by CSIS weren't translated verbatim and, in most cases, conversations were paraphrased, posing the possibility that nuances had been missed altogether along with key evidence that may have seemed irrelevant to transcribers at first glance. Those were major gaps. Still, enough remained to paint an enticing picture of what may have happened. In some cases the partial picture would also prove misleading, since CSIS had not taped other associates and that created a massive blind spot on the activities of other involved. Who were they talking to and recruiting would remain unknown.

For instance, the CSIS intercepts shed some light on the long-sought identity of Mr. X. During an intercepted conversation between Parmar and ticket agent Pawa on June 6, Pawa asked Parmar where Sukhdev Singh was since the airline wanted his tickets. Parmar replied that Sukhdev Singh was not at home and had his tickets with him. The RCMP concluded Mr. X was known as Sukhdev Singh, and was possibly from Toronto. But tracking him down would prove impossible (Reyat had earlier identified the visitor to his home as Surjit Singh, who he thought was from eastern Canada).

The chain of tantalizing conversations began on June 12, 1985, the day the RCMP and the U.S. Secret Service warned Parmar and Gill about making any moves against Gandhi during his visit to Washington. The surveillance suggests Gill, Parmar, and Pawa had quite different reactions to the cautionary visit. Parmar now appeared to be more interested in meeting with his ticket man Pawa in person. CSIS agents tailed Parmar to an area near Kingsway and Joyce Street in Vancouver and observed Pawa joining him in the car. The two talked for about four minutes before Pawa drove off in his own car and Parmar left in his vehicle. This was stealth; driving up in a car, meeting a source, all in a matter of minutes. Surreptitious indeed.

Surjan Singh Gill's reaction was captured in the following conversation intercepted by CSIS:

"On the twelfth of June, 1985 at 1233 hours, a telephone conversation between Talwinder Singh Parmar and Surjan Singh Gill was intercepted. Mr. Gill questioned how this problem (the police) came to them. He advised that first two and then four members of the RCMP attended his residence and that they had many things, including photographs. Mr. Parmar advised Mr. Gill that the four had already visited him. The police also asked him about his trip to

Toronto. (Parmar had flown to Toronto with Ajaib Singh Bagri on June 9 for a brief visit) Mr. Gill asked what he wanted him to do with the money. Mr. Parmar told Mr. Gill to cash the cheque and to convert the cash into one hundred dollar bills. Mr. Gill asked why he wanted that and Mr. Parmar angrily said that he did not want to go into that over the phone."

On June 16, 1985, six days before the bags were checked in at the airport, a conversation between Parmar and Pawa appeared to be about the timing of bookings for the Air India planes. Parmar phoned his travel agent Pawa and asked when he was going to India. Pawa replied "in a day or two."

Parmar replied, "Plan to go to India as soon as possible." Pawa was not going anywhere. I saw him at the Air India office on the morning of June 23, 1985!

On the evening of June 18, csis surveillance observed a car belonging to Malik park in front of Parmar's home. A few minutes later, Johal also arrived. csis took pictures of both Malik and Johal as they went into the house. Johal was carrying a briefcase, Malik what looked like a camera (no one knows for certain what they discussed—alternative explanations that can't be refuted can ruin the best supposition made by eager cops. At that time, Hayer was being sued by Parmar, Johal, Malik as well as Surjan Singh Gill. The meeting may have been called to discuss the lawsuit). There was also a non-BK man, a Dr. Khalsa, invited but he did not attend. Parmar had already met with Pawa and Gill to settle monies owing for tickets that Pawa would book for Parmar and others who needed to travel. However, when Parmar's son, Jaswinder, phoned Gill's home in the evening, his daughter replied he could not come to the meeting since he was sick. RCMP thought this was the first signal that Gill was considering getting out of the BK, which he did three days later.

On June 19, csis intercepted a coded conversation between Johal and Parmar. Its meaning would become evident when police finally compared the time of this call in relation to the time the tickets were booked. And it was significant to cops that the this call would come one day after the meeting between him and Parmar at the BK leader's home.

"On the nineteenth of June, 1985 at 1715 hours, a telephone conversation from Talwinder Singh Parmar to Hardial Singh Johal was intercepted by CSIS monitors. Mr. Parmar asked Mr. Johal if he had 'written the story yet.' Mr. Johal replied that he had not. Mr. Parmar suggested that Mr. Johal should do that work first."

The key message here was "write the story."

According to telephone logs, within minutes—shortly after 6:15 p.m.—CP Air agent Martine Donahue received a call from a Mr. Singh to book two tickets for flights that would connect with Air India. The unknown person who booked the tickets left behind a telephone number. The number, it turned out, had belonged to Johal until a few months before (Johal had moved, but his phone number still had the same last four digits as his previous number and the number that was left behind with CP Air was Johal's former number not his present one).

Shortly after the call with CP Air ended, CSIS monitors picked up another conversation at Parmar's home. This time, it was Johal calling. He told Parmar he had "written the story" and asked if Parmar wanted to come over to see the "story." Parmar said he would come over and CSIS observed him leave his home and drive in the general direction of Johal's house. There was no mobile surveillance, so no one followed Parmar to see where he actually went. However, shortly after Parmar left for Johal's place, another call was made to CP Air and some changes were made to the tickets. The RCMP reasonably inferred from this that Parmar had wanted some changes made to the bookings.

The problem Parmar and Johal and their travel agent Pawa faced in my opinion was that the first booking by phone had resulted in a confirmed flight to Dorval Airport near Montreal. But Air India would be flying from Mirabel Airport—some distance away from Dorval. And that would mean the passenger would have to physically pick up his bag at Dorval and then transfer to Mirabel, which would upset the plan since the intention was to board a bag in Vancouver but not for anyone to travel with that bag.

So Parmar had instructed Johal to make the change: fly to Toronto and connect with Air India Flight 182 at Lester B. Pearson Airport. The very next day a man wearing a net over his beard and a large turban went to CP Air's downtown office, paid more than $3,000 in cash in a bundle of large bills. He also carried written instructions for some more changes. The first bookings made by phone were for passengers named Mohinderbell Singh and Jaswand Singh. The man had those names changed to M. Singh and L. Singh. He also asked for a change in the contact phone number first left behind during the telephoned bookings. The contact telephone number traceable to Johal was now changed to a number belonging to the home of Sodhi Singh Sodhi– the man who had attacked the consulate of India with swords. Incredibly, Sodhi's phone number was only one digit different from the previous number traceable to Johal. The last digit of Sodhi's phone number was just number lower than Johal's.

On June 21, CSIS surveillance personnel observed Surjan Singh Gill arrive at Parmar's residence. Gill gave Parmar a manila envelope and left after a few minutes. During an unrelated search months later at the home of BK member Gurmit Singh Gill in Kamloops, RCMP discovered a letter written by Surjan Singh Gill in which he had indicated he was no longer a member of the BK organization. The RCMP made the assumption the envelope given to Parmar by Surjan Singh Gill contained his letter of resignation. Once again, the RCMP were drawing an inference about the contents of the envelop handed by Gill to Parmar.

Also on the same day, Parmar had telephoned Surjan Singh Gill and asked him whether he had delivered "those papers" and when Gill confirmed he had delivered them, Parmar instructed Gill to deliver the "clothes" to the same place. Police said on their affidavit they believed the "papers" referred to the airline tickets and the "clothes" referred to suitcases that would later carry the bombs. It was once again and unsubstantiated inference that could not be backed up by any evidence.

On Saturday, June 22, 1985, on the day the bombs were being checked in, CSIS intercepted a call from Kulwaran Parmar, the rebel leader's brother, who asked "whether that work has been done yet."

Parmar replied, "Not yet."

Local Sikh and former New Westminster Sikh temple leader Raghbir Singh Grewal (see chapter 5) had been at Vancouver Airport on the morning of June 22, 1985. As he waited for his brother to get to the airport, he had run into Johal: it was a damning experience for Johal to be spotted at the scene of the crime. Later, Grewal, who lost his brother-in-law in the Air India bombing, would tell the story of the chance meeting with Johal.

But more information of what Johal was up to, apart from his presence at the airport and his phone number on the initial ticket bookings and his contacts with Reyat and Parmar, was coming in. I had asked Sodhi Singh Sodhi to ask Johal for me why he had been at the airport around the same time as the first fatal bag was being checked in. Sodhi phoned back to say Johal was not denying he was there, but he said he had gone there because he had some immigration questions to ask officers working at the airport. It was a bogus excuse but it had confirmed for me the story that Grewal had told the cops about Johal's presence at the airport.

So after being seen at the airport in the morning, Johal and Parmar had a conversation that afternoon on Saturday, June 22, 1985, shortly after both bags had been checked in. CSIS tapes were picking up the conversation.

Parmar asked Johal if he had "mailed the letters." Then the two of them agreed to meet in person to discuss the mailing of the letters! RCMP and I inferred that meant the bombs were code-named "letters." Why would two people meet to discuss the mailing of letters? Was it not a correct inference to draw that Parmar wanted to be briefed in person about the bags being checked in? I thought that was the correct conclusion to draw. RCMP became frustrated when they found out CSIS had not kept a copy of this conversation, but merely made a transcript and logged the time of the call.

And there was more bad news for the RCMP. Amazingly, on that critical Saturday June 22, 1985, for the first time in several days, CSIS had neither physical surveillance nor an observation post to monitor the comings and goings at Parmar's home. With the infamous anniversary of the Golden Temple attack having past two weeks earlier and Rajiv Gandhi safely home from New York, the agency felt the high-level alert was unnecessary. CSIS had other priorities to which it devoted its limited resources. And they decided that the danger had passed since nothing happened during the anniversary of the attack or during the visit by Gandhi.

In an internal memo dated February 9, 1989, Russell Weaver Upton, CSIS coordinator for counter terrorism in B.C., outlined the weaknesses CSIS had in dealing with Sikh extremism. He said the months of March and April 1985 were extremely busy, chaotic, and unsettled.

"In my opinion, we did not have a complete analysis of Sikh terrorist developments in Canada leading up to the Air India and Narita Airport explosions. This area of terrorism was a new one to us. We possessed limited understanding of this complex subject. Our resources were limited, both from the stand point of field sources and resources and headquarters' analytical expertise."

He added, "We had extremely limited technical coverage of the subject area and reliable, well-placed human source coverage was almost non-existent."

After the Air India bombing, CSIS's greatest "problem remained a lack of trustworthy and reliable human sources able to elaborate and/or corroborate the mixed and questionable conversations of technical targets, most of whom were extremely security conscious."

On Sunday June 23, 1985, as news of the Air India disaster echoed around the world, CSIS agents rushed back to take their position outside Parmar's home. CSIS agent Raymond Kobzey returned home from his vacation and called the home of his partner David Ayres. Ayer's wife told him an Air India plane had been downed. Kobzey rushed to work where his colleague was already busy answering calls from CSIS headquarters. Kobzey told RCMP during an interview that his first thoughts were that Parmar had done it. Kobzey later returned to work for the RCMP, having quit his job at CSIS.

As news began filtering out in Vancouver on Sunday that a plane had been downed and a bag had exploded in Tokyo, Parmar phoned his friend Surjit Singh Gill (not Surjan Singh Gill) about what time the priests were coming to his home. Was Parmar going to have prayers for the souls of those lost aboard Air India? Or was it a religious celebration of success? To thank God for making the unholy terror work?

On the same day, a Sunday, Parmar's wife called Malik to inquire when he would be coming over. Malik replied he would be there around 6 p.m. While the priests wearing colourful robes were seen arriving, it was not clear if Malik attended. But it seemed several people were attending the prayer session to be held at Parmar's home on June 23, as the wanton destruction of Air India became clear. CSIS agents had now rushed back to stand outside Parmar's home after a day's absence.

Despite those amazing telephone tracks, however, the RCMP's investigation appeared stuck for answers. Memos written by RCMP investigators in British Columbia to headquarters in Ottawa facing a squeeze from Air India victim families were vague about the status of their investigation. The reports spoke of no concrete evidence against key suspects, but instead talked about their "possible" involvement.

Frustrated in their attempts to get anything from the community, the investigators continued to beat their heads against the brick wall of the core suspects. What they should have done was to talk to others who were removed from the centre of religious gravity. On the outer circles, there was full knowledge of what had happened and religious sentiments were not as strong as they were within the core of the BK. Another error made by both CSIS and the RCMP was the mistaken belief that there was no sharing of tasks between the BK and other Sikh militant groups in Canada. It was believed that an operation carried out by Parmar would only involve BK members. But at that time, it was clear to me that sometimes recruits for operations came from several different militant groups regardless of which group was primarily responsible for an attack. I believe some of the participants in the plot were brought in from Toronto and were not members of the BK, but possibly belonged to non-aligned Sikh terrorist groups whose services were available to any Sikh militant organization caring to recruit them. And I still believe that the ISYF supplied some members from B.C. to assist the BK in executing the plot. RCMP Staff-Sergeant Bob Wall had told me many years earlier that one of their intercepts showed that Parmar had said, "The youth can be quite useful." Wall said the conversation was deemed to have been a reference to the ISYF.

A month before the tenth anniversary of the Air India bombing, the RCMP were trying to breathe new life into their dying investigation. On May 17, 1995, Sergeant Bob Stubbings (now retired from the force) and Corporal Cunningham (now an inspector in an intelligence section) visited Reyat in the warden's office of the high-security Matsqui institution. They made small talk with Reyat, first inquiring about how his mother was doing following her stroke and the right-side paralysis that she had suffered (it had been more than mercy that had prompted police to allow Reyat an escorted visit to his mom in hospital). Reyat said she was still in poor condition.

The two veteran Air India investigators then switched to the real purpose of the visit, telling Reyat that with the tenth anniversary of the disaster approaching, family members were still living in agony, and he could help them. In return, they would give him immunity from prosecution and other concessions.

But Reyat could not be bought. He continued to maintain that Mr. X was on holidays and had stayed less than a week at his home. He had given him the tuner and had no idea what happened to it. Stubbings then asked if Reyat had made the bomb. Reyat said he did not.

Reyat expressed his sense of betrayal over Officer Doug Henderson's conduct, having first come to his home in 1985 as a friend, then, later, arresting him. He was bitter that Henderson had dinner with him and his family before he turned on him, taking him into custody, and questioning him for hours. He said he told Henderson lies during the 1985 interview out of frustration. He described how he had known Parmar for six years prior to the bombing and had met him at prayer sessions where he played drums and his wife sang hymns. In short, not only was Reyat failing to confirm anything new, he was backtracking. He even floated Parmar's old farrago about there being no bomb at all aboard Air India 182. When asked by the two officers visiting him in jail what had happened to the plane, Reyat had suggested it had been an accident: "Maybe the door came off." The two officers reported in their notes that he "still denied Sikhs necessarily did this, no proof—show him proof."

Then Reyat asked them, "Who built the bomb? Who put the bomb in the suitcase?" Now Reyat was asking the questions. If the officers knew the answers, they would not have been here with him in the first place. Nevertheless, I believe Reyat had posed valid questions to which the RCMP would not have an answer for twenty years—perhaps, never.

Reyat said his wife, son, and three daughters had lived in a house belonging to the Khalsa School run by Malik but the two officers told him the home was owned by Johal, the man who had been identified as being at the airport when bags were checked in. Reyat appeared to be protecting Johal rather than Malik. He said Malik visited him on occasion but he had no contact with Surjan Singh Gill (who was now keeping his distance from everyone except Malik).

After they left, the officers noted that Reyat was "in complete denial," that the explosion in the woods in Duncan had been a rifle shot, that he did not know the identity of Mr. X, that Parmar never asked him to construct bombs, nor did he make them. He even denied he attempted to get dynamite. The notes reveal the Mounties' frustration:

"He had no knowledge that Ajaib Singh Bagri took bags to the airport. And he said Bagri was not even in Vancouver at the time of the bombing." (The whereabouts of Bagri at the time of the bombing would become a very important point later at trial. What Reyat was saying may have had merit).

Reyat had also made it clear he was comfortable in jail and growing in spirituality. It was another disappointment for the police as their probe continued to falter.

Reyat's brother Awatar was keen to see his brother out of jail and he blamed the other suspects for his predicament. He told me he confronted Bagri in full view of the congregation at a Surrey Sikh temple. He told me he wanted me to meet with his brother since he believed more charges would come and Reyat would take yet another fall while the others stayed free. But Reyat would not agree to talk with me or grant me an interview, despite Awatar's best efforts.

That was the state of affairs in 1995. The investigation was at an impasse. It had been on a treadmill since Reyat's conviction. Three years of banging heads on brick walls. But once again, events in Punjab would have a ripple effect in Canada. The Sikh insurgency had staggered to a bloody end the previous year with upwards of thirty-six thousand dead in the eleven years that it had lasted. Punjab police chief K.P.S. Gill had, in effect, cut the head from the snake and the body eventually had died. The collapse of the struggle for Khalistan nationhood mirrored the new geo-political situation on the continent. The Cold War was over and the flow of cheap U.S. arms and cash into the region had dried up. The Soviets had long fled Afghanistan and now Washington was concerned about the growing power of a group called the Taliban. In Vancouver, the end of the insurgency of violence eased the tensions that had divided the Sikh community. Police hoped people with knowledge of what had happened in the Air India bombings might be more willing to talk.

In June of 1995, the RCMP and the Solicitor General's office were under pressure from a coalition of victims' families to hold a public inquiry. Internal RCMP documents show that the RCMP still hoped to move forward with the Air India investigation and asked for the appointment of a prosecutor to assist them. The RCMP in B.C. told the Solicitor General's office that an inquiry would be inappropriate when there was still hope of bringing the perpetrators to trial. The talk with Reyat had convinced the RCMP something new had to be injected into the investigation to rejuvenate it. At that time, brass at Vancouver RCMP brought in a tough but compassionate cop to man-handle the investigation back on track. Doug Henderson, who had extracted the few concessions from Reyat during the interview conducted at the police cell in Duncan, was appointed chief of the task force. Henderson, by now a staff-sergeant in rank, decided one of the key faults of the investigation had been that it had been treated like an intelligence gathering operation rather than a plain, old-fashioned murder probe. Again, Henderson, I thought, had failed to factor in religious zeal that had motivated the crime, and solving it in my opinion would require injecting a source into the Sikh mili-tant group's periphery or into its central core.

Four weeks into his tenure, a heart-wrenching personal tragedy struck. Henderson's sixteen-year-old son, Tom, was killed by a hit-and-run driver. Henderson, his wife, and their surviving children were devastated.

Even before his son's tragic death, Henderson had expressed remorse that the victims of the Air India bombing had basically been left to fend for themselves. His own tragedy propelled him to action: he made arrangements for the first official meeting with the families of the victims in Ottawa. The meeting was with twenty-five family members in the presence of RCMP "white shirts" and Henderson felt it was a too political and too charged with formality and tension.

"I was appalled by the lack of contact when I took over," said Henderson. "I said we don't have any contact with the victims.

"As a country we didn't do anything, as RCMP we didn't do anything (for the victims), it was wrong, we could have done much more" he said as he bulldozed his way past objections at headquarters for more informal settings for the meetings with victims of the disaster. "I mean, I was a lowly staff-sergeant and there was concern something wrong could be said—it was highly political."

So he set up more meetings with families in Toronto, Ottawa, and Montreal. For the first time, victims were talking heart-to-heart with a man who seemed to care.

"At first they vented on me. 'Why did the prime minister of Canada send his condolences to India?' And I said, let's get past the politics and deal with this. I said, let's not dwell on the past, let's not just complain about the past, I am not a politician. I'm just a cop."

They talked about their tragedy and Henderson said it ripped apart his still-raw heart over the tragic death of his own son. I could see how much his son had meant to him. Tom's smiling face beamed back at Henderson from a picture in his office. His voice broke when he talked about Tom.

"It broke me; talking to the victims just broke me; it would kill me. When I finished and came back from Ottawa I was just drained. It killed me; it just killed me."

From that time on, however, Henderson and other investigators made it a point to reach out to the families.

Henderson had decided on a $1-million reward to rejuvenate the probe. Just a few weeks before he announced it, Henderson called and asked if I could go over to RCMP headquarters for an informal chat. I agreed and was ushered into a room where several other officers were gathered around. Henderson said he was contemplating a $1-million reward and wondered first if it would have an impact and, second, how best to approach the community with the new inducement.

I scratched my head for a second. I was not sure there was information in the community at large. Perhaps at the outer circles of the fundamentalist group one could find takers

"I think you should get Hardial Singh Johal to assist you in distributing pamphlets asking for Sikhs to help in the Air India investigation. It would be fantastic if Hardial was standing at the Sikh temple with a police officer advertising the reward," I joked.

Henderson, always on the lookout for tricks, appeared amused.

"It could piss off some of the others and they would wonder if Johal had turned," I added.

"Goddamn it, Jiwa, you should have been a Mountie," he said after the meeting.

"You wouldn't have paid me as much as *The Province* pays me," I said. "Besides, Sikhs talk to me more than they talk to cops."

On June 23, 1995, the tenth anniversary of the Air India bombing, the RCMP made headlines by announcing a million bucks cash for anyone who brought information forward that would result in an arrest. I got an exclusive composite drawing of M. Singh who had checked in the bag and a composite drawing of the turbaned man who had picked up the tickets to terror The two composite pictures were handed to me by Sergeant Peter Montague, a close contact of mine, after I convinced him the drawings could jog some memories along with the reward money. M. Singh's composite drawing was made from Jeanne Adam's description of the man who made a fuss to check in the bag and that of the man who paid cash and picked up the tickets came from CP Air agent Gerald Duncan. More than one hundred new tips poured in, but not many that they could take to the bank. And one would come in free of charge that would steer the investigation straight into the ditch.

TEN
THE BROWN VAN:
1995 to 2003

Following the tenth anniversary of the bombings and the announcement of the $1-million reward in mid 1995, a few promising tips came in that gave investigators their first glimmer of hope since the conviction of Reyat on May 19, 1991. But even as the RCMP and the Crown slowly built their case, there was abundant evidence that Canada's law enforcement agencies were still getting their signals crossed.

I witnessed one such communication breakdown at a party thrown by members of the Overseas Congress Party (an extension of India's Congress Party) in Vancouver. Ostensibly to honour Jawahar Lal, the new consul-general of India, the festivities took place at a restaurant on Kingsway in Vancouver. My wife Mina, and I sat at the head table opposite Lal and were introduced to the consul-general's wife, Rita. I was chatting with Mina and sipping a drink when I looked up to see Ripudaman Singh Malik taking his seat at the head table next to the consul-general. I almost choked. What was Malik doing here, right next to the Indian government's representative in Vancouver? He had arrived with Guru Raj Kaur Khalsa, a white woman who had converted and become a devoted Sikh, and she was seated next to him. I nudged Mina with my elbow.

Rita Lal then turned to me.

"What is the situation with Sikh militants in Vancouver nowadays?" she asked.

I looked carefully at Malik who was busy talking with Khalsa.

"Ask him," I told her, pointing to Malik.

Rita Lal frowned, confused. Obviously, she had no clue she was seated next to a man who had years ago donated money to Parmar while getting a $2-million loan from the India's state bank. Talwinder Singh Parmar's brother, Kulwaran, entered at that moment. He took his seat at a table reserved for other officials of the Indian consul, some distance away from the head table.

This was unreal. I looked around and spotted several guys who looked like plainclothes cops. But they were seated some distance away from the head table. None of the cops appeared to have noticed the arrival of the same two men a law enforcement task force had spent a more than a decade investigating.

Overseas Congress Party executive member Malkit Singh Parhar and OCP president Mohan Singh Baria had thrown this party to fete Lal and welcome him to his new post. But Parhar was also playing a sort of middleman in a bid to introduce both Kulwaran Parmar and Malik to the new consul-general. Parhar was related through marriage to the Parmar family. His brother-in-law, Swaran Singh Manhas, was actually married to two of Parmar's sisters at the same time (he had first married Parmar's older sister, Sarwan Kaur, but the marriage had failed to produce children, so his wife had suggested he marry her younger sister, Mahinder Kaur). Parhar often visited Parmar's home because of this family tie.

Baria had maintained good relations with successive Indian consuls. Following the Golden Temple attack, Consul-General Jagdish Sharma had revealed to him film footage produced by the Indian government supposedly demonstrating the heavy fortifications surrounding the Golden Temple as well as the imposing stockpile of armaments militants had allegedly collected prior to the assault by the Army. Baria had agreed to distribute about one hundred copies of the film within the Sikh community in Vancouver, a move which enraged Sikh militants. Baria continued to attend Indian diplomatic soirees and had seen Air India suspect Johal and Vice-Consul Gurinder Singh together at several of these parties.

Parhar admitted later that the private agenda at this public celebration was to introduce Malik and Kulwaran Parmar to Jawahar Lal and make it easier for both of them to get visas to India.

"Kulwaran wanted a visa and they would not give it to him, so we thought we would introduce him to consulate staff," he said.

After this astonishing gathering at the head table, I was so amused I called Staff-Sergeant John Schneider, who had taken over as Air India task force chief when Henderson had moved to a unit investigating unsolved homicides.

"So where was VIP security yesterday?" I asked, describing the guest list at the party for the consul general. (RCMP's have a special section which protects dignitaries and foreign officials stationed in Canada. The unit is known as VIP Protection.)

VIP security was stunned when they heard about this. They had been completely unaware of the presence of the brother of the man India had killed or Malik at the dinner. (The only reason I mention this incident is that when Malik was finally arrested, the security precautions in effect portrayed a picture of such grave danger while in fact these individuals had been living within our every day life as normal people going about their normal lives. It would seem odd later that the RCMP and Crown would portray Malik as such a dangerous terrorist, who had blown up a plane, and guard the Air India courtroom with such elaborate security that people had to go through metal detecting gates).

A few months after the party, Jawahar Lal used his good offices to allow Malik to travel to India not once, but twice. Whereas his friend Parmar was tortured and shot by Indian police the second he was caught in the country, Malik now roamed India untouched. Like Malik, Johal also had free access to India and that was a little bewildering to me. Malik was the man who had received a $2-million loan from the State Bank of India using a typewriter, an old station wagon, and a few other items as collateral, just three months before the Golden Temple attack in 1984. People of interest to the RCMP were free to roam India, yet, New Delhi daily put pressure on Canada to solve the Air India case.

While some Canadian officials were baffled by the ease with which Malik and Johal toured India, others attributed the lack of interest by Indian authorities to a decision by the government to put the insurgency behind them and to work on reconciliation. Many militants, including Dr. Chauhan and even General Bhullar, who had advised Canadian Sikhs to wage war against India, had returned to India and were living peacefully in the once-again prosperous

Punjab (which had recovered after the decade-long insurgency that collapsed in 1994).

It appeared the Indian path to reconciliation included at least one unannounced amnesty. Maloy Dhar, former joint director of the Indian Intelligence Bureau (and an officer at India's high commission in Ottawa before that), explained to me in an e-mail recently that the government had high hopes the rapprochement would succeed mostly because the insurgency was "homegrown." The logic appeared to be that despite the violence a large majority of Sikhs had remained loyal to India and it was best to allow some militants to come back home and re-integrate into Punjab society. To achieve lasting peace in the Punjab, even senior militants were allowed to return and resettle, unmolested. In addition, the government has taken several measures to answer grievances of the excessive use of force by police and to address the ill-feelings among Sikhs of the Delhi massacres of innocents following Indira Gandhi's assassination in 1984. To date, it appeared to have worked and had helped restore a sense of fair play among disaffected Sikhs. By first brandishing the stick of brutal law enforcement and then dangling the carrot of reconciliation, India brought the Sikh insurgency under control.

With the end of the struggle for Khalistan nationhood, Sikh politics in Vancouver shifted from the crusade for independence to matters of religious orthodoxy. In 1998, there had been an upsurge of violence in many temples across Canada and the U.S. over what might strike an outsider as an unremarkable element of temple doctrine: a demand by fundamentalists that the faithful sit on the floor to eat their temple-cooked meals. An edict was issued in May 1998 by the high priest of the Akal Takht, *Jathedar* Ranjit Singh, that furniture be removed from the temples by May 29, 1998. This was known as a *hukamnama* (a binding religious edict). Sikhs who disobeyed faced excommunication. High Priest Ranjit Singh was a staunch fundamentalist and had spent ten years in prison for killing a man considered a heretic before his appointment as head of the Akal Takht.

The moderates, who were in majority control again at most temples, revolted. They were initially supported at Ross Street Temple by past president Daljit Singh Sandhu.

But traditionalist Surjit Singh Gill (elected on a slate comprising mostly moderate Sikhs) was president of the Ross Street Temple in 1998 (societies run the temples and those holding elected office are known as temple presidents) as the row over tables and chairs broke out. He took a stance in favour of obeying the edict on furniture, and headed for a confrontation over the matter with the rest of the executive of the temple. Soon, some sixty priests across British Columbia went on strike in support of the high priest's edict. A scuffle broke out at Ross Street. Traditionalists at the Abbotsford Temple were even bolder; they brought in a truck in the middle of the night and carted the furniture away. Tensions had boiled over in a similar way at the Surrey Sikh Temple in January 1997 and several people lay bloodied after *kirpans* were used during a riot.

Police officers fearing a repeat of the bloody fracas at the Surrey temple turned out to in force to guard the temples in major centres across B.C. For months, they stood guard to ensure there was no further violence. But they couldn't be everywhere and the doctrinal war between moderates and fundamentalists would claim at least one prominent victim.

For *Indo-Canadian Times* publisher Tara Singh Hayer the dream of a separate Sikh state which he had backed from the beginning was over. Now the prevailing winds had shifted in favour of moderates who had seized control of the temples. Hayer was quick to side with the moderate faction as it tried to fight off the edict about sitting on the floor to eat temple meals. Moderates co-opted him quickly. Hayer began to run abusive tirades against the high priest's order for Sikh faithful to sit on the floor to eat their meals. His tirades against the high priest once again focused the attention of his former fundamentalist friends on him. Hayer, in their opinion, had become a traitor to their cause. Once again it seemed to me the biggest curse for the editor was that he talked in inappropriate language about the high priest, who had a following of millions. Following a fracas at the Abbotsford Temple where there had been a fight, Hayer wrote an article for a Punjabi newspaper published in India. In it, he said, "Abbotsford Temple *Jathedar* Ranjit Singh's followers beaten like jackals." It was a bad choice of words to say that the high priest's followers had been beaten like jackals. Once again, Hayer was appearing to be gleeful about violence.

High Priest Ranjit Singh ordered the excommunication of Hayer and several other Sikhs in B.C. And the anger in Canada's traditionalist community against Hayer had begun to mount. One militant in Edmonton told me he had sent Hayer a fax telling him he would soon be in diapers again (a reference to his paralysis) and may need more than one wheelchair to get around. I received word that across Canada, remnants of the ISYF were collecting some $50,000 to kill Hayer. I warned the cops that Hayer was being targeted. But no additional security precautions were taken, apart from videocamera surveillance at his Surrey home.

I talked with Hayer almost every day during this turmoil. He said to me the traditionalists wanted to "create violence and bloodshed in the Sikh community in Canada" and believed militants had engineered the issue to regain control of the temples.

To me, it appeared the silent engine behind this upsurge of fundamentalism was Johal. For an ally, he had Daljit Singh Sandhu, who had switched sides knowing the high stakes of disobeying a religious edict. At the behest of his friends, Sandhu took to the airwaves on a Punjabi radio station urging devoted Sikhs support the *hukamnama*. He said he'd made a mistake by not supporting it before, when he had stood on top of a table and in the temple to reject the edict to remove the furniture.

On November 18, 1998, at the end of a long work day, Hayer said goodbye to his colleagues–having declined an invitation to go out for a beer–and headed home. He opened his garage door and struggled to get his partially paralysed body out of the car, two waiting gunmen opened fire. Upstairs, his wife heard the shots.

She found him lying in a pool of blood, dead.

Tara Singh Hayer's funeral was held on November 28, 1998 at the Valley View Funeral Home in Surrey. As I stood at the casket for a moment to say goodbye to a man I had known for eighteen years, I thought about how Hayer had supported, nurtured and glorified violence for so long. He had written a book on Sikh rebel Jarnail Singh Bhindranwale, calling him the greatest Sikh of the twentieth century, he had endorsed the sword attack on the Indian consulate in Vancouver, he had called the killers of Mrs. Gandhi martyrs; and now he lay dead, a victim of violence too.

Yet, I felt pained as I looked at his face in death. We had talked so often in the eighteen-years that I had known him and he was a source of information for me—sometimes that information worked and sometimes it was dubious. I felt sorry that two merciless gunmen had killed him. It was a primitive response to settle scores through violence.

But nations and individuals have often paid the price for supporting violence, particularly for fanning religious extremism. K.P.S. Gill, the hard-nosed, no-nonsense, Punjab cop, had repeatedly advised nations confronting terrorism to take a more aggressive and proactive role nipping militant movements at the root.

"For decades," he wrote recently on the Web site of his think-tank called the Institute for Conflict Management, "the rich nations of the world have purchased a kind of immunity from terrorist actions, even as they tolerated and sometimes encouraged, terrorist movements in other and distant parts of the world—and Canada has certainly been prominent among these. Recent history has, however, repeatedly demonstrated that the chickens, eventually, come home to roost and that societies that have encouraged such movements 'far away'—or offered their soil as a safe haven to actors in such apparently remote movements—have eventually become targets of terror themselves. "

History is, unfortunately, replete with examples of the bite-back factor for nations who ignore the growth of militancy. Pakistan and the U.S. poured vast amounts of money to help the Taliban and Islamic Jihadists to defeat the Soviets in Afghanistan. U.S. congressmen and President Jimmy Carter's national security advisor, Zbigniew Brzezinski, went to Pakistan in January 1980 and then on to the area of the Khyber Pass. To bring down the Soviet Bear, Brzezinski felt it was necessary to turn this war between Islamic fighters and the Soviet occupiers in to "God's cause" to galvanize the Afghans and to draw other Muslims and Arabs into this *jihad* against Russia.

Brzezinski, in that now-famous quote made in front of Afghan rebels said, "We know of their deep belief in God and we are confident that their struggle will succeed. That land, over there, is yours. You will go back to it one day, because your fight will prevail and you'll have your homes and your mosques back again, because your cause is just and God is on your side."

As the Soviet empire crumbled, the U.S. no longer needed Islamic militants to fight their doctrinal war of containing communists. And Afghanistan was left in tatters, allowing the same violent Jihadists to begin building a state of terror which ultimately attacked the U.S. on Sept. 11, 2001. Pakistan, which nurtured the Taliban, also faced the same backlash as President Pervez Musharraf began backing away from the militants who had at least two terror training camps within Pakistan itself as late as 2001 (the fact that Islamic terror camps existed in Pakistan I gleaned from the confession of Algerian terrorist Ahmed Ressam to the FBI. Ressam had tried to enter the U.S. in December 1999 from Vancouver with bomb-making materials). The Jihadists Musharaff's government provided succour to prior to Sept. 11 tried to kill him, not once but twice. On the Pakistan-Afghan border, these mujahideen of old are still holding out, killing Pakistani troops and launching forays into Afghanistan to torment Canadian, U.S., and other NATO troops stationed there.

During a summer 2005 investigation on behalf of ABC Television News I-Team, I was asked to make a determination of how top Jihadists travelled and raised funds with the full knowledge of the government of the United States during the 1980 and early 1990s. I found that the very man who had formulated al-Qaeda's ideology of killing Americans and Jews, a man known as Dr. Abdallah Azzam had given pro-Afghan mujahideen speeches in the mosques at Davis, California, in Sacramento, California, and in many other places in the U.S. while raising funds for the fight against the Soviets. And five years after the war with the Soviets was over, top Jihadists–including Dr. Ayman al-Zawahri–currently Osama bin Laden's number two man visited the U.S. twice. I interviewed a top Muslim leader who runs an Islamic Institution in Sacramento. He told me he welcomed al-Zawahri and others because the Reagan administration encouraged Americans to support the mujahideen. What he said to me was: "These guys were our friends." I even got a letter written by him to U.S. authorities outlining why top bin

Laden aide's were welcomed by Muslims living in the U.S. because Muslims in the U.S. were under the impression their government supported the *jihad* in Afghanistan against the Soviets.

K.P.S. Gill's theory that the chickens of terrorism sooner or later come home to roost is absolutely correct in my opinion. In my mind, Sept. 11 was evidence of that.

Hayer's death in 1998 came three years after he signed a sworn affidavit declaring to the Air India task force that he had overhead Bagri in November 1985 in London admitting to having taken bags containing bombs to Vancouver Airport. He had signed the affidavit knowing that the man he claimed had also heard that conversation, fellow London Punjabi newspaper editor Tarsem Singh Purewal had been shot dead in 1995. Purewal published the *Des Pardesh* newspaper in London. He was killed as he left his office in London.

Hayer had told me in 1988 that Purewal overheard Bagri claim that he had taken the Air India bags to Vancouver Airport. But Hayer never mentioned that he, himself had been present with Purewal and had overheard the same conversation. He had added that Bagri told the London editor that the plan was not to blow up people in the air but things went wrong when the aircraft was delayed in leaving Canada–a fact that I had asserted in my book, *The Death of Air India Flight 182*.

Purewal denied the story that he had overheard Bagri admit to his role, as did several others who Hayer claimed had heard the same thing. Hayer insisted that one of those present during this conversation was Rajwant Virk.

RCMP Air India task force member Corporal Bart Blachford and a London police officer visited the *Des Pardesh* offices on November 12, 1996, to interview him. According to Blanchford, "Virk was questioned about the allegation that members of the BK had admitted responsibility in the disaster. Virk denied any knowledge of this information. It was put to Virk that he was present when Bagri admitted his involvement in the Air India disaster while talking to Purewal in the office of the *Des Pardesh*. Virk again stated this was not true and questioned when this occurred. When told it happened in November of 1985 Virk advised that he did not arrive in England until January 13, 1986."

Virk had directly undercut the veracity of Hayer's claim. He was not even a resident of the U.K. when the conversation allegedly took place.

A Vancouver newspaper nevertheless repeatedly tried to link the murder of Purewal in London to that of Hayer in Vancouver, suggesting both had been shot because they were aware of Bagri's role in the air disaster. However, the RCMP promptly denied there was any connection between the two slayings. It is believed Purewal was killed as a result of a private dispute while Hayer died because of his row with the traditionalists over the furniture in temples struggle and for bad-mouthing the high priest, which had resulted in many threats against the editor. Scotland Yard, in an interview with the BBC, also insisted that any suggestion that Purewal's murder in England was motivated by his knowledge of the Air India bombing, was purely "speculation" fuelled by the media.

By 1999, my sources in the RCMP were hinting at charges being laid in the Air India bombings. As a sign of what was to come, both Malik and Johal again found it difficult to get visas to visit India because of pressure from Canadian External Affairs. And for the first time, I saw Malik take part in a Sikh demonstration in front of the Indian consulate on March 26, 2000.

The demonstration had been called to protest the massacre of thirty-five Sikhs in Kashmir on March 20, 2000 by some forty gunmen purported to be Kashmiri Islamic insurgents. Many Sikhs at the demonstration claimed the government of India orchestrated these deaths because former President Bill Clinton was visiting India at the time and India wanted to highlight the danger of Islamic militants. Malik observed a minute of silence and then caught my eye. He gestured with his head as though summoning me to come over. When I approached him, he suggested we go for coffee. We walked towards the Waterfront Centre Hotel and down an escalator that led to the foodcourt. Malik asked if Starbucks coffee was okay and I said that sounded good enough to me. I insisted on paying but Malik was faster on the draw. We sat down at a table, I took a sip, then looked up and posed a question which I thought would unsettle him a bit.

"What will you do if they pick you up," I asked Malik.

"Pick me up for what?" Malik replied, looking at me a little quizzically.

"For giving the money to Parmar," I replied, watching him intently.

Malik said nothing. Then he nodded and reached into his pocket. He fished out a little black diary. He laid it on the table and turned the pages, each page had a notation of a name and alongside the names were figures ranging from several hundred to a thousand dollars. "The Rupee Man" was the right moniker for him. These were donations from him in just the last few days, he said. I already knew from sources that he had donated thousands to the Indian consul-general's fund for earthquake relief. That donation may not have been entirely for altruistic reasons—but more to secure a visa to travel to India.

"People chase me for money, Salim. Everywhere I go they ask for money. 'Malik, please donate to this.' 'Donate to that.' I don't ask them what they do with it. I give because I think it will be used for a good cause," he said. "People think Malik is a mint."

Indeed he was, with a net worth of over $11 million. Malik did not deny giving money to Parmar in 1985. He told me he gave money to support only Parmar's religious cause. He had never denied that, not even during my visit to his office before the Commonwealth Heads of Government meeting. If there was a cause to give to, he gave. That was apparent. And I knew there was absolutely no evidence anywhere in the possession of RCMP or CSIS that he had paid for the tickets for Air India. There was no proof of that allegation, only conjecture brought on by his wealth. He had become the target of speculation over his donations to the Babbar Khalsa Society, which was a registered charitable institution in B.C., but that did not mean he had financed the Air India disaster. In fact, just two days before the disaster Malik had been asking Parmar for a loan of $100,000 for which Malik said he would pay Parmar a better rate then the bank gave him. It seemed some of the transactions between the two were purely for business, since Parmar had already joined the millionaire club by June 1985, having gone from working in a mill to a real estate developer. It was astonishing that Parmar was now playing banker to Malik!

The public perception was different. Malik was rich and terrorism costs a lot of money. He associates with Parmar, so he must have financed it. Preconceived notions drove this case for the RCMP as well.

"Fair enough," I said, as Malik put the black book of charity back in his pocket.

Once again, Malik simply nodded his head.

Malik was driven by religious work and by his desire to set up Sikh community institutions. His Satnam Trust at first sold trinkets and Sikh religious items at the Ross Street *Gurudwara* and then later he set up the Satnam Education Society where he poured tens of thousands of dollars to set up a school for Sikhs. The first Khalsa School opened in Vancouver in 1986. Values of the Sikh faith, its history and practice would be taught along with the normal academic curriculum. In the same year, Malik, along with a group of his allies set up the first branch of the Khalsa Credit Union. Both ventures grew and today the Khalsa school branch in Surrey has an enrolment of over 1,300 students and is highly regarded by educational authorities as a first-rate school. The Khalsa Credit Union now has five branches and assets in the millions of dollars. Sikhs acknowledge that these ventures were Malik's initiatives. Malik became an icon in the Sikh traditionalist community but as his influence grew from the relatively unknown businessman in 1985 to a patriarch of schools and the credit union the list of his enemies also grew. He had dished out money and favours and jobs. Some of his friends turned against him for various reasons. Some were business spats others personal and some both. Most involved money.

One such bitter enemy of Malik surfaced in January 1998. She blew into media circles like a tornado bent on damaging Malik's credibility and community standing he had worked for years to build. Later, she would become known by her courtroom name Ms. D.

I first heard about her towards the end of 1997. She had been fired from Malik's Khalsa School in Surrey where she had headed the preschool since her hiring in 1992. I heard of her because she was making the rounds of local journalists, including some who had worked part-time on the Air India story. One of the first people she approached was my source and Punjabi-newspaper writer

Sukhminder Singh Cheema, who had written several Punjabi-language articles about the bombings. Cheema and I had first met around 1992.

In mid–January, a woman left me two voice messages asking why I was not writing stories about Malik, his Khalsa School and the Khalsa Credit Union. She suggested I should dig into it, but left no name or phone number. I asked Cheema who this woman calling me was and he gave me her name and phone number. I called her at her home and told her there was no need to leave anonymous messages: I was available if she wanted to speak with me. Ms. D admitted she had left the messages.

A few days later, in early February 1998, she came to my office building. We picked up a sandwich from a restaurant downstairs and since she feared being seen in public and wanted to talk to me in private, we drove to Stanley Park in my car. She was articulate, bright, and gracious. But it seemed to me that throughout our meeting, which lasted an hour, she was confused about her relationship with Malik. She would talk about alleged criminal activity on his part and in the same breath talk about protecting him because she still liked him. She painted herself as a close confidante of Malik and someone who had his ear and often travelled with him on camping trips for children that Malik's school organized.

We sat at in my car at Brockton Point in Stanley Park. It was obvious she had come with a laundry list of questions relating to the Air India bombing. I was not under any impression that she was to be a witness later in the Air India trial. But I had been aware that she was the most likely source of a series of stories that had turned up in a daily newspaper in Vancouver relating to problems at the Khalsa School and the Khalsa Credit Union, which Malik had founded. I had felt the woman was instrumental in supplying information for these stories. So at this point, my impression of the woman was that she had a major axe to grind against Malik.

She started asking questions as she bit into her sandwich. Who booked the tickets? Who picked them up? Who took the bags to the airport? I saw no danger in telling her some of the many scenarios and names that existed publicly over the years, since what I had seen of the stories she had inspired did not pertain to the Air India bombing. I talked to her about the fact that the man who picked up the tickets had a ring on his finger. She wanted to know who I knew at the RCMP.

Then she dropped a bombshell.

"Salim, I have information that would make someone millions of dollars."

Here it comes, I thought.

I asked her if the information had come from Malik, since she was gung-ho about bringing him down. "Yes," she replied.

"And when was that?"

"One night when we were going to Vancouver Island," she said. Had she told this to the cops?

"No, I don't want to get the poor fellow into that much trouble, I have to protect him, I still like him," she said.

Shortly after this, we drove back toward the office. On the way, I stopped the car to get coffee. And when we came back, I gave her the keys so she could sit in the car while I went back to the stall.

"You guys always give me your car keys, Malik always does the same thing," she said.

She told me she had met Staff-Sergeant John Schneider in a restaurant and when he came in she told a friend, "Watch, John always forgets his keys in the car, and sure enough John came in and he was red in the face, and he had forgotten his keys inside the car."

I dropped her off and watched her head into the SkyTrain station. Later I phoned Schneider to rib him about her comment that he always forgot his keys in the car.

I also told him she mentioned she knows about Air India. Schneider was nonplussed. "Oh, she told you that, eh?"

From then on, Ms. D and I talked almost every day. Much of the time she came up with information about the goings-on at Malik's school and many times about his activities and whereabouts. It seemed to me someone was feeding her information about the whereabouts of Malik. That became apparent as well in the logs kept by Staff-Sergeant Schneider and Corporal Doug Best who had been assigned to her. She appeared to report to them on a daily basis about what Malik was doing, where he was holding meetings, and what kinds of vehicles were parked outside his home. Later, I would determine who was doing this spying for her by looking at those RCMP logs.

Our conversations continued on a daily basis, sometimes we would talk two to three times a day, both on the phone from my office and at home since I had given her my home phone number as well.

In mid–April, she phoned me at the office with something different.

"Guess where I am?" she said.

"You tell me," I replied.

"I am at Hardial Singh Johal's campaign," she said.

At the time Johal was running against Malik for the chairmanship of the Khalsa Credit Union.

"Why are you at Hardial's campaign?" I asked, thinking it strange indeed that she was with the biggest surviving fish in the Air India investigation following Parmar's death.

"I am trying to help him win the election. It will be good if he defeats Malik," she said. I thought that was very odd that she would be helping a man I considered a terrorist win an election against Malik.

Once she phoned up and said she was frightened because her home had been pelted with eggs. Later in April, she called again to say she had decided to become a witness. She asked me how that would affect her. I told her that the cops were desperate and if she had said anything to them about Air India she could bet that she would be a witness whether she liked it or not. I told her that life in witness protection would not be easy. But I also told her that if I had incriminating evidence I would give it to the cops.

Police statements that I saw later also indicated that it was on April 27, 1998, that she decided to provide a detailed statement about an alleged confession Malik had made to her detailing the Air India plot. Months had passed since she had first started talking to the RCMP, CSIS, and journalists about Malik's activities completely unrelated to Air India. By this time she had also filed a lawsuit against Malik and his school for firing her and calling her a "slut." There had been enough time for her to gather information in the public domain about Air India, the names of the suspects, and the roles that the key players had supposedly played—most of it speculation not backed by evidence. I felt badly that I had also said things to her about people possibly involved with Air India.

Later still, she phoned to say she had been moved by the police to a different location. This was when she was put into witness protection. It was odd for someone in the program to have called a reporter.

In the fall of 2000, there was growing buzz within the policing community about arrests finally being made in the case. During the week of October 20 I had gone to lunch with two police officers who were part of the Air India task force. The two officers were all smiles. And in not so many words told me things were going to happen.

I was primed to break the story—after all, I had worked on it nonstop for fifteen years. Then, on the morning of Friday, October 27, 2000, two top RCMP officers called me to their office and tipped me they were going to make arrests at around 2 p.m. that day. (The police like picking people up on Fridays, since it gives them some breathing time before they present the accused in court on Mondays.) They were going to pick up Malik and Bagri, they said. Some people they wanted to interview were not in town, particularly Surjan Singh Gill, who was now living in the U.K.

I was a bit pissed off at this. I had written this story the previous evening, but RCMP Superintendent Gary Bass had called and asked me not to run with it. I had agreed to hold off on putting the story in Friday morning's paper with the consent of my editor-in-chief. I didn't want to ruin the investigation with a premature article. But the call from the cops on Friday morning and the tip they were after all going to lay charges was bad timing for the paper. Friday is the black hole at *The Province*. There is no Saturday edition and anything that happens on Friday is old news by the time the Sunday paper hits the streets. But I wasn't going to let a little thing like no paper stop me from breaking the story—not in the age of the Internet. We broke an exclusive story on *The Province* Web site. My supervisor, Fabian Dawson, called several news outlets to tell them to check out the breaking news on our site. News that arrests were being made began flashing around the world, quoting *The Province*.

By early afternoon, Malik and Bagri had been taken into custody. Johal was later arrested but not charged. The man at the centre of this crime, Johal, was still a free man, even though his telephone number was on the ticket bookings and he was positively identified as being at the airport.

On Monday, October 30, 2000, I sat in the court room and watched as Bagri and Malik made a brief appearance on the following counts: one count each of first degree murder of 329 Air India passengers, one count each of first degree murder of Japanese baggage handler Ideharu Koda, one count each of first degree murder of Japanese baggage handler Hideo Asano, and one count each of conspiracy to commit murder. Together Bagri and Mail faced eight separate charges in total.

With all the available forensic evidence in 1991, Reyat had only been convicted of manslaughter of the two baggage handlers in the case of that bomb that exploded in Japan. How the Crown was planning to prove first-degree murder in the Air India case, I had no idea, but I thought it was a substantial stretch. Reyat still could not be charged at the same time that Malik and Bagri since he had been extradited from the U.K. with the understanding that he would not face additional offences without permission of the British. Adding him to the same indictment would take several months of negotiations with the British. At the same time as the Air India charges were laid, Bagri also was slapped with a count of conspiracy to commit murder dating back to the 1988 attack on Hayer that was carried out by the emotionally charged youth Harkirat Singh Bagga. But this charge was far-fetched and would prove unsustainable for lack of any credible evidence and was soon dropped. A witness who had first told me in 1992 that he had been present at a meeting of several Sikh traditionalists at Bear Creek Park had finally been upfront with the cops around 1997 about what he had told me several years earlier. He had said while sitting with the men he heard two people discuss financial debts related to the Hayer shooting of 1988 by Harkirat Bagga. However, close to the time of the Air India trial the witness had lied in an unrelated court case and his credibility went out of the window. Since he was a key to prosecuting Bagri on the charge of conspiracy to kill Hayer, the charge was no longer sustainable. I met with prosecutor Richard Cairns to confirm that I had been told about this Bear Creek Park event by the witness back in 1992. And that I had at that time told the police about this evidence. Nevertheless, Cairns said he felt that he could not proceed because the credibility of the witness was now in serious question. The witness had told a provable untruth under oath. And that was fatal in any future court appearance where an entire case hinged on his credibility.

But the current scene in the courtroom as Malik and Bagri were presented before a judge was tragically comic. Malik, the proud Sikh who always wore a black turban with a metal badge on its front, had a shower cap over his head. Both Sikhs had been forced to remove their turbans in transit from jail to the courthouse, but were given the option of putting them back on once the appeared before the judge. Bagri had managed to get his back on in time, but Malik for some reason opted for a shower cap. Now, he looked absurd standing there with this unorthodox headgear as the charges were read out in court. When this was reported in the papers, there was an instant backlash from traditionalists who accused the police of violating his rights. The constant publicity surrounding his school and credit union had already created the impression the media were hounding an honourable Sikh. He had become an icon of the Khalsa, lionized beyond his true importance in the Sikh community. This press hysteria and public lashing of Malik would work against the Crown and the RCMP during the case, as people who previously might have helped turned against them. What police and reporters forgot was that the Air India disaster wasn't a recent event; it happened almost twenty years ago. In 1985, Malik was a nobody when it came to Sikh militancy. Later he had grown wealthy and his school for Sikh children had become a focal point for some traditionalists including a turbaned police officer working on the Air India task force who sent his children to Malik's school.

When senior Crown prosecutor Bob Wright provided an overview of his case against Malik and Bagri in the B.C. Supreme Court, it became abundantly clear that his case hinged on the word of Ms. D, the woman with whom I had talked in Stanley Park. The fragile case appeared to be entirely based on an alleged confession made to Ms. D by Malik. She had also alleged that Malik's close confidante, Balwant Singh Bandher had driven the bombs to the Vancouver Airport in a brown van. The existence of the brown van was to be proven by the testimony of one Narinder Singh Gill, a man who I had yet to meet. He had apparently travelled in the brown van to Seattle from Vancouver around the time of the bombing.

It seemed to me that some of Ms. D's allegations were already in the public domain and included what we had talked about at Stanley Park. She could have easily fished out the rest of it from books, articles, the Internet, and the reporters she had met with to discuss the Air India bombing.

I came out of the court room in a bit of daze. After twenty years, that was all they had? Was any of this even true? Years of public information was being repeated by a witness. Where was the evidence about the two helpers Reyat had in Duncan? Where was the name of Mr. X we had been looking for? Where were the real names of the two people who checked in the bags?

I did several interviews with radio and television, including the CBC, expressing serious doubt about the evidence, calling it fundamentally flawed and easy to trash. It was all based on hearsay. With no corroborating evidence, I felt all along this was doomed to fail. There was no forensic evidence, no wiretaps, no confessions—just the word of a woman who had even tried to help terrorist Hardial Singh Johal win a contest for the leadership of the Khalsa bank to wrest it away from Malik.

Something was wrong here. It seemed to me that the woman had told the cops where to go for confirmation about the brown van story. It did not seem likely to me that a man like Malik would rattle off a bunch of names of people who did chores in the Air India bombing and then in a tense conversation add the bomb went to the airport in a brown van. Who talks like that? Certainly not the Malik I knew well. Where had the brown van come from? Where did it go afterwards?

I phoned my journalist friend Cheema (also a former leader in the ISYF) to see if a meeting could be arranged with Narinder Singh Gill. He knew Gill well and set up a rendezvous.

The meeting at Gill's Surrey house was a revelation. He confirmed that he lived in Calgary in 1985 and attended meetings where militants talked about various options to damage India. There'd been trips to Calgary by Parmar. But Gill made no mention that Malik was in attendance at any meeting in "Cowtown".

Gill said a discussion occurred at the Calgary Sikh temple and people were talking about shooting a plane down. He said the final plan agreed to by some people was to blow up an Air India plane on the ground. He said Malik did not book the tickets as Ms. D was alleging; that had been done with the help of Pawa, the travel agent. He was then asked about exactly when he went to Seattle with another Calgary man, Balwant Singh Bandher who Ms. D was blaming for driving the bombs to the airport. Gill said it was after June 14, 1985, that he had travelled with Bandher to Vancouver and then to Seattle. But he could not be sure just how many days after that date he left on his trip to the west coast.

He remembered leaving Calgary with Balwant Singh Bandher, who years later moved to live in the Vancouver area. The two of them drove to Vancouver along with Bandher's wife and children, and then on to Blaine, Washington where they picked up Bhai Jeevan Singh, Malik's spiritual leader in the AKJ movement. Jeevan Singh had been waiting at a small cabin owned by a Sikh who was a friend of Malik and Johal. Gill, Bandher, and Bhai Jeevan Singh were joined by Bandher's wife and three children and the group went to Seattle, where local Sikhs were running a small temple. After they got there, another group of Sikhs arrived from Vancouver. Parmar, Malik, Reyat, Bagri, and several others had come in their cars. Gill rattled off the types of vehicles they were all driving, including the colours and even the fact that some were rented. I thought he had a fantastic memory.

Gill also he recalled he had left Calgary sometime after the birth of a friend's son on June 14, 1985, since he had taken the mom-to-be to hospital. He said he stayed at the Seattle temple because he had back pain caused by an accident, but others were moving back and forth from Vancouver to Seattle.

"Can you tell me where you were on June 22, 1985 and June 23, 1985?" I asked him. These were the two key days when bags were checked in and the Air India explosion occurred.

Gill's eyes started darting back and forth from Cheema to me.

"I don't remember," he said. "Perhaps my wife can tell me, or it may be in my diary."

"Hard to forget a day like that. I was a young kid when Kennedy died and I remember where I was. You came here after hearing discussions about Air India. You went to Seattle and remember what cars they were driving. I don't understand how you could not remember where you were on that day," I said. "You drove back to Calgary with your friend Bandher. You must have talked about what happened to Air India."

Gill's incredibly clear memory had suddenly grown foggy. I pressed him.

"I mean, your other friend (Ms. D) is saying Bandher took the bags to the airport in a brown van. If that is the case, you were with him all the way back to Calgary. You didn't talk about the destruction of the airplane?"

He said there was no discussion during the trip back to Calgary between himself and Bandher about Air India Flight 182. He said he could not remember where he was on the day the aircraft blew up because he was on pain medication. He said the drug had affected his memory.

When we left the meeting, I stopped my car a few blocks away from Gill's home. I went over to Cheema's vehicle.

"Do you remember every word he said to us?" I asked.

"Yes, every word. It's amazing. What are the cops doing?"

"Not much," I replied. "Remember what Gill said. We were asking more questions than the police did. He said police did not ask all these questions."

The police had simply confined their questioning to confirming the existence of the brown van. Yet, the fact that the brown van had not just existed in Vancouver was important. I doubted if the cops had given any thought to the fact the allegation now was that the brown van had actually arrived from Calgary, and that put a whole new spin on the story of how it had turned up at Vancouver Airport laden with bombs. There were many more issues now than just a brown van being driven to the airport allegedly by Bandher. Now, one had to look for evidence of when this van came from Calgary, when it went to Seattle, when it went to the airport, and when it returned to Calgary. Bandher and Gill were not residents of Vancouver, as the cops had assumed after hearing Ms. D's story.

It threw a lot of Ms. D's evidence into doubt, I thought. Malik was not even in Calgary when the alleged conversations about blowing up a plane had occurred. Ms. D had told the cops Malik had been there during discussions about blowing up the aircraft. Gill's version of events, and Ms. D's, appeared to clash in some areas and overlap in others. Gill had claimed to be present at the very birth of the Air India conspiracy, yet said he couldn't remember where he was when the bombs had exploded. None of that was in the transcript of the police interview I had read. It raised questions about the depth of the police investigation, Gill's reliability as a witness, (because of pain medication that caused a foggy memory) and the credibility of Ms. D's evidence.

The next day I phoned Schneider and told him I was going to be doing a story on my conversation with Gill once I had corroborated it. I told him what Gill had said. I had written down everything he'd told me and I thought it was important for Schneider to know what had happened. The Air India investigation was not an ordinary story. It carried an enormous burden for me as a journalist. I wanted this case solved desperately. But I was also interested in seeing that it was solved in a just manner, consistent with fundamental principles of fair play in Canada's justice system. I told him I would do a story about this after first going to Seattle to find out from people there if they could remember seeing the Air India suspects in their town.

Schneider was astounded because during their questioning of Gill, the police had failed to ask for details about the history of where that van had come from and where it had gone back to after the air disaster. Now we even had the name of the person Gill said the vehicle had finally been given to many years later.

Schneider was red in the face.

"The Crown will shit their pants. They are not going to like this," he said.

"Yep," I said. "I imagine the Crown will shit their pants."

Schneider, I felt, knew the perils of getting the full story from Gill. It would seriously affect the makeup of Ms. D's so-called confession from Malik. And it could raise serious issues of where Ms. D was getting her information from about Malik.

Refusing to let matters rest, Cheema and I headed to Seattle to check out Gill's story. We found the cabin that Gill had described on the border with Canada some miles from the border town of Blaine along Zero Avenue, the dividing line between Canada and the U.S. I called a friend of mine at the border patrol who confirmed Sikhs used to use the cabin as a temple around that time and there was a small Sikh flag there as well. He said border patrol agents considered the cabin and its backyard an entry point for illegal traffic in and out of Canada. We also found the temple in Seattle, which was now used as a daycare and church.

Cheema and I interviewed prominent local Sikhs who were in leadership positions at the temple around that time. They remembered a trip by Sikhs from Canada, but it was impossible to say when it had happened. But a new name surfaced: "Talk to Mahinder Singh Sidhu. He knows."

We finally went to the home of Mahinder Singh Sidhu, who ran a landscaping business.

Sidhu, a fair-skinned, polished, intelligent man, said there was no way Malik would ever participate in a scheme of terror. He is not a hands-on person, and he is not brave, he said. Sidhu admitted to being a long-time friend of Malik's, but said Johal was an even better friend. He confirmed that both Malik and Johal had visited in the mid–1980s, but the only meeting at that time he could remember was a separatists gathering held in Seattle that Hayer had attended, but from which Malik, Johal, and others had been absent. He said Hayer even visited his home around June 1985. Hayer had asked to use the phone and Sidhu overheard him asking Chauhan for more funds to support the Khalistan movement. A later check in Hayer's paper confirmed he had given a speech around June 1985 at the Seattle-area temple that was published in his paper on June 10. During the speech at the temple, Hayer had declared war on India, saying Sikhs would fight India in the alleys and villages.

Sidhu's landscaping business had employed the brother of FBI-hunted Amand Singh. Amand had later died in a car crash.

We felt Sidhu had been honest with us. There really was no way of establishing the precise timeline of the trip to Seattle in the brown van that Gill and Ms. D had described. It had happened. But it had no relationship to the Air India timeline.

Later, checking csis surveillance reports and intercepts, particularly in reference to where Parmar was on each given day in June 1985, it became apparent that he had not travelled to Seattle around that time. He never once talked about Seattle on his phone, but did discuss going to Toronto and other cities in Canada (csis transcribers had been told to keep a particular eye on travel plans and would have recorded it if he had talked about going to Seattle). So for the entire period in June 1985, Parmar was heard talking on his phone at home or was on view of csis surveillance parked outside his home. The only time he left was when he went to Duncan on June 4, 1985, then to Toronto on June 9, and a trip to Kamloops on June 14. But there was no trip to Seattle.

The lack of evidence of a trip to Seattle during the critical time frame dispelled the notion that a brown van took bag bombs to the airport. Perhaps Gill had really been affected by the pain killers as he had said. Meanwhile, innocent people had been maligned and named as suspects. In my opinion, there was no evidence to suggest Balwant Singh Bandher had come to B.C. from Calgary and taken bag bombs to the airport in the company of Bagri and others. The available evidence did not support this theory. Some informed sources now suggest there is a possibility this trip occurred much earlier than June 1985 or much later. Some law enforcement sources suggest it was around June 1984 after the Golden Temple attack.

The rest of the story of the Air India Flight 182 disaster—a trial debacle of historic proportions watched by anguished relatives of victims brought from all over the world inside a specially built multi-million dollar courtroom—would play out before one of the most astute and reasonable jurists in Canada, Justice Ian Bruce Josephson of the Supreme Court of British Columbia. His twenty-nine years of experience as a judge would stand him in good stead as he surgically peeled off the layers of the Crown case and got to its hollow core.

ELEVEN

THE DAY OF JUDGMENT:
2003 to 2005

Ripudaman Singh Malik and Ajaib Singh Bagri sat in their cells for almost thirty months before their trial began before Justice Bruce Ian Josephson on April 28, 2003.

Many months before the trial commenced, I told senior investigators that I felt many of their witnesses would not tell the whole truth on the witness stand. And sure enough, it proved to be an absurd arena of justice filled with comically tragic theatrics, dubious witnesses, blatant lies, and legal landmines that blew up in the Crown's face.

Even before the trial of Malik and Bagri began, the RCMP had been left scratching their heads after a handshake agreement between Reyat's lawyer, David Gibbons, and Chief Crown Prosecutor Bob Wright, reportedly over lunch. Reyat agreed to plead guilty to a much-reduced charge of manslaughter over his role in the bombing of Flight 182. The Crown had charged him with first-degree murder. Reyat's culpability was much higher in this case than any other suspect since his purchase of parts for an explosive made him the only accused against whom there was any physical evidence of any sort. The case against Malik and Bagri was based solely on witnesses who would claim to have obtained admissions from the pair. This made for a highly precarious state of affairs for the Crown. The sole determining factor in the case against Malik and Bagri would therefore be the credibility of witnesses—and part of the collection of characters the Crown had accumulated here would make anyone wonder in retrospect how this had even gone to court in the first place.

It had taken nearly six months to add Reyat to the list of the accused who had conspired with the late-terrorist Talwinder Singh

Parmar. There were also more delays caused by tardy disclosure of vital exculpatory evidence by the Crown, as well as pre–trial motions and admissions.

The Crown appeared somewhat surprised when the issue of adding Reyat to the indictment arose and it was discovered that permission would have to be obtained from Britain to add him to the list. There had been no forethought given to that aspect. But that was only the beginning of a series of drawbacks.

The Crown's admission of how weak their case against Reyat truly was became clear in their submission to Justice Donald I. Brenner, and one wondered why the man was even charged with first-degree murder in the first place. In accepting Reyat's plea agreement, the Crown conceded it could not prove that Reyat had even made the bomb that downed Air India Flight 182. The so-called bomb maker had now become merely a foot soldier who collected bomb parts for others to make the devices. And the Crown said Reyat had no idea who had made the bombs, nor any idea that its intended target was an aircraft. The Crown was in no position to challenge that.

"In his submissions, Mr. Wright stated that the RCMP has never stopped (working) in this case. Since June 1985, they have been at work and they have aggressively pursued all instigative leads. As a result of that investigation, which I think can only be described as exhaustive, the evidence available to the Crown supports nothing further than the charge of manslaughter, the specific charge of aiding and abetting with which Mr. Reyat is charged before the court."

Gone were the counts of making a bomb and premeditated murder, charges that I had always felt were highly inflated. Now it was a count of manslaughter, in essence, of aiding and abetting The Crown had even surrendered any notion that Reyat knew who made the bombs or who checked them aboard the aircraft. That, I thought, was the price to be paid for not having tracked down a minimum of three and as many as five individuals vital to this case. The missing persons without whom you could not form the thread of continuity in this plot were the two people who checked in the bags and the Mr. X who had gone to Reyat's home with Parmar on June 4, 1985. There were others who had never been identified, such as the two men who had gone to Woolworths on June 5 and picked up the stereo that exploded in Tokyo. They did not wear turbans, unlike Mr. X. The employee who identified them did not think either of the two men was in fact Reyat, although the receipt was made out in Reyat's name. It was devastating that in eighteen years of investigation, the RCMP did not have the faintest clue about these missing characters; a fatal flaw that would leave the Crown in the completely helpless position of having to admit critical shortcomings in their evidence.

If that sounded surprising, the wording of the agreed statement of fact on Reyat's plea was even more brutal on the shortage of information about his role in the conspiracy. The Crown was forced to agree that "although Mr. Reyat acquired materials for this purpose, he did not make or arm an explosive device, nor did he place an explosive device on an airplane, nor does he know who did or did not do so. At no time did Mr. Reyat intend by his actions to cause death or believe that such consequences were likely to occur." Further, the Crown agreed that Reyat believed the explosive devices would be used in India to blow up "something heavy" like a car or a bridge. The statement also cleared Reyat of any foreknowledge of the conspiracy, stating "unbeknownst to Mr. Reyat, the items that he acquired were used by other person or persons to help make an explosive device that on or about June 23, 1985, destroyed Air India Flight 182 killing all 329 people on board."

I thought that was a damning and spectacular admission by the Crown that they knew nothing beyond what the police had uncovered in November 1985, some eighteen years earlier. Accepting this evidence raised the spectre that Reyat had been double-crossed by someone. Who? Hardial Singh Johal? Who had timed the bombs? Did someone change the timing?

The startling admission of facts left some police in the court room feeling betrayed. Some felt the Crown should have consulted them far more than they were in terms of the wording of this admission. And it raised the question of why the Crown had not insisted on getting from Reyat the name of the person or persons to whom he gave these bomb parts. Why was he in Vancouver prior to the bags being loaded and why did he go to buy a battery after one bag was checked in? However, Wright did not have answers to those questions since the police had not found them.

But some investigators believe Wright should have at least forced Reyat to name Mr. X before letting him off with a legal slap on the wrist: a five-year additional sentence for pleading guilty to one count of manslaughter of 329 people. The plea agreement raised more questions than it answered. In fact, it was now completely baffling as to what he was even pleading guilty to.

I thought the Crown was hoping that with the weak evidence they had against Malik and Bagri, at least one conviction in the bag would help. It was face-saving at best. They also thought they could now call Reyat to the stand and extract key information from him under oath. But earlier interviews with Reyat had made it clear he had already taken a higher oath of silence to God. Calling Reyat to the stand later would prove disastrous, but for me the writing was on the wall already.

On February 10, 2003, Justice Brenner sentenced Reyat to five years in addition to the time he had already served. It amounted to a total of twenty-five years in jail, including the time he had spent incarcerated in the U.K. in 1988. Justice Brenner would also recommend that Reyat spend those five years at the minimum-security Ferndale Institution, a luxury resort in comparison to the harsh conditions at maximum-security institutions. As well, he banned Reyat from possessing explosives or firearms for the rest of his life.

But this fiasco was a portent of a bigger disaster to come in the case that had been heralded in with such fanfare and the culmination of an "exhaustive" police investigation costing $100 million. Combined with the cost of the trial that figure would rise to more than $140 million, not counting the construction of a $6-million special court room with bullet-proof glass for two men who had freely roamed the world for fifteen years before their arrest.

The Crown called Reyat as a witness during Malik and Bagri's trial in a bid to see if his evidence could shore up the case against the pair. However, it was more of a fishing trip than a realistic expectation that Reyat would finally divulge information after holding steadfast for years and years. Any hope that the deal he'd cut would move him to cooperate with the Crown swiftly vanished. He stated that Parmar asked him to make an explosive device that would be used in India, a position the Crown had agreed to earlier. Reyat also claimed to have taken the early morning ferry from the island to Vancouver on June 22, 1985. The rest of his testimony was a mix of evasiveness, memory loss, and invention. He could not explain telephone calls between his home and Johal's house made the night before and the day of the bombings. He claimed the real purpose of Parmar's June 4, 1985 trip to Duncan had been to learn about propane conversion for his car , despite the fact that Parmar had not even brought the vehicle on the trip, travelling to the island by ferry, and being picked up and driven to Reyat's home by third party.

Reyat was not a reluctant witness. He was a witness determined to lie. It was so bad that the Crown requested permission to question him as a hostile witness. Justice Josephson denied this request. It was clear Josephson felt that would not assist the Crown or the court. The court would have simply heard more lies, a point Josephson would make forcefully in his final judgment against Malik and Bagri at the end of the trial.

"Mr. Reyat's credibility on the witness stand is also of little moment in relation to the outcome of this trial. That said, it is without hesitation that I find him to be an unmitigated liar under oath. Mr. Reyat endeavoured to reveal as little information as possible regarding the complicity of himself and others in the offences, while attempting unsuccessfully to craft a story consistent with his plea to manslaughter and his admissions of fact in that connection," said Josephson.

Reyat had repeated many of his lies from his 1985 and 1995 interviews with the Mounties prior to charges being laid, saying the explosive device that was tested on June 4, 1985 in front of Parmar was useless; that he had been a mere assistant to Mr. X, who was going to gather materials in Duncan to make the device. When caught out, Reyat feigned memory loss or made up yet another wild story.

"Much of his evidence was improbable in the extreme and entirely inconsistent with common sense," ruled Josephson. "His hollow expression of remorse must have been a bitter pill for the families of the victims. If he harboured even the slightest degree of genuine remorse, he would have been more forthcoming,"

Indeed, when he was sentenced on the reduced charge, Reyat had pumped the hands of lawyers and smiled jubilantly. It was not fun to watch this gleeful zealot's reaction. He was the man, I believed, who had the blood of 331 people on his hands.

The trial of Malik and Bagri commenced in B.C. Supreme Court in the Arthur Erickson-designed Vancouver courthouse on April 28, 2003, just over two months after Reyat's plea bargain had been approved. Presiding over this high-profile and controversial case was the Honourable Mr. Justice I. Bruce Josephson, a respected and experienced judge who had earned his law degree at the University of Saskatchewan. He had been appointed a B.C. Supreme Court Justice in 1990 and was the right choice to officiate what would prove to be a complex, exhausting trial that would take nineteen months to complete, with 230 trial days and endless legal manoeu-vring. The high-security courtroom was packed by victim's families; supporters of Malik, Reyat, and Bagri; members of the public; and the media. The court heard days of intricate technical testimony from competing experts and, in all, 115 witnesses would take the stand. The majority of the witnesses had no bearing on the outcome of the trial. Most were technical experts and some were from Ireland where the human tragedy had landed in the wake of the bombing.

But for all that, the Crown's case against Malik rested solely on the credibility of Ms. D, who cannot be identified by court order and is in the witness protection program. She was the hub of the case against Malik. Without her evidence everything else would hang like loose threads. Inconsistencies, theatrics, and a malleable memory severely undercut her credibility in the eyes of the court, along with her professed love for the man she was testifying against.

When she walked in to testify for the first time, the Crown's star witness was full of theatrics fit for a Bollywood soap opera. She bowed to Malik, and then took the stand to testify how, while employed at the Khalsa School, Malik expressed his feelings of love for her in January 1995. This made her happy, but she was unable to express her own feelings to him in return. They hugged, they held hands, but they never kissed or had sex, she testified. Malik

wanted to make love with her, but was afraid that this breach of
Sikh principles, if ever discovered, would ruin him. She went on to
testify that she had great love for Malik that remained to this day,
even as she tried to send him to jail for life.

This professed love proved to be the decisive struggle between
the prosecution and the defence team. Justice Josephson picked a
portion of Ms. D's testimony to illustrate this clash of love on the
one hand and an attempt to convict Malik of murder on the other.
It seemed to illustrate the height of duplicity.

Q: [Ms. D], today do you hate Mr. Malik?
A: I could never hate him. Never.
Q: Do you want to take revenge against Mr. Malik?
A: Oh lord, never. Never.
Q: What are your feelings for him today?
A: I still love him. I still respect him. I miss him. And I hate
being here. I just wish I wasn't here.
Q: Did you ever make a promise to Mr. Malik about your
love for him?
A: Yes, I did.
Q: What did you promise him?
A: I promised him no matter what, no matter where,
regardless what, I'll always love you, always respect you,
and if I can, I will always be there to help you...

Justice Josephson used another portion of Ms. D's testimony to illustrate this contradiction between her professed love and her actions:

Q: Do you feel that by giving evidence for the Crown you
are breaking that promise?
A: Of course, yes.
Q: And how does that make you feel today?
A: Oh, don't know how horrible I feel. If there was any
way, anything, I wouldn't be here. I just don't want to.
It's a betrayal that is so insulting to me. I just–I just don't
want to.

Josephson saw Ms. D's claim of love on the one hand and her actions on the other as a glaring contradiction of normal human behaviour. Malik's defence team would feed on this contradiction. They pointed to the human rights complaint Ms. D had filed against Malik and the Satnam Education Society which runs the Khalsa School for which she worked in May 1996. Although she later withdrew the complaint, the defence argued that such an action was an embarrassment to Malik and did not speak of love: on the contrary, it pointed to a deterioration of relations between the two much earlier than the alleged confession made to her by Malik.

Ms. D's relations with key Malik confidantes Balwant Singh Bandher—a former resident of Calgary who at one time owned a brown van—and Aniljit Uppal soured for several reasons, including accusations she was a CSIS spy. Faced with conflicts with his confidantes, Malik finally fired Ms. D on November 1, 1997. In January 1998, she filed a wrongful dismissal suit naming Malik, Bandher, Uppal, and his education society as defendants. She had claimed she had been called a "slut" by Malik. She settled out of court for $12,000.

About one month before she was fired, Ms. D had telephoned CSIS agent Nick Rowe and later met with him at a coffee shop. She claimed she contacted CSIS because Bandher had been spreading rumours in the school she was a spy for the security service. During several meetings with Rowe, she made a litany of allegations against Malik: that he was a thief, a fraudster, participated in immigration scams, misappropriated money, and treated children and employees at the school poorly.

She made no mention to CSIS that she had any knowledge that Malik had participated in a plot to blow up Air India Flight 182, despite the fact that she met with Rowe many times and related many other types of criminal conduct.

Rowe decided much of what she had said related to claimed criminal activity was not in CSIS's domain, and he called RCMP Corporal Doug Best, a former CSIS agent. Best was on the RCMP's Air India task force and later interviewed Rowe about his dealings with Ms. D. The CSIS agent told him about their several meetings in October 1997. He said she had recounted numerous nefarious activities by Malik and he felt she was "in some respects anxious to get back at him."

Best then interviewed Ms. D. Again, she made no mention of an admission by Malik to her about playing a role in the Air India bombing.

On November 2, 1997, Schneider, Inspector Gary Bass, and Best met Ms. D at the Surrey RCMP detachment. She had piqued their interest: Malik had been an Air India suspect since 1985, he was an associate of Parmar and Johal, and there was the ever-present rumour in the community that he had financed the Air India project. The three Mounties asked Ms. D if she would go back to the school the next day carrying a panic button and a radio transmitter in her purse. She was to push the button if she felt she was in any danger.

Ms. D squeezed the button very shortly after she got back into the school on Monday morning. The police rushed to the scene and arrested Bandher, who she said had come close to her but did not actually appear to have threatened her. Uppal on the other hand told the police she had been fired and should leave the school property, which she did. What purpose this little scheme would serve the RCMP is not clear. In effect though, Ms. D had become an agent of the RCMP by carrying out their instructions and participating in a sting operation—a powerful hint of her desire to "get back" at Malik and his people.

On the same day, she gave the RCMP her first statement that related to anything remotely resembling Malik's role in Air India. Even that was fraught with problems with wording; exactly what he said would be debatable. It related to an event that had occurred almost two years ago as she spoke about it for the first time to the officers. If she had believed what he had said, one wonders why she remained a terrorist's girlfriend for so long after.

Ms. D claimed that on May 8, 1996, during a discussion about a Khalsa school child who had attempted suicide, Malik had asked Ms. D not to fret. Malik told her: "If one child dies, so what?" and "1982, 328 people died. So what? Air India crashed. We had Air India crashed. So what?"

But during her testimony in court, the exact meaning of what he had said remained doubtful, because her version of their conversation changed a number of times. Could he have said "when" instead of "we'd?"

On November 7, 1997, RCMP asked Ms. D point-blank during a recorded interview if there had been any other references about Air India during her life at the school. The question was clear and simple. And she gave a simple answer:

Q: Are there any other references that you can recall or that you have a note on where Mr. Malik specifically made reference to Air India?

A: No.

Ms. D would wait another five months during which she talked extensively to reporters, police, and her other associates (including witnesses who would also testify for the Crown) before making another revelation about a critical conversation with Malik. This was the most detailed statement she had made about Malik's purported confession which occurred under bizarre circumstances.

She told police that in March or April 1997, she confronted Malik about an article that had appeared in Punjabi–language newspaper *Awaaz*. Written by Sukhminder Singh Cheema, the March 28, 1997 story said police were closing in on several suspects in the Air India bombing. The article had stated several Sikhs would be arrested by police. The article mentioned Reyat, Johal, Bagri, Surjan Singh Gill, and "a prominent West End Sikh," an indirect reference to Malik (published in Punjabi, the article also demonstrated my contention that a large majority of Sikhs in B.C. were well-informed for years about the names of RCMP suspects. Many of the same people had been picked up by the RCMP on several occasions beginning in November 1985, their pictures had appeared in newspapers, and the suspects, including Malik, had been talked about in books as well as the national media).

Around the time she was fired in November 1997, one of the first people Ms. D contacted was Cheema. They stood near a Sikh temple and discussed the article and the list of names he had published and she sought information from him about these people he had named.

In her statement implicating Malik, Ms. D claimed she put Cheema's article in front of him at his desk in his school office. She demanded he explain what it meant. Malik, her boss, caved in and gave her a detailed explanation. In itself, the manner in which she obtained the confession appeared suspect. This was not "pillow talk." It was simply a demand for an explanation from a man she claimed was enamoured with her, but against whom she had filed a complaint with the Human Rights Board just a year earlier. Desperate police looking for answers had long suspended disbelief; as the rest of the trial would prove.

Malik, Ms. D said, told her that each person in the Air India plot had been assigned a task and he had been in charge of overseeing the project. In effect, he had admitted he was the project manager. According to Ms. D, Malik said he had called "Canadian Airlines" and booked the first ticket for a flight from Vancouver to India with connections in Japan and Bangkok. He then booked a second flight from Vancouver to India, with a connection in Montreal. But he had been concerned about the second ticket as it would mean a transfer from a smaller airport to a larger airport so he called to change the connection from Montreal to Toronto. (*The Death of Air India Flight 182*, published in 1986, had carried a detailed "verbatim" statement from CP Air agent Martine Donahue and another agent about the various configurations for tickets that a caller had tried during a phone call on June 19, 1985. A flight to Dorval domestic airport from Vancouver would have meant a passenger would have had to take his bag to Mirabel for the international flight via Air India Flight 182. This would have been impractical since no one was going to board any flight with the bomb-laden bag. This was made clear in the book. However, Ms. D denied having read it.)

Ms. D further claimed that Malik said that during his telephone call to book the tickets, he'd told the ticket agent he would arrange to have the ticket picked up (again, the book mentioned the caller had said he was quite close to CP Air's offices and he would have the tickets picked up). She further claimed that Malik had instructed Daljit Singh Sandhu (well known to the community as a person who was pro–Khalistan and wore a net on his beard) to pick up the ticket. Malik allegedly said to her that Sandhu was dressed up, wore his beard in a net and had a "fancy ring" on when he picked up the tickets. Malik said Sandhu then changed the telephone number on the ticket booking to one of the temple. (In fact, the phone number left behind by the person who booked the tickets by phone was a number traceable to Johal. The person who picked up the ticket then changed the phone number to a number belonging to Sodhi Singh Sodhi, which was only one digit different from the number originally left behind.)

My book, included detailed statement from CP Air ticket agents as well as Gerald Duncan, the airline agent from whom the flight tickets had been picked up. The book had also mentioned that a ticket booked around the middle of June for an A. Singh flying to Tokyo via CP Air and then Air India for an onward destination had never been picked up. But the caller had left a number for the Ross Street Sikh Temple. This initial booking had raised a query to the Vancouver Air India office from their Tokyo office about a missing A. Singh who had booked but not bought a ticket. It appeared that several attempts had been made to book tickets under various names and the terrorists had finally settled on the names L. Singh and M. Singh as the bogus travellers. Gerald Duncan's statement contained in the book mentioned Duncan recalling under hypnosis that the man who picked up the ticket was wearing a large diamond ring. Further, the ring had been mentioned in my book as well as my conversation with Ms. D in Stanley Park. At the time the book was published, there was no entity known as Canadian Airlines, and *The Death of Air India Flight 182* referred to bookings being made via CP Air. But a later book by another author referred to the airline in question as Canadian Airlines. This suggests Ms. D had read that book and repeated the mistake, a clear migration of errors in public sources that had made their way into her "confession" yarn.

It was inconceivable that the so-called project manager of Air India bombing plot would make such errors, since he would have a vivid memory of his deeds, including the persons associated with the plot and the details of how it worked.

Ms. D also went on to state that Malik had told her that Johal had gone to the airport and was part of the group that delivered suitcases loaded with bombs. Malik had further told her Bandher (who had lived in Calgary at the time) had gone to the airport in a brown van along with Bagri and another man to deliver the fatal bags.

She also claimed that Malik had told her that Surjan Singh Gill had worked hard on the project, but had changed his mind about participating in the plan. This was another factor well-rumoured in the community (it was common knowledge that Surjan Singh Gill had resigned from the BK before the disaster) and also known to her close friend, Narinder Singh Gill. (Gill had told me she had talked to him about Air India on several occasions.)

Later, Ms. D would add more information to this confession. She said Malik, Parmar, and Malik's spiritual guide, Bhai Jiwan Singh, had made a trip to Seattle prior to the bombings and that the spiritual leader had blessed the Air India bombing during the meeting in Seattle. This new information would appear to Justice Josephson to be attempts to add meat to her confession story, an attempt to lend it credibility, but it had a negative effect in the final analysis.

Malik's confession got better and better as time went by, with Ms. D adding more details (as they became available to her) and she added more people to the plot. Justice Josephson would call this the evolution of her evidence.

"Ms. D was cross-examined about inconsistencies in her evidence regarding the Seattle trip and the fact that she had not revealed Mr. Malik's statements in that regard until a Crown interview on October 30, 2003, the day before she commenced her evidence in these proceedings," said Justice Josephson.

That would make it more than five years after she first gave police information about Malik's so-called confession back in April 1988.

The Seattle-trip story added to Malik's confession raised more questions for Justice Josephson.

"Ms. D was uncertain with respect to the timing of her conversation with Mr. Malik about this trip. She was also questioned about her statement to the Crown about having discussed the trip with Narinder Gill on three separate occasions. She replied that she could no longer remember discussing this issue with him, nor could she recall that portion of the Crown interview from a few weeks earlier," said the judge, about her seemingly selective memory of collaboration with Gill.

Another major area where Ms. D clearly lied was a conversation she alleged she had overheard between Malik and Mindy Bandher (son of Balwant Singh Bandher). She said she overheard the conversation in April 1997. The two were allegedly talking about some chatter in the community about the Air India bombing. The defence produced Mindy Bandher as a witness, along with documented evidence he was out of the country for a major part of that period of time. At first, the Crown ridiculed Bandher during cross examination but later was forced to concede he indeed was out of the country at the time.

With so many inconsistencies in her statement, with so much in her evidence consistent with public domain information or information in possession of her good friend Narinder Gill and another witness, with her attempts to conceal her hatred for Malik by claiming to love him even as she testified against him and hyping the confession several times, it was plain that no judge would accept the testimony of a witness so badly tainted, or severely confused emotionally.

To make matters worse, at one point she even turned on Crown Counsel Joe Bellows, a respected veteran prosecutor, accusing him of putting words in her mouth and getting things wrong. The Crown had announced with great certainty at a bail hearing that Ms. D had made notations about Malik's main Air India confession in her journal. However, she said in court she never wrote anything about Air India in her journal. This had led to a defence request to see the Crown's notes.

It was a bizarre incident that further undermined Ms. D's credibility. The position of Malik's lawyers on the contradiction between the Crown's bail hearing statement and the reversal that she did not write about the Air India confession in the journal was summed up by Justice Josephson as follows:

"The Crown relied on this entry at the bail hearing as independent confirmatory evidence of the Newspaper Confession. Once Ms. D realized that the dates in her journal did not fit with the date of the *Awaaz* article, she began to resile from her earlier position. Her subsequent explanation to Corporal Best that there was another occasion within two months involving a similar confrontation with

Mr. Malik after reviewing an article with Mrs. Reyat is implausible. It would be remarkable for her to have forgotten about making a reference in her journal to her confrontation with Mr. Malik which she described as a shocking revelation."

Daljit Singh Sandhu, who she had said was the man who picked up the tickets while wearing a "fancy ring," defended himself against the allegation on the stand as a defence witness. It is my belief he would not have testified had he really been involved, since he had no idea what ammunition the Crown could fire at him. Sandhu testified he had never worn a ring in his entire life. He appeared with a collection of his photos from the past showing no ring on his hands (Sandhu told me he did not even wear a ring on his wedding day). He testified he did not pick up the tickets, nor did CP Air agent Gerald Duncan identify him as the man who had. There was nothing to corroborate his role apart from the claimed confession. Sandhu was rumoured for years to be the man who had picked up the tickets, a rumour fed by moderates in the community who detested his support for Khalistan and traditionalist Sikh values, as well as his role in the furniture controversy (some Sikh moderates came to my home during the trial to ask me how they could bolster the evidence against Malik, since it appeared the Crown's case was weak). Justice Josephson doubted whether a prominent man in the Sikh community would consent to carry out the very public job of picking up the tickets.

Narinder Gill's testimony added more nails to the Crown's coffin. He could not remember the exact timing of his trips to Vancouver or to Seattle in the company of Balwant Singh Bandher, who Ms. D had named as a suspect. The defence produced documented medical information to show Gill was in Calgary on June 24, 1985 and Bandher's children were in school until after the air disaster. As well, Bandher had seen a doctor in Calgary on June 21, 1985.

The judge said Ms. D had first disclosed having had a conversation with Malik about the Seattle trip just before appearing in court to testify.

"Ms. D first disclosed having had this conversation with Mr. Malik in a Crown interview on the eve of her testimony. In that interview, she acknowledged having spoken to Narinder Gill about this trip on three prior occasions, who, by this time, had completed his testimony. When cross-examined about this Crown interview, she claimed a surprising lack of recall about what had been discussed," Josephson said.

"I am satisfied that no such Seattle meeting took place prior to the time of the alleged offences," he ruled.

Even if one argued that medical and school records could have been doctored, then one still had to discount unassailable evidence in CSIS records. I searched CSIS intercepts for the month of June along with mobile CSIS surveillance records and the records of the observation post which was outside Parmar's home during June. At no time did Parmar talk about a trip to Seattle during his phone conversations with others but on several occasions talked of trips to other cities such as Toronto. CSIS followed him to Kamloops on one occasion. He did travel to Toronto and his trail was picked up from airport to airport. Parmar was proven to be in Vancouver at all other times and could not have possibly gone to Seattle prior to the Air India bombing.

Another man known to both Ms. D and Narinder Gill–a man referred to as Mr. B because he is in witness protection as well–told police in 1997 that Malik had approached him prior to the Air India disaster and effectively asked him to become a suicide bomber. He said he had wanted a loan of $40,000 to avoid foreclosure of his home. Malik asked him to take a suitcase with a bomb to India. Mr. B said Malik told him if something happened to him in transit then he would be considered a martyr.

Mr. B had severe credibility problems and had lied under oath before. He had a major grudge against Malik and had not gone to police for twelve years or told anyone about his evidence until he read about a million-dollar reward in a Punjabi newspaper.

"Mr. B believed that he had been cheated and thwarted at every turn on many occasions over many years by Mr. Malik, leaving him in a state of financial ruin. In addition to his lawsuit against Mr. Malik, his outrage at this treatment culminated one day when he informed Mr. Malik that he would 'beat him up' and ruin his reputation. It was later that same day that he made his first disclosure to police. This occurred one week after a Punjabi newspaper published notice of a $1-million reward related to the Air India investigation," said Justice Josephson.

It would appear Narinder Gill had known about Mr. B's statement and it seemed whatever Gill knew, Ms. D also knew. It was Gill who directed Ms. D to take Mr. B to her lawyer since he was also having problems with Malik. Mr. B mentioned the issue of being asked to take a bag bomb to India in front of Ms. D at her lawyer's office. It would reinforce a defence suggestion of collusion among witnesses.

The Crown's case had been weak from the beginning. The majority of people Ms. D had named as being involved in the conspiracy by Malik had not even been charged, an indication the Crown was in no position to back up her allegations about others with corroborating evidence. Her evidence could be used only against Malik since what he said to her about others was hearsay (a point some seasoned journalists seemed to miss; in one newspaper account, a reporter even described Daljit Singh Sandhu as a co-conspirator even though he had not been indicted).

In my twenty-five years of covering crime and courts, I have rarely seen a judge shred the evidence of a Crown witness in the manner in which Justice Josephson dealt with Ms. D in his judgment.

"Surprising were Ms. D's adamant protestations of on-going love, respect, and longing for Mr. Malik, a man whom she claims admitted his complicity in the senseless mass murder of hundreds of complete innocents. Of her being a witness, she testified:

'Oh, don't know how horrible I feel. If there was any way, anything, I wouldn't be here. I just don't want to. It's a betrayal that is so insulting to me...'

"When one adds to that her evidence of his treatment of the student Cudail, (a child who attempted suicide), his illegal activities and, ultimately, his cruel treatment and firing of her from a position that was a central part of her life, that surprise edges towards incredulity."

Josephson also found that while she testified that she talked to Malik almost everyday, police wiretaps between September 1996 and January 1997 found Ms. D had talked to Malik only once on the phone during that period. This lack of telephone contact that she had insisted existed on a daily basis would make her claim of love and devotion a mere fantasy.

"Either this mature, intelligent, and strong-willed person has abandoned all she believes in because of overwhelming and unreasoning emotions of the heart, or she is misleading the Court by claiming to be his loving confidante in an attempt to blunt the inevitable credibility attack based on her animus towards Mr. Malik. This latter possibility would also better provide some explanation for the apparent unlikelihood of Mr. Malik having chosen to provide her with such a detailed confession.

"I find that Ms. D was not a credible witness. The concerns regarding the Newspaper Confession alone raise serious issues with respect to her veracity and motivations. Having found that Ms. D was not truthful with respect to the core of her testimony against Mr. Malik, it would be wholly unsafe to rely on her other evidence tending to incriminate Mr. Malik."

In effect the judge called Ms. D a liar. Just how fundamental Ms. D's testimony was to the case against Malik was underscored by Josephson's judgment in finding Malik not guilty:

"Having made these findings regarding the credibility of the main witnesses against Mr. Malik, there can be no conclusion other than that the Crown has not proved its case against him beyond a reasonable doubt. Even if I were to accept all of the Crown's submissions regarding the inferences to be drawn from the balance of the evidence in this case, there is simply no evidence tending to point to the role that Mr. Malik may have played in the conspiracy to place bombs on Air India planes. It follows that the Crown has not proved its case against Mr. Malik beyond a reasonable doubt with respect to his being a member of the alleged conspiracy or a party to the alleged offences and, accordingly, I find him not guilty on each count of the Indictment," Justice Josephson ruled.

Equally disastrous was the evidence against Bagri. The Crown's case was once again undermined by questionable witnesses and a lack of legwork on the part of the RCMP. The worst things for the Crown are surprises. But it seemed that in this case, one of historic proportions for the country, surprises abounded.

Bagri had been indisputably a long-time advocate for an armed struggle to establish Khalistan and a member of the BK. While not unique at that time, Bagri's speech at Madison Square Garden in July 1984 and his many speeches in British Columbia and Ontario temples clearly indicated the mindset of a man bent on bloody vengeance for the attack on the Golden Temple.

A New York man, known as "John" was the key witness against Bagri. But he had been convicted of killing his own brother in India and had lied in sworn statements during his applications to stay in the United States. According to the Crown, John had been paid US $300,000 for his protection to be a witness against Bagri. But it soon became apparent that John wanted more money–$200,000 more–on the eve of the trial. Not for protection, but for testifying.

John had been one of the kingpins of the Dasmesh Regiment (Lal Singh's group), an organization the FBI chased during the 1985 assassination attempt on Indian cabinet minister Bhajan Lal in New Orleans. It was a group that had sent several men to a mercenary training school in Alabama and discussed acts of terror, including chemical warfare.

John lived in New York during the 1980s and had become an FBI informant after the failure of the Dasmesh Regiment's 1985 New Orleans assassination plot. Lal Singh and Amand Singh, both of whom he knew, had fled. John had aided Lal and Amand's flight from justice, but had never been charged with being an accessory after the fact.

John testified that he received a call from a friend two weeks after the Air India disaster. The friend asked him to go to a gas station in New Jersey to meet with Bagri, who was in town. A friend drove him to the gas station where several members of the BK from Ontario were present, including Hamilton resident Tejinder Singh Kaloe.

John took Bagri aside and expressed concerns that the Dashmesh Regiment was being blamed for the Air India bombing (at that time, Lal Singh and Amand Singh had been suspected of being linked to the disaster). Bagri's response, according to John, was: "Why the fuck they bother you? We did this."

He claimed to have spoken with Bagri at two other venues during 1987. On one occasion, Bagri was reluctant to discuss the Air India bombing, saying "walls have ears. Only two of us know; a third person will know, for this we can go in jail."

During cross-examination, the timing of this New Jersey confession became critical. When asked what he meant by a couple of weeks after the Air India bombing, John replied that could mean anything over one week. It could be two weeks or ten or twenty.

He also indicated that at one meeting in an apartment in New York, Bagri met with Lal Singh and Birk, the leader of the New Orleans conspiracy. John said he also talked with Bagri after Reyat's arrest in England in 1988. When he asked Bagri if Reyat could talk to the police, Bagri said, "Don't worry, he fucking don't know nothing."

But it appeared John's key character flaw was his greed. He haggled with the RCMP over the price of his testimony. He wanted US $500,000 to implicate Bagri. Just before his scheduled testimony, John took off to India, causing some panic among the Mounties. They had paid him $300,000. John faxed them, demanding another US $200,000 to attend the trial. The fax in John's broken English read in part, "If you want me testify please I want my 2 hundred thousands to sent to me and nothing else… Yours very obedient and truthful, John."

Bagri's lawyers successfully attacked John as "an infamous human being–a person of the most base character capable of engaging in atrocious behaviour." He was a man convicted of murdering his own brother for which he had spent time in an Indian jail, and later acquitted on a second charge of attempted murder. During his various U.S. immigration applications he had lied under oath and fabricated his concerns during an asylum request. His attempt to blackmail the cops for an additional $200,000 on the eve of his testimony also showed him to be a man motivated by greed to give false testimony. In helping Lal Singh and Amand Singh flee a charge of conspiracy to murder the Indian cabinet minister, John, in effect was culpable of a charge of accessory after the fact. The defence said he had turned on Bagri to avoid being charged.

Bagri's lawyers pointed out that their client's work records indicated he was at his job in Kamloops, B.C., during the whole of

September. Further, CSIS and the RCMP had been actively surveying Bagri and others, and it was clear Bagri was not in the New York area during that time. Records seized by the RCMP from Pawa's travel agency in Vancouver show he did not travel to New Jersey at the time in question.

Josephson's conclusions regarding John's character were damning.

"Mr. (John) C, I conclude, is a person driven by self-interest, not conscience or altruism as he testified. The extent to which his actions have been motivated and coloured by that self-interest was evident from his testimony and raises serious, if not overwhelming, concerns with respect to his credibility as a witness.

"Mr. C (John) is an individual driven by self-interest. His past conduct demonstrates a willingness to engage in deception, even under oath, to advance that self-interest. It was also self-interest that motivated him to become an informant to the FBI. He hoped that his status as an informant would assist him in avoiding deportation as an illegal immigrant, arrest in relation to the New Orleans incident, and later, implication in the Air India/Narita explosions."

Further, if as he alleged, the conversation occurred two weeks after the bombing, the gas station had not been acquired by his friend until September, evidence showed. And Bagri's work records show he was in Kamloops, British Columbia during the entire month of September.

The police, it seemed, had bought a pack of lies for US $300,000. Unfortunately for Canadian taxpayers, John is also eligible to collect a portion of the $1-million award advertised by the RCMP since the reward was offered to anyone whose information would lead to an arrest, not necessarily a conviction.

Another witness fraught with difficulties from the outset was Ms. E, a seamstress, who seemed to have been Bagri's girlfriend. This relationship had caused some other baptised Sikhs in the BK to raise concerns with Parmar. During a visit to Kamloops in June 1985, it seems Parmar went to the home of BK member Satnam Singh Khun Khun as opposed to Bagri's home. Ms. E's identity was known to investigators, including myself, as early as 1985.

Her testimony at trial was evasive. She did not wish to cooperate with the Crown and court was forced to accept the hearsay testimony of former CSIS agent William Laurie who had switched back to the RCMP some years later.

Laurie had managed to visit the woman, bought some drapes from her, and coaxed her into telling him that on the evening before the explosions, Bagri had gone to her home to borrow her car. Bagri had told her he was going to the airport but he was not travelling. Only the bags were going, he said. The admission to Laurie was made in September 1987. The RCMP had earlier visited to clarify who the individual was who had attended her home on June 9, 1985 based on CSIS surveillance that showed Bagri had been dropped off at her home following his return from the Toronto trip with Parmar.

During 1985, Ms. E had lived in a basement suite while her own home was under construction. Bagri had asked his distant relative, Daljit Sandhu, to help with the construction and during this period Bagri kept in close contact with both Ms. E and Sandhu.

Ms. E testified she did not recall any instance when Bagri talked about airplanes or baggage. She said she believed CSIS surveillance had the date of the visit to her apartment. This was on June 9, 1985, many days before the bombing. During cross-examination she continued to maintain there had been only one late-night visit by Bagri during June. That is all she recalled. She had no recollection of a visit on the night before the explosions.

Laurie later testified that he had destroyed audio recordings and notes he had made of his visits with Ms. E. This led to a ruling that his actions violated Bagri's rights under the charter since he had no ability to glean exculpatory evidence from those records.

"In her statements to Mr. Laurie, Ms. E consistently described Mr. Bagri's visit as having occurred the evening before the Air India explosion. In her evidence at trial, however, she generally associated that event with CSIS surveillance, which placed the visit on June 9, 1985. Looking at the evidence as a whole as I must do in assessing ultimate reliability, what is troubling is that throughout her evidence and her prior statements, Ms. E never described a second late night visit by Mr. Bagri in June 1985. This anomaly would have properly been the subject of rigorous cross-examination at trial to explore the possibility of mistaken recollection or fabrication. The defence, however, was denied this opportunity because of what I find to have been feigned memory loss on the part of Ms. E," ruled Justice Josephson.

"Thus, proof of Mr. Bagri's guilt beyond a reasonable doubt rests upon hearsay statements for which there is no reliable confirmatory evidence," the judge ruled.

"Considering the evidence as a whole, I find that the Crown has not proved its case against Mr. Bagri beyond a reasonable doubt with respect to his being a member of the alleged conspiracy or a party to the alleged offences and, accordingly, I find him not guilty on each count of the Indictment."

Another thought that occurred to me about Ms. E's alleged statement to Laurie about Bagri's supposed visit on the "evening before the disaster" was that the bombing had happened on Sunday, June 23, 1985. Ms. E would have heard the news in the morning on Sunday. The evening before that would have been Saturday. By that time, both bombs had already been checked in several hours before the alleged visit by Bagri to borrow her car.

Arguments in the Air India trial ended on December 3, 2004. Three-and-a-half months later, the inconsistencies, lack of evidence, and, above all, absence of credible witnesses would come home to roost when the judge delivered his verdict. The agony of the families of the victims and the Canadian public in general was reflected in Justice Josephson's devastating conclusion.

"I began by describing the horrific nature of these cruel acts of terrorism, acts which cry out for justice. Justice is not achieved, however, if persons are convicted on anything less than the requisite standard of proof beyond a reasonable doubt. Despite what appear to have been the best and most earnest of efforts by the police and the Crown, the evidence has fallen markedly short of that standard."

Malik and Bagri walked out free men after having spent four years in jail.

Outside the courthouse, after the verdict, there were swirling crowds of media interviewing lawyers, Crown counsel, and victim families. One radio reporter wanted an answer from me as the author of a previous book on this episode of terrorism. He stuck his microphone in my face and asked me if justice had been done.

Several television and radio shows would want to know the same thing from me over the next few days.

Yes, I said, justice had been done. It would be injustice to send someone to jail for life based on evidence beyond reasonable doubt and the testimony of such horrendously dubious witnesses. Compounding the injustice of terrorism with another injustice would just double our agony as a nation. We have convicted people before on flimsy beliefs and regretted it later; just ask David Milgaard how it feels to spend twenty-two years of your life behind bars for murder he did not commit.

TWELVE

THE DEATH OF AN INVESTIGATION:
A Post-mortem

The spectacular collapse of the case against Ripudaman Singh Malik and Ajaib Singh Bagri led to an outcry from the families of victims, and a call for a national inquiry into the Air India bombing.

Many family members believed the case had been mishandled, both by the RCMP and CSIS, which they said had erased evidence that could have been used in the proceedings against Malik and Bagri. Others unfairly blamed the judge for not believing Ms. D.

The distress of family members was evident on March 16, 2005, as they streamed from the courthouse in tears. I watched in grim silence as Eddie Madon and his sister Natasha walked out, supporting their mother Perviz, as they slowly made their way to the parking lot. It was a painful sight. I remember thinking that this could be described as the second Air India disaster—an agonizing unearthing of buried memories along with an overwhelming sense of justice delayed and then denied. I had talked to Perviz and her children many times since 1985. At this moment, though, I decided intruding into her grief for a response to the verdict was an invasion of privacy. The anguish etched on her face told a story that a million words could not express.

Many victim families had been flown in to see justice being done. Some had come from half-a-world away, and watched proceedings in the ultra-costly $7-million courtroom specially built for the case. Their expectations had been raised disproportionately to the reality of the Crown's fragile case. I wondered if anyone had told them not to hold high hopes. I doubted if this kind of caution would have come from Crown lawyers who were so certain of a conviction they had arranged a party for cops and themselves for that night. This sudden let-down resulted in the families pouring out blame—bitterly blasting the Canadian government for a series of failures, including but not limited to what they considered unconscionable bungling by the RCMP and CSIS. A few blamed racism. They believed the police had not worked hard enough because the victims were Indo-Canadians.

That was—to me—an unfair charge, but emotions were running high. In my many years dealing with dozens of RCMP officers assigned to the Air India bombing, officers with whom I had the closest contact of any reporter in Canada, I never witnessed nor had any indication of even a hint of racism. The officers I knew had spent hundreds and hundreds of hours dedicated to finding and ulti-mately to convicting the guilty. It was not because of a lack of personal commitment that the investigation had failed. Mistakes were made, perhaps too many. There *were* many instances of sloppy or incomplete work by law enforcement and intelligence service investigators, including failures to follow up on tempting leads and an overreliance on polygraphs to rule out suspects, rather than using "old fashioned" legwork.

The RCMP suffered from a simple—and perhaps, in retrospect, an inexcusable—indifference to Canada's diverse cultures. It was an institutional failure. With few Indo-Canadian officers compared to the population, law enforcement was virtually handicapped in any effort to penetrate or infiltrate militant groups. It could not be done by white cops. It seemed to me, as well, that despite oftentimes heroic efforts on the part of some officers, the mood too often was to sit back and wait for evidence to come to them. But I never saw a tinge of racism.

Having said that, I must acknowledge—and applaud—the brilliant investigation by RCMP at the outset of the probe that resulted in the conviction of Reyat. He was convicted for his role in the Narita explosion and also in the case of the Air India Flight 182 bombing, two intertwined crimes. It was hard work done on sniffing out forensic evidence in the 1980s that had led to this, and Reyat will have spent a life-term in jail on both convictions by the time he is freed in 2008. Unfortunately, the committed effort seemed to slacken when what had been a criminal investigation morphed into an intelligence gathering operation.

Setting aside, if one can, the emotional responses of the victims, it must be acknowledged that terrorism trials are notoriously hard to prosecute–most especially in developed democracies with legal systems that respect the law and rules of evidence. K.P.S. Gill–the tough Punjab cop–scoffs at legal systems such as Canada's that strictly adhere to points of "legal formalism, such a ritualistic commitment to procedures." These systems, he argues, are doomed to defeat at the hands of terrorism.

After the verdict, I phoned him at his home in New Delhi for comment. He posed a rhetorical question: "How will democracies fight terrorism? Tell me."

Gill had harsh words for Canada and its "permissive" legal system and lax intelligence and law enforcement services.

Indeed, he complained bitterly that Indian intelligence and enforcement agencies had repeatedly provided hard evidence to Canadian intelligence and enforcement agencies on the activities of Sikh terrorists in Canada, but to no avail. It was, in fact, only after the 9/11 events in the U.S., he claimed, that Canada woke up to the reality of terrorism. In a sense this was true. It was not until after the 9/11 tragedies that Canada finally banned the BK and the ISYF as terrorist entities and made it illegal for anyone to assist the two organizations or finance them.

However, when I told Gill that his own country had allowed both Ripudaman Singh Malik and Hardial Singh Johal free passes to travel throughout India–despite ample warnings–Gill admitted, somewhat sheepishly, that he had not been aware of such a security breach. And Gill said he was not aware either of the fact that the State Bank of India branch in Vancouver had given Malik a $2-million loan at a favourable rate in 1984, at a time when Malik had already demonstrated close proximity to Parmar, a fact known to Indian agents in Vancouver.

Gill insisted that a "scorched earth" approach to rooting out terrorists had worked in the Punjab and nothing short of a similar policy in North America would work. He had nothing but disdain for the more congenial and less aggressive techniques that characterized Canadian law enforcement.

"They should have put the suspects through tough interrogation," he suggested of the RCMP.

As if to support his charge, I recalled that when Hardial Singh Johal was arrested and questioned in November 2000, RCMP interrogators practically fell over themselves in attempts to lay out a welcome mat. They began their interrogation by offering the suspect a muffin and a bagel. An observer may well have wondered whether Johal was under interrogation in connection to one of history's most brutal acts of terrorism, or had been cordially invited to a tea party.

If the RCMP strategy was to disarm through kindness the man I considered the mastermind of the bombing, it failed famously.

The interview with Malik had been even more relaxed. The cops talked and talked while Malik gently parried. What might have been a bare-knuckles interrogation–along the lines advocated by Gill– had turned into a complex but slow-moving dance or a surreal game of cat-and-mouse. The question became, however, who was the cat and who the mouse? Too often sloppy questioning allowed the interrogated to seize the upper hand.

At one point when interrogators were questioning Malik, for instance, they unadvisedly, and falsely, suggested that Surjan Singh Gill had been a CSIS agent. This was a charge Malik would never believe about a man who had been a close friend of his, and the cops should have known that. Instead of luring him in, they put him on his guard and seemed at a loss about how to proceed with the interrogation to a conclusive end. Somewhat desperately, they offered Malik a deal: a walk in exchange for information.

But Malik knew from their demeanour that there was no compelling evidence tending to implicate him, so the "walk" offer rang hollow. He seemed to be more concerned about the length of the trial and how it would affect his multi-million-dollar business rather than the strength of the evidence against him. At one point Malik suggested that if the allegation against him was that he gave Parmar money, then why was Inderjit Singh Reyat buying parts for a bomb on his Visa card?

One cop in the interview room could not even pronounce Ripudaman Malik's first name, and erroneously kept referring to him as "Daman." At the very least, it showed careless preparation. And the tea-party atmosphere continued.

Cop: Do you want another cookie before we go?

Malik: Okay, Sure.

Malik grew so comfortable that at one point—apparently exhausted and in need of relief from the ordeal—he asked if he could take a shower. Astonishingly, the interrogators agreed. When Malik returned, he appeared—not surprisingly—refreshed and completely at ease!

"Now," he commented airily, "where were we, guys?"

Back in the Punjab, Malik's family had nicknamed him "Machoo," which means fish, since he wiggled like an eel rather than crawl like other babies.

It is fair to debate the value or efficacy of K.P.S. Gill's methods. Western democracies cherish their traditions of law and order and do not take the suspension of civil liberties lightly. On the other hand, seldom have Western democracies experienced the levels of civil unrest and violence as has India, for instance, where as many as 36,000 people have died in the Punjab.

One can only wonder how law-abiding Canadians would react to hundreds—thousands—of their fellow citizens being gunned down in the streets, or blown up in restaurants.

In the wake of the acquittals in the Air India case, I have often thought about the question I was asked by a reporter outside the Vancouver courthouse: had justice been done?

Inderjit Singh Reyat had been convicted. I knew that some had taken solace in the violent death of Parmar at the hands of the Indian police. What's more, the B.C. Supreme Court had ruled, based on salvage operations carried out by the RCMP in which they had retrieved 5 per cent of the Air India plane and expert evidence, that a bomb had indeed destroyed the plane. This was the first time a legal tribunal had made that ruling in Canada.

Progress, perhaps, but justice?

My answer *then* was the same as it is *now*. One man had been convicted and two others against whom there had been no believable evidence had been acquitted. The legal system had worked as it was designed to. Justice *had been* done. My answer, I felt, reflected the ambivalence I always felt in this case. On the one hand I understood and felt the pain of the victim families, yet, I had to often set those conflicting emotions aside and do my job as a reporter. And that sometimes meant writing about the violation of fundamental rights of individuals like Reyat. My job was to remain as dispassionate as possible.

There is a pledge, a solemn commitment in the Canadian Charter of Rights which states, "Everyone has the right to life, liberty and security of the person and the right not to be deprived thereof except in accordance with the principles of fundamental justice."

That guarantee that the liberty of individuals cannot be taken away except in accordance with the principles of fundamental justice was sometimes forgotten by reporters as well as they let their emotions dictate the tone of their stories. This was Canada, not K.P.S. Gill's India. I chose to live in Canada, and made this country my home, because of the selfsame guarantees of fundamental human rights that Gill held in such contempt. As a reporter who had been on the case continuously from the very beginning, I was only too aware of the extremely complicated nature of the Air India case. Ultimately, casting aside my emotions, I could not then nor can I now contemplate a verdict different from the one handed down by Justice Josephson. Emotion cannot play a role in the administration of justice. What is your evidence? That is the only mantra the justice system understands. Justice Josephson made this very point in his ruling. No matter how dastardly the crime, the standard of proof required to convict cannot be lowered. In this case, as he so poignantly pointed out, evidence had fallen "markedly short."

I wonder still why the case had gone to court when it was so weak, and so fraught with so many credibility problems. It cruelly raised expectations among grieving family members who believed they had been denied justice for so very long.

There are many in law enforcement and the public who liken the fight against terrorism as a war, where the fundamental guarantees ordained by the Canadian Charter of Rights and Freedoms should not apply. When I left Tanzania in 1976, no proof was required to jail a citizen. Freedom could be taken away for arbitrary reasons. Dissent was not tolerated. Knowing how many journalists were in "preventive detention" in Tanzania for raising issues the government did not like to hear about, I am convinced that there is no threat so serious–not even terrorism–to justify setting aside or suspending constitutional guarantees and the right to a fair trial.

The fight against terrorism does not have to resort to extrajudicial or extraconstitutional concepts. I don't see the fight against terrorism as a war. I believe it can be won–but painfully and inevitably over time–by a commitment to traditional and time-honoured techniques of law enforcement. The failure in the Air India case was not a failure of the system; it was a failure to carry out a comprehensive investigation.

Despite twenty years of investigation by the RCMP, comprehensive knowledge of what happened in the Air India bombing remained sketchy and rudimentary.

There were only three suspects we could–with anything like certainty–know were involved in the bombing: Reyat, Johal and Parmar. I was also almost certain about Amarjit Singh Pawa's involvement, the ticketing agent for Parmar I had seen sitting at the Air India office on that tragic day on June 23, 1985.

Reyat had acknowledged his role testing the makeshift bombs, as well as having purchased bomb parts. As a result, he pleaded guilty to manslaughter in the Air India Flight 182 case. It was his testimony that Parmar had asked him to make bombs to do a "big job." Parmar most definitely monitored the progress of Reyat while he perfected the bomb. Parmar also fled Canada–most likely with the knowledge that he might be next–when he learned of the law enforcement attempt to extradite Reyat.

I was convinced as well that Johal was the brain "inside" the Air India bombing. It was Johal who had introduced Parmar to Reyat. Further, Reyat and Johal were fundamentalist members of the same prayer group. It was a phone number traceable to Johal that was left behind when a man booked tickets for the Air India flight. He was independently identified as being present at the airport when the suspect bags were being checked in. Around the same time the explosives were being delivered to Vancouver by Reyat, there were back-and-forth calls from Reyat's home in Duncan to Johal's home in Vancouver. We had heard from good Sikh contacts that Johal had helped store the bombs at an empty school early on Saturday June 22, 1985, just before they had been dispatched. That made sense to me. Such deadly bombs made by an amateur bomb-maker that Reyat was, would hardly be trusted to be stored at someone's home.

I remain convinced that Parmar–the man I had come to know thoroughly–lacked the brains to conjure up such a diabolically clever plot. Others more clever than he manipulated him, I believe. The person who directed him, I strongly suspect, was Johal. All the intercepts and activities show that Johal did more work and coordinated more activities related to this bombing than anyone else, including picking timetables, liaising with travel agent Pawa, booking tickets, housing Reyat in Vancouver, and supervising the bag check-ins. Pawa had earlier also diverted the son of a friend from flying aboard Air India on June 22, 1985. The least that can be said from this is that Pawa was coordinating with Johal on the ticket bookings and flight time-tables so critical to the success of this plot.

By the end of 2005, there was simply no hard evidence against anyone else. Yes, many people had proximity to Parmar and Johal, but association did not equate to participation in a conspiracy. A Sikh of my acquaintance confirmed to me that he had warned people from his temple not to travel by Air India just a few days before the explosion. And when people at the Sikh temple in Vancouver gathered around to talk about the tragedy on Sunday, June 23, 1985, this man went around proclaiming, "We told you not to travel by Air India." There is also an intercept from a bug in Parmar's home that is in police custody that has not been made public. The gist of the conversation by a group of men was this: if no one talks, how will they catch us? Pre-knowledge or post-crime knowledge, of course, does not equate to participation. It is not an offence to know about a conspiracy. It is an offence to participate in one.

One of the key failures in the Air India bombing was the fact that many of the men under suspicion had remained unidentified. This proved fatal to the Crown's case. It was a key hindrance to providing supporting evidence that could have backed up witnesses. Who was the mysterious Mr. X who went to the island with Parmar on June 4, 1985, to watch the bomb-experiment in the woods? Who were the other two men seen at the Woolworths store in Duncan picking out the stereo that was delivered to Reyat? Who picked up the tickets? Who stuffed the bombs inside a bag? Who bought the bags? Who timed the devices? Who was the man with Reyat when he went to Auto Marine Electric in Burnaby on June 22, 1985, while Reyat bought a battery for the Tokyo bomb and asked for an employee discount? Who were the two who checked in the bags–the so-called L. Singh and M. Singh? We don't even know what L. Singh looked like because he checked in the bag with a confirmed ticket and there was no fuss over that bag that went to Tokyo.

Many Sikh militants whom I visited at their homes had whispered names of people who they said were involved. Some told me whom to chase to identify Mr. X–that fellow from Toronto as Parmar's kids had called him–but over the years we could not find confirmatory evidence. I also had names of people Sikh friends insisted had checked in the bags, or picked up the tickets. But there was an absence of concrete proof. I felt the RCMP were never able to exploit this knowledge that had been passed on to them as well.

But in the absence of useable evidence, we had for years been guessing endlessly about the roles of individuals who we felt were close to Parmar and Johal–the sense that we all knew what happened had collared our thought patterns. Preconceived notions also destroyed the RCMP's ability to be open minded.

Part of the reason the RCMP were tunnelled into simple perceptions were the CSIS wiretaps and surveillance of Parmar. The thinking of the RCMP was that all the evidence had to tie in with Parmar. He had been construed as the hub from which all other spokes of this conspiracy radiated. Preconceived notions–such as CSIS's belief that the major danger during "Black June" (the anniversary of the Golden Temple attack) was a possible attack on Gandhi during his Washington, DC. trip–turned out to be false. It allowed people to execute a terrorist bombing under the noses of our spies. While they sat outside and listened to Parmar's calls, he was able to commit a crime of horrendous proportions. It was also an assumption based on a partial picture that had led CSIS to conclude the blast they heard in the woods on June 4, 1985, was a gunshot.

But the critical fact of this case was that neither the RCMP nor CSIS had a panoramic view of the other key plotters. Hardial Singh Johal had such a pivotal role in this that he may have recruited the people who checked in the bags. But the RCMP did not pay as much attention to Johal as they paid to Malik. A media blitz aided by Ms. D had left the impression with cops that Malik was a real big fish. This attention focussed on Malik resulted in a substantial waste of time and money as well as resources between 1997 and 2005. The cops became obsessed with Malik, just as much as Ms. D was.

Since most CSIS tapes were destroyed, only paraphrased transcripts remained, often not even verbatim, the RCMP had a narrow view through a peephole into the life of Parmar. Retention of the tapes could have given investigators more information, since CSIS did not initially even realize the relevance of Parmar's conversations. Post-crash analysis could have given new meaning to conversation discarded as useless.

The threshold of evidence required for conviction was far from satisfied in this case. There was strong reason to believe the evidence against Malik was based on a composite story gathered from several different sources rather than straight from the horse's mouth. To convict a man on the basis of the testimony of such a witness is to court the huge danger of a miscarriage of justice. There was also, and there always had been, a lack of corroborating evidence against Malik although investigators had viewed him with great suspicion for many years. Association and proximity do not equate to participation in a crime. It was clear from our many years of investigating Malik's life that he was a friend of Parmar's and even Reyat and that the families of both men called on him often for support. After Reyat was convicted, Malik provided his wife with assistance, but so did dozens of other devoted Sikhs. This financial support of Parmar or Reyat's families meant little and no inferences can be drawn from it.

In a meeting I had with Chief Prosecutor Bob Wright prior to the commencement of trial, I had pointed out, when asked, that the nature of the evidence was that Malik, for no explainable reason, had blurted out the names of a group of men who had been tasked with specific functions. And that confession had been given to a woman who hugged him but did not kiss him. She made it clear this was not pillow talk.

If Malik had been involved in this crime as project manager (as Ms. D described him) and had rattled off a bunch of names, including the names of people who had gone to the airport with bag bombs, then I would be looking for some key indicators of truthfulness, I told Wright.

Nowhere in Ms. D's information did we see the names of at least three of the mystery people who we had hunted for so many years, yet remained unidentified despite the so-called confession. For example, who were the two men who checked in the bags? Who was Mr. X who went to Vancouver Island? If Malik had played the key role she attributed to him, and had gone so far as to describe the names of the people who took the bags to the airport, then why would he stop there? Why not go on and name two more names of the people who actually boarded the bags? Why would he not name the mystery man Mr. X if he was in the mood to rattle off names and jobs carried out by each? If the confession was so detailed that it included the colour of a van that went to the airport, I did not see why the three men whose names were not in the public domain were not identified.

The other names Ms. D obtained were in the public domain, including the name of Daljit Singh Sandhu, who some moderates in the community whispered about. Justice Josephson cleared Sandhu, saying he doubted if a man with such a high profile in the Sikh community would get involved so publicly in picking up tickets. Sandhu was no doubt looked at during the investigation, yet there was not a shred of corroborative evidence against him. I talked to him often. I knew why he had surfaced as a suspect—as a community leader he rushed to get legal counsel for Reyat when he was first arrested in 1985. Someone saw him sitting at lawyer David Gibbons' office and began circulating rumours about him. Helping someone get a lawyer cannot be read under any situation as participation in a crime. But this is how desperate this investigation was. There is no one that I know of today who can even begin to speculate about who picked up those tickets. Many militant Sikhs wore the same kind of net around the beard that Sandhu did. Also, ticket agent Gerald Duncan did not identify Sandhu as the man who picked up the tickets. For me, it was important that Sandhu had testified for the defence during this trial. In my opinion, Sandhu would have never agreed to take the stand not knowing what mud the prosecution could throw at him. It was Sandhu's way of telling the Crown and the cops, "Hey, I am here in the witness box, now put up or shut up."

"Do you believe her?" lead prosecutor Bob Wright asked me about Ms. D during our meeting prior to the trial.

"No, I don't," I had said, as we sipped coffee in the cafeteria at RCMP headquarters in Vancouver.

"Well, we'll see," he replied. "She is sticking to her story."

Sadly, three years later, Justice Bruce Josephson would tell Wright the same thing as I had.

By accepting Ms. D's story that Malik had booked the tickets, the RCMP had discarded their own evidence. In fact, they had overlooked some potent evidence against Johal. Going beyond what the evidence shows you is highly dangerous and takes you dead in the centre of a destructive minefield of speculation.

The allegation that Malik booked the tickets flew in the face of evidence police had believed for the longest period of time; that Hardial Singh Johal had booked the tickets and left behind a phone number that had been his just a few months before. This phone number had two characteristics traceable to Johal. First, it had been Johal's actual phone number prior to his move in 1984. Second, the last four digits of his new phone number had remained the same even after he moved. When a person is suddenly asked for a phone number, that person is likely to leave behind a familiar phone number. Only Johal would have remembered his own recent phone number in an instant that it took him to respond to the question from the ticket agent with whom he was on the phone.

The RCMP belief that Johal booked the tickets was supported by the fact that Parmar had phoned him on June 19, 1985, and asked him to "write the story." Within minutes of that call, tickets had been booked by a caller who phoned CP Air's reservations number. Then Johal called Parmar back to say he had "written the story" and asked if Parmar would go over and look at it. During the time Parmar's phone calls were monitored, there were plenty of evidence of coded conversations between Parmar and Johal and others. But no coded conversations were noted between Parmar and Malik. While Parmar often referred to Johal by his nickname—Dyal (a short form for Hardial), indicating a degree of familiarity and camaraderie between the two hardliners—Parmar's references to Malik were almost always more formal. He called him Mr. Malik. As for the issue of financing the tickets, it appeared Malik was the one who was asking for a loan of $100,000 from Parmar around that time, an indication that Parmar could handle the cost of some $3,500 to blow up two airplanes. Further, it was highly unlikely the RCMP would find a slip of paper that would show who paid for the tickets. It was a futile avenue of investigation. Only a few days before the tickets were paid for and picked up, a conversation on Parmar's phone was intercepted. Parmar had asked an associate to get him large bills. That is the form the payment for the tickets took: cold cash. And it is evident that cold cash was in Parmar's hands in hundred-dollar bills just days before the tickets were picked up with wads of cash, in large bills.

Johal was also the person independently identified as being at Vancouver Airport on June 22, 1985. His presence at the scene of the crime was another key indicator corroborating his central role in the Air India bombing. Further, telephone calls to and from Reyat's home at a time when Reyat was not in Duncan on the evening of June 21, and the daylight hours of June 22, 1985, indicated that family members left behind in Duncan were aware that their contact point for Reyat was Johal's home phone number in Vancouver. This was during the crucial hours when bombs were being loaded into bags in preparation for boarding and a few hours after the bombs had been dispatched.

On the day the bombs were checked in, Parmar telephoned Johal to ask if he had "mailed the letters," to which Johal replied he had "mailed the letters." The two then met to discuss the "mailing of the letters." That was incredible. Who would meet to discuss the mailing of letters? What they really wanted to discuss was sending off the bombs and how that had worked out at the airport.

It was clear who the RCMP suspected of booking the tickets: Johal.

A June 28, 1995, memo from Staff-Sergeant Don Brost that lists RCMP suspects, reads, "Hardial Singh Johal, currently residing in Vancouver. Was an associate of Parmar's prior to the bombing. Prior to the bombing the plane ticket reservations utilized the phone number of Johal's. When the tickets were picked up the phone number was changed. The registered owner of the new number was an associate of Johal's."

In an affidavit to obtain wiretap authorization, the requesting officer wrote, "I strongly suspect that, given that the targets of this affidavit frequently spoke in codes and the circumstances of the timing of the calls, the hypothesis that the phone calls from Mr. Johal to Mr. Parmar represent communications regarding the booking of the tickets is not only viable, it is highly probable."

In 1985, Hardial Singh Johal had a track record of Sikh activism and militancy. As stated earlier, even during his youth, Johal had been so vigorous in making demands for Sikh rights that he landed in jail several times in India, the first time when he was only fourteen. He went to jail in India a total of eight times. He had also been heavily involved in making sure that Sikhs who entered the temple at Ross Street wore head-coverings. In short, he was a fanatical political activist. Johal was also heavily involved in the politics of the Punjab while he lived in Canada and was active in the executive of the Ross Street temple.

For me and for many cops with whom I carried out a postmortem following the verdict, it was clear that all the tracks from Parmar's home led to Johal's, from ticket bookings to supervision of the bag check-in to even possibly housing the bag bombs at a school where he was working the night shift at the time of the bombings. All the telephone tracks from the suspected bombmaker, Reyat, also led directly to Johal's home on two crucial days of June 21, and June 22, 1985. There were no calls to Malik from Reyat's home during that significant time period.

When I asked Johal how he first learned of the explosions, he told me he kept his radio tuned to the BBC World Service, which broadcasts out of London. He heard the news while most people in Vancouver were still in bed. To me that was a telling sign. He was tuned to London. He knew where the first news of an explosion aboard Air India Flight 182 (which would have made a stopover in London) would come from. I strongly believe that the bomb was timed to explode at Heathrow Airport while the aircraft was on the ground. It blew up in the air because it was delayed leaving Canada.

Since there was corroborating evidence against Johal, he should have been snared in a conspiracy charge. However, he was not charged and I suspect that was because if he was in the dock, the Crown would have to assert his role in booking the tickets. But that would have taken away from the evidence of Ms. D that it was Malik who had done the deed.

Since the 1991 conviction of Reyat in relation to the Tokyo bomb, the RCMP had become stuck. It was Willy Laurie of CSIS who first obtained information from Bagri's friend–the so-called Ms. E. The RCMP's attempt to talk to her in 1985 produced no results. It was the FBI that forwarded the source–"John" of New York–to testify about Bagri's alleged "we did it" story.

Even the unbelievable Ms. D, had been forwarded to RCMP by CSIS.

Now, since they had failed to find anyone in all these years, once they got these so-called witnesses from other agencies, it seemed the RCMP had failed to collate and collect all possible evidence respecting their new-found sources. The legwork was absent. Elementary things such as whether suspects had alibis were not thoroughly checked out, their investigation of Ms. D's statement was not thorough, their probe of Narinder Gill's story that tended to corroborate some of what Ms. D said, and their line of questioning of him almost amateurish about the travels of the brown van. In short, their investigation was so incomplete that the Crown had been forced to absorb serious body blows from a pummelling by defence lawyers.

Many top cops, some retired, agreed on the general scale of failures. The most serious shortcoming was a failure to do legwork. There was no corroborating evidence obtained to support any of Ms. D's allegations, the police conceded. Many promising suspects were abandoned or discarded for no better reason than that they passed lie detectors. Conversely, the stories of many witnesses were adopted as "gospel" even though their lie detector results suggested their information or credibility was "iffy."

Notwithstanding the fact that it was a new agency still finding it's feet, CSIS had failed dramatically. Its failure to translate eighty-one tapes of Parmar's conversations from a two-month period in 1985 for over five months after the bombing was just one of many blunders. Why monitor conversations of terrorists if no one has any intention of actually listening to the tapes?

The scale of the failure was even more spectacular when one takes into account how careless the terrorists were in planning the attack: the paper trail was a mile long! Bomb parts were purchased with credit cards. Suspects even asked for employee discounts while making incriminating purchases!

What professional terrorist would wait to book tickets until three days prior to the arranged date? What kind of experienced terrorist would show up with a bomb in his bag and not even know for sure if his reservation on the same flight was confirmed? What if Jeanne Adams had stuck to her guns and refused to check in the bag? Is that why Reyat had gone out and bought a second battery because if the first check-in failed then he could have re-timed the device for dispatch to Tokyo? If that was the thinking on his part, then we could have ended up with one bomb rather than two.

The Air India bombing almost didn't happen but for a series of human errors. It was only the scale of the tragedy that made it seem the work of a large experienced criminal organization.

One of the key questions posed throughout the period from 1985 to 2005 was whether Indian government agents had carried out this act by using one of their agent provocateurs within the BK and its allied groups.

I met with senior aides to former Ontario Premier Bob Rae who was tasked by the former Liberal government to decide if a national inquiry was merited in the case. Air India Review Secretariat officers Michelle Sample and Taleeb Noormohamed sat with me at my home for almost two hours. They were looking for guidance about what Rae should be looking for in the event that he recommended to the government of Canada a national inquiry into the tragedy. What, they asked, were the outstanding issues? I pointed out that one of the allegations in the Sikh community was that Indian government agents were involved in the bombing and that it was important that an inquiry put this to rest. CSIS had conducted a comprehensive investigation of Indian government agents in Canada using some of their best counter-intelligence abilities. Following this investigation, they concluded that the agents of

R&AW and India's Intelligence Bureau who were stationed in Canada played no role in the bombing. CSIS had extensive surveillance on Indian spies in the mid-1980s and fourteen agents—based on that surveillance—were expelled and returned to India.

Those agents included Gurinder Singh and Harkishen Singh, his assistant in Vancouver. In Toronto, CSIS fingered R&AW agent S. Grewal and, in Ottawa, Indian agent Sunder Kumar among others. Canada did this quietly, so as not to disrupt friendly relations with India. Canada signed an intelligence sharing agreement with India to make it unnecessary for India to send spies here surreptitiously. However, a constant stream of agents continued to come in as diplomats, until the Sikh insurgency was brought under control. Many Canadian Sikhs are still on blacklists and cannot go to India.

The RCMP told me some of the suspects appeared to have counter-intelligence ability, I said to Sample and Noormohamed. The RCMP watched in awe as a suspect in whose car they planted a bug, parked it two days later and took off the car plates. Then, when the Mounties removed the bug upon expiry of their warrant, the suspect promptly put the plates back on and merrily drove away. The cop who told me this said there is no way the suspect could have discovered that they were planting the bugs. It would lead to suspicion that a translator at RCMP headquarters may have been leaking information since he was found to be a distant relative of one of the suspects. Cops don't like talking about this episode publicly, but one source said the translator was let go. Another cop said the investigation of whether there was a leak at headquarters was handed to RCMP's major crime section but nothing came of it.

I told the two members of Rae's team that I talked with Gurinder Singh about the issue of any Indian involvement as the Sikh community was full of chatter about this and a book had been written in Canada blaming the bombing on Indian agents.

"The prime minister would never approve such a project," said Gurinder Singh, adding a project of such horrendous proportions would have never been sanctioned by any government of India. Consul-general Jagdish Sharma was asked about this too. His response was "CSIS did it."

Government sources attribute meetings between Gurinder Singh and Johal to an agent's search for answers in the attack on one of their planes and the deaths of one hundred Indians aboard the aircraft. Gurinder Singh was doing what agents do—recruiting informants. The RCMP would have gladly recruited Johal. CSIS would have done so too. And I know Gurinder Singh gave me a list of names of people who worked at Vancouver Airport with access to secure areas even though they had relatives or friends suspected of terrorism. The two names of suspects Gurinder Singh had told me were available with newspaper editor Tara Singh Hayer were people who had worked at Vancouver Airport. But police had dismissed them as suspects after investigating and taking them in for polygraphs.

Many of the claims of government of India involvement in Air India came from the Sikh militant lobby, since the incident brought incredible pressure on them from law enforcement agencies in the West. To that end, the claim would appear to be a self-serving attempt to deflect blame. It was important to hear from CSIS publicly about their findings on this issue, I said.

I also told the pair that Rae should hold a focussed inquiry rather than a broad-ranging one. I told them I did not believe an inquiry can find people criminally responsible. Under our constitution, I said it would be unconscionable if a public inquiry attempted to second-guess findings made in our courts. Clearly, outstanding issues include the working relationship between CSIS and the RCMP; the overlap of anti-terrorism work; the question of how to make sure our security service was not dragged into the courts every time a terrorist crime occurred; and how CSIS warrants can, and whether they should, even be used in our courts.

On November 23, 2005, I was pleased to see Bob Rae's recommendations to the government in a report entitled "Lessons to Be Learned."

He had wisely not made it an open-ended inquiry but focussed his attention in areas where deficiencies have come to light. Much of this book deals with those deficiencies. We need to sort out how we will deal with future threats if the RCMP and CSIS continue to tread on each other's toes. We need to prepare for the bigger threat of Islamic fundamentalism that we now face as a nation. I was also glad that Rae understood he cannot undertake to "convict" anyone. Rae said in his report to then Deputy Prime Minister Anne McLellan that in his meetings with relatives he was most often confronted with the demand that he find out who did this and bring them to justice. But others told him that what we need to as a nation is find out what went wrong and correct those issues that led to the disaster.

In summing up his call for a focussed national inquiry, Rae told the government, "The inquiry I am recommending will not provide 'closure' for the families or for anyone else. But it should provide us with further insight and better practices."

McLellan accepted the recommendations made by Rae and appointed him to conduct an inquest into key areas where failures occurred in the functioning of the RCMP and CSIS, into transportation security, financing of terrorism, and witness protection. The new minister of justice, Vic Toews, said in March 2006 that his government is looking at whether to call a full-blown judicial inquiry, as opposed to the limited probe authorized by the former Liberal government. I know that the prospect of a judicial inquiry is something the RCMP, CSIS as well as Crown counsel dread. It could be highly damaging to wash the dirty laundry of public institutions before a judicial inquiry.

As the dust settled from the Air India trial debacle, the RCMP got together a think-tank to analyze what had gone wrong. One of the conclusions was that a failure to find corroborating evidence and Ms. D's inconsistency on the witness stand had accounted for a failure to convict. The RCMP also decided to appoint veteran investigator Inspector Dan Bond to head a small task force of eight cops to review the evidence without preconceived notions. What could they do next in an investigation that had stretched twenty years and was now littered with dead suspects and dead witnesses as well as two who had been acquitted?

I thought Bond was a thinking man who understood clearly the direction the RCMP needed to take to tackle the many outstanding suspects who could be pursued. The task was to figure out who could be cultivated to get information that we knew existed in some areas about the identifies of the missing suspects such as Mr. X and the two men who checked in the bags.

But there was also a realization among top cops that the passing of so much time had caused enormous damage to the investigation.

For the most part the trail that once may have been red hot had gone–for all intents and purposes–ice cold. Travel agent Amarjit Singh Pawa was dead. Hardial Singh Johal died a few months after his arrest and release in November 2000. Babbar Khalsa operative Avtar Singh Narwal, who turned up at Parmar's home on the eve of the bag check-ins in Bagri's borrowed car, had also died. Narwal died in a mysterious car crash in the B.C. in 1998. While driving in broad daylight his car drifted onto the side of the road and went into Nicola Lake near Merritt. Witnesses said he made no effort to get out as his car sank. When he was dragged to the surface by a motorist after fifteen minutes, he was dead. A cop who worked on the investigation said the manner in which the car went into the water–"for no apparent reason"–raised eyebrows. Narwal's insurance company was suspicious, too, especially as he had had only recently taken out a large policy.

I was unable to confirm the outcome of the insurance company's internal investigation, but the police officer's report on the scene said it was broad daylight when the car slowly drifted onto the side and into the water. There was no mechanical problem with the car, he said.

I phoned Narwal's home in Kamloops, and a family member ruled out suicide, adding, "only *Wahe Guru* (God) knows what happened."

Parmar was killed by police in India in 1992.

Still, all was not lost. It was worth revisiting some of the people who had been approached in the past and one of the people the RCMP continued to be interested in was Parmar's brother, Kulwarn, who had turned up on some interesting CSIS intercepts.

For example, Kulwarn had called his brother on June 22, 1985 and asked if that work had been done. Parmar had replied, "Not yet." This conversation turned up on an RCMP affidavit showing clearly they were interested in what he was asking about. A few hours before the June 4, 1985 incident when the mysterious Mr. X had emerged from Parmar's house and was then followed to Duncan for that blast in the woods, there had been a few interesting calls from Talwinder Singh Parmar's home to airline offices and to ticket agent Pawa's office about a flight arriving from Toronto. Police believed Parmar's family was inquiring about a flight that carried Mr. X to Vancouver.

CSIS picked up a curious conversation at approximately 3 a.m. on June 4. Parmar phoned his younger brother Kulwarn at his home and asked him for a ride to the airport to pick up a visitor. Parmar instructed Kulwarn that he would have to go inside the terminal building and pick up the visitor. The RCMP think the man picked up on that flight from Toronto was Mr. X. Once again, this information was laid out in RCMP affidavits showing their interest in whom Kulwarn Parmar picked up at the airport in the company of his brother.

In November 2005, the Superintendent of Financial Institutions, W. Alan Clark, removed Malik from the board of directors of the Khalsa Credit Union, which Malik had founded. One of the reasons was the allegation that Malik had provided funds to Parmar and that, allegedly, constituted support for terrorism, according to Clark. Malik challenged this decision in the Supreme Court of B.C. Documents I searched that Malik had filed showed the superintendent of financial institutions was also concerned about Malik's purported application to join the BK group in 1985–at a time when it was a charitable society incorporated by the B.C. government. The application form to join the BK was seemingly signed by Malik. His friends say the application form to join the BK was a forgery and Malik said he was never a member of any terrorist organization as alleged by the financial institution. According to documents filed in the B.C. Supreme Court, the information used by the superintendent of financial institutions used to oust Malik from the credit union had come from Kulwarn Parmar, who had earlier attempted to run against Malik for directorship of the Khalsa Credit Union. It was a sign that former friends were now at loggerheads.

By February 2006, the RCMP had multiple little projects on the go in an effort to snare many of the other conspirators who existed. The stinging rebuke from the court had caused the cops to scratch their heads and go back to the drawing board. A realization had set in that some fresh ideas were needed to snare people who had so far remained out of police sights but people who should have been targeted earlier. There was a realization finally that many people had played small but important supporting roles in the terrorist episode, for example, helping to drive people around to carry out tasks related to the conspiracy. These folks were important to chase, even if their roles were minor compared to some of the terrorists who had died over the long investigative period.

On another front, Inderjit Singh Reyat and his lawyer John Hill of Toronto were getting ready for a National Parole Board hearing to decide if it was safe to let Reyat out of prison after serving two-thirds of his sentence of five years that he had been given with the plea agreement that crown had gleefully signed and probably regretted later. Crown's dream team had not figured out what I had about Reyat when they signed the deal in the hope he would testify truthfully in court while under oath. They had even failed to get him to sign on to a statement about what he would say if he was called to testify. And a part of the agreement between the Crown and Reyat was that he would not even be required to talk to the Crown or police before his testimony. That is as naïve as it gets. Now the Crown needed a comeback of some sort to save face.

On February 17, 2006, Inderjit Singh Reyat got a rude shock. He was charged with perjury—an offence rarely laid despite the fact that dozens of people testifying on witness stands every day lie in their testimony. During my long years covering trials, I have seen even police officers tell less than the full truth on the stand.

Crown Counsel Spokesman Geoff Gaul was adamant this was not about sour grapes, but lawyer John Hill was livid. He called the charges political window dressing aimed at placating the victim families and pointing a picture of cops hard at work to solve one of the worst cases of terrorism ever in the world. Gaul made public the charge, which accused Reyat of lying in at least twenty-seven instances during his testimony between September 10 and September 15, 2003. Most of these lies dealt with Reyat's dealings with Parmar: his testimony that he had not used dynamite during the test explosions in Duncan in June of 1985; that Parmar had asked him to make only one bomb as opposed to two; and that he had not discussed with Parmar what the bombs were going to be used for. The other allegations against him dealt with his dealing with Mr. X, who still remained unidentified at the time the perjury charge was laid against Reyat.

The fact that twenty-seven areas of false testimony had been alleged against Reyat was more of an indictment of the Crown than the accused. The Crown had originally charged Reyat with conspiracy to commit first-degree murder. And clearly they did not have the evidence to back it up—hence the plea agreement on a reduced charge of manslaughter of 329 people and a light prison term of five years. But now the Crown was claiming to have evidence that Reyat lied on crucial matters that indicated participation with knowledge and premeditation in the offence. And that totally backed up my assertion earlier that the charge of first-degree murder was highly inflated by an over-zealous Crown team.

As Reyat prepared for a bid to gain early release, his Toronto lawyer Hill had hired the services of forensic psychiatrist Dr. Karen De Freitas to carry out an in-prison assessment of Reyat. She met with him for nearly two hours. Reyat was warned by De Freitas that she was hired as an impartial assessor of his mindset and that no doctor-patient privilege applied in his conversations with her and any conversation he had with her could be used by the authorities against him. I don't know whether either De Freitas or Reyat were aware of the minefield they were walking through with this interview or even whether De Freitas will be called to testify in Reyat's perjury trial. But it seems to me that professionals need to pay heed to the dangers that exist with new laws that can be used to compel people with knowledge of terrorism to be brought before a judge to testify about their knowledge. This danger was particularly apparent in the case of De Freitas's conversation with Reyat since no privilege applied. The evidence she obtained is therefore useable in court against Reyat. The danger clearly exists that both Reyat and De Freitas had walked into peril by talking about a crime. De Freitas can be compelled to testify if the Crown so chooses.

Reyat made some startling admissions to her—admissions that went beyond his testimony at trial. I obtained a copy of her assessment report of the interview she carried out on January 12, 2006.

DeFreitas reports, "Mr. Reyat stated that in 1985 he was approached by Mr. Parmar, who was an acquaintance of his, and asked to help fellow Sikhs in India by helping to obtain explosives. Mr. Reyat stated that he initially told Mr. Parmar that he could not do this, but that Mr. Parmar continued to 'push' him."

Reyat stated to her that he eventually agreed to buy some parts to assist Mr. Parmar in making an explosive device. She said Reyat told her that he gave the parts to Parmar and his friend (Mr. X) and said to them, "Take those parts and do it yourself."

"Mr. Reyat stated that Mr. Parmar told him that he wanted to damage property such as cars and bridges in India, but that he would ensure that no one would be hurt," said De Freitas.

"I wasn't 100 per cent agreed...I took it maybe he knows what he is doing...if he wants the property to be damaged that's his choice," she said Reyat told her. Further, Reyat added Parmar told him that "I am positive no one would be hurt."

Reyat added that Parmar appeared sincere to him. "He was very sincere from his heart. I believed him." When people died, Reyat told the psychiatrist he then prayed daily for them. He felt he had been "duped" by Parmar. He also agreed the attack on the temple had been his motivation in helping Parmar in relation to obtaining parts for bombs.

Asked by De Freitas why he had been picked, Reyat responded that perhaps that was because he was an electrician. Reyat added, "People sometimes mislead you and that is that. I had to open my eyes up, be careful not to help people like that."

Reyat also revealed his father had committed suicide, perhaps because Reyat was incarcerated and unable to help his family. Reyat also said his mother had passed away while he was in custody and unable to help her during her last days. His wife was being called the "bomber's wife" and that he had paid the greatest penalty of all in the case.

Reyat had just walked down a slippery slope. All these things he said to De Freitas could be used against him in a charge of perjury, I felt. However, if the Crown uses this evidence, lawyers will have a field day about violations of Reyat's rights. Was he made completely aware that what he was saying could be used against him? That the psychiatrist's report could place him in serious jeopardy of a criminal charge? That question will have to be answered by the courts.

After the charge was laid, Reyat authorized his lawyer to send me a letter Reyat had written about alleged wrongdoings by police and Crown counsel, violations of his rights and harassment of his family, including his eldest daughter while she was at work.

One key issue he shed light on about why the Crown so eagerly gave him a deal was the fact that during his trial in 1991 on charges connected with the Tokyo bomb, Woolworths saleswoman Karen Smith had positively told the cops that it was not Reyat who had picked up the stereo tuner of the type that exploded at Tokyo. Yet, that exculpatory evidence was not made available to Reyat's lawyer at the time. A receipt for the tuner was found in Reyat's home with his name on it. But Smith's non-identification of Reyat was crucial evidence that should have been properly turned over to his defence team.

During preparation for his trial on the new charges related to Air India in 2001, his legal team turned up police documentation that showed that he had not been identified as the man who picked up the tuner and yet the judge in Reyat's previous trial in 1991 had been led to believe that this was the case. Reyat said his legal team began discussing this violation of his rights with Crown counsel Bob Wright who was the lead Crown attorney in the Air India case.

"During the Air India trial in 2001, when Karen Smith's evidence was referred to by my legal team, the prosecution immediately consulted them and offered me a deal as they did not want this evidence exposed nor did they want to bring James W. Jardine (prosecutor in 1991 case) on the stand for cross-examination," Reyat said in his letter.

"James Jardine is now a judge so this exposure would have been a huge embarrassment to the Canadian justice system," Reyat wrote in his letter. Court transcripts show that Jardine's associate Crown Counsel Richard Cairns carefully avoided asking Smith any questions about the identity of the man who picked up the tuner. Smith was not asked to point out the man who bought the tuner since Cairns knew she could not point to Reyat. And the defence was too afraid to ask her about the identity of the person who picked up that tuner, just in case she pointed to Reyat. Defence lawyers will not ask a question to which they don't know the answer.

Reyat also said that in February 1997, his daughter was alone at home when RCMP entered to retrieve a bug. Reyat said his daughter Pritpal Kaur was frightened by her face-to-face encounter with strangers.

"They lied to her claiming that they were responding to a burglar alarm," Reyat said. His home did not have a burglar alarm, he added. Ten months later RCMP apologized to him and said they had entered to retrieve a bug after a warrant to intercept conversations had expired. Now, if RCMP entered his home to get a bug out, they would normally have a warrant. Without it, the entry would be considered a burglary. Police sources said they would not enter a home without proper authorization but it seemed to me the cops had failed to make sure no one was home when this was done. Apparently Reyat's daughter was in the shower and the police thought their path was clear. A mistake had been made by the officers but I doubt if the entry was illegal. Every cop knows that a sure path to jail is to break into someone's home without a lawful warrant. I write off that incident as another example of poor preparation on the part of the cops in not making sure they entered when no one was home.

Reyat said two cops visited him in prison in Kingston, Ont., on December 12, 2005. They threatened to take his family to court and told Reyat "it was up to him" to make sure this did not happen. Clearly Reyat was being squeezed by the police.

Later two officers went to a location in Surrey, B.C., where Reyat's eldest daughter, Charanjit Kaur Reyat, worked. The cops, said Reyat, followed her into the parking lot and told her they wanted to talk to her about her father's "life after prison." She declined to talk to the two cops. This episode leaves a bit of bad taste in the mouth. Family members of suspects need not face harassment such as this. It was not the fault of his wife or daughters or son that Reyat had committed this grave offence, and in my mind it was unfair to use them as pressure points.

During his parole hearing On March 3, 2005, Inderjit Singh Reyat made a "heartfelt" apology to victims of the Air India bombing, who had turned up at his hearing to speak out about the carnage that he had caused. It was clear to me, though, that Reyat still had not cleansed his soul by not telling the truth about the Air India bombing. Telling the truth, in my mind, would amount to an ultimate apology.

One of the speakers at his hearing was Toronto's Lata Pada—an acclaimed dance choreographer. She had been waiting in Bombay for her husband Vishnu, and daughters Brinda and Arti to arrive. They died aboard Air India Flight 182 and Reyat had contributed to their deaths.

Her words were poignant. They came from her heart and her soul. "Over twenty years ago, a horrific and unimaginable darkness engulfed me. Waiting excitedly for Vishnu, Brinda, and Arti in Bombay to arrive on the Air India flight from Toronto and spend a glorious summer vacation with family, a phone call jolted me with the life-altering news: they had been killed in the Air India explosion off the coast of Ireland. Nothing in life can prepare anyone for such a totally crippling event, the snuffing out of one's entire family in such a sudden and horrific way is an act of cruelty one can never imagine, let alone experience. I died while still being alive, my life and that of my immediate family was never the same again.

"Twenty years is a lifetime, an eternity for the families who have waited with trust and faith in the justice system. They have been patient, dignified and hopeful while coping with unimaginable pain that the rest of Canada has forgotten about."

She asked that Reyat not be given early release. The parole board declined Reyat's release application.

I had seen this resilience demonstrated by members of the families of people killed in the Air India bombing. They had come back from their tears and fought to re-establish their lives but still hungered for justice that the investigation had not provided. So I remain hopeful about the more recent progress made by cops, but I must also be mindful that too many suspects have died and others are untouchable.

For me, there was only one comfort in these twenty years of terror.

It was the remarkable human spirit of the families who triumphed over the terror and the tears.

Mrs. Amarjit Kaur Bhinder, who faced debilitating initial devastation to the point where she carried her husband's clothes with her wherever she went, showed me that the human spirit cannot be brought to its knees by cowards who attack unarmed civilians.

Recently while she was travelling in Singapore, I talked to her over the phone. She told me she had put together the pieces of her life after Captain Satwinder Singh Bhinder's death and faced an excruciating battle to overcome her loneliness in bringing up her two young children. Ashamdip Singh was only seven at the time and her daughter Jasleen was ten.

Ever since Ashamdip was three, he had been telling his dad that one day they would fly together as a team. "From the very childhood, the day he started speaking, [Ashamdip] wanted to be a pilot like his dad," Amarjit said. "The day he started speaking and he saw his dad in Air India uniform, he said he wanted to be a pilot, too. He used to tell his dad, 'One day I will fly with you as your co-pilot.'"

As a widow with children to raise, she had to find a way to work if she was to help her son fulfill that promise to dad. Air India hired her, offered her training and a first job in Bombay. A year later, she moved to Chandigarh, where she had family. Eventually, she was station head for Air India in Kuala Lumpur.

Today, Captain Ashamdip Singh Bhinder pilots an Indian Airlines Airbus 320 between Bombay and the Middle East. He has triumphed over tragedy and the effects of losing his father to terrorism. They brought his dad down, but another Bhinder has taken to the skies.

Jasleen went on to marry a pilot too. Her husband, Captain Pritpal Singh Bhandal, works for Singapore Airlines. She teaches school in Singapore.

The children remember their father well, Amarjit Bhinder said. "And of course we talk a lot about him. He's not a closed chapter in our lives—we often discuss him."

The tragic tale of Air India Flight 182 will never be a closed book in the hearts of those of us who were touched by it. It must remain open for future generations of Canadians.

To learn how to deal with the growing threat of global terrorism, Canada must learn from what went wrong yesterday.

SALIM JIWA:

Salim Jiwa is an award-winning senior investigative reporter with *The Province* newspaper in Vancouver. He began investigating Sikh militancy in Vancouver in 1981. He met the key players who would later become the targets of the international investigation into the tragic bombing of Air India Flight 182. Jiwa introduced the prime suspect, Talwinder Singh Parmar, to the world over twenty-four years ago. He has carried out an in-depth investigation of the bombing for over two decades. He has written extensively on terrorism for major newspapers around the world and appeared on numerous television and radio programs as an analyst and commentator. He has also worked as a terrorism consultant for the New York-based ABC television network and carried out wide-ranging investigations into the activities of al-Qaeda in the U.S. and Canada. Jiwa's 1986 book, *The Death of Air India Flight 182,* published only seven months after the bombings, provided an inside look at the RCMP's investigation. In this new account of the disaster, he shares his own experiences and examines the events leading up to this haunting episode that led to the death of 331 people, the majority of them Canadians. This is an authentic and critical account of Canada's failures in dealing with the tragedy.

DONALD J. HAUKA:

Don Hauka has worked as a journalist, screenwriter, playwright, and college instructor. He was Jiwa's colleague at *The Province* newspaper for nearly twenty years, covering B.C. and Canadian politics. He was story editor for Jiwa's *The Death of Air India Flight 182.* He adapted his first novel, *Mr. Jinnah: Securities,* into a TV movie for CBC, broadcast in October 2003. The first Jinnah MOW, *Pizza 911,* was nominated for a Gemini Award for best TV movie (Hakeem Jinnah is, of course, modeled on Jiwa). A writer for radio as well as television, Hauka's first non-fiction work, *McGowan's War,* was released in 2003 by New Star Books.